A DIRECTOR CALLS

A DIRECTOR CALLS *Wendy Lesser*

University of California Press

Berkeley   Los Angeles

University of California Press
Berkeley and Los Angeles, California

Published by arrangement with Faber & Faber Limited

Library of Congress Cataloging-in-Publication Data

Lesser, Wendy.
    A director calls / Wendy Lesser.
      p. cm.
    Includes bibliographical references and index.
    ISBN 0-520-21206-1 (cloth : alk. paper). — ISBN 0-520-21262-2
(pbk. : alk. paper)
    1. Daldry, Stephen.   2. Theatrical producers and directors—Great
Britain—Biography.   I. Title.
PN2598.D22L47   1997
792'.0233'092
[B]—DC21   97-20476

Printed in the United States of America

9 8 7 6 5 4 3 2 1

The paper used in this publication is acid-free. It meets the minimum require-
ments of American Standard for Information Sciences—Permanence of Paper
for Printed Library Materials, ANSI Z 39.48-1984.

For Thom Gunn

Contents

Acknowledgments

This book would not have been possible without the generosity and openness of Stephen Daldry, who gave me access without imposing any restrictions or obligations. Nor could I have written it without the miracle-working kindness of Marieke Spencer, the helpful informativeness of Anne Mayer, and the warm assistance of everyone else at the Royal Court. The list of those who, over the last few years, have spoken to me about the theatre, about directing, or about Stephen Daldry is too long to give in full, and I hope they will all accept my undesignated gratitude, but I would like to single out Chris Barton, John Castle, Annie Castledine, Cherry Daldry, Tony Doyle, Bill Dudley, Stephen Evans, Rick Fisher, Raeda Ghazaleh, Stella Hall, Caroline Harker, Tony Hudson, Ron Hutchinson, Tony Kushner, David Lan, Alastair Macaulay, James Macdonald, Ian MacNeil, Meredith Oakes, Irene Oppenheim, Pearce Quigley, Ian Rickson, Kate Rowland, David Saltz, Prunella Scales, Rufus Sewell, Richard Seyd, Steve Tompkins, Johanna Town, Steve Vineberg, Stephen Warbeck, Julian Webber, and Nicholas Woodeson. For their astute reading and their helpful comments on the manuscript, I am deeply indebted to Stephen Greenblatt, Lisa Michaels and, above all, Arthur Lubow. I am grateful for the inventiveness of Christopher Ricks and Graham Whybrow, who simultaneously but separately came up with the book's title. And, as always, I am enormously thankful for the theatre-going companionship, thoughtful conversation, and boundless good humour of my husband, Richard Rizzo, and my son, Nicholas Rizzo.

A grant from the American Council of Learned Societies supported the writing of this book.

1 Why Stephen Daldry?

There is a companion question, which might be formulated: Why *any* theatre director? I will attempt to answer both, but in my case the particular comes first. That is, I was not aware of having any ideas about theatre directing, or any questions about those ideas, until I first saw Stephen Daldry's production of *An Inspector Calls* at the Royal National Theatre in June 1993.

I went to it cold. I had never seen or read the play – or, for that matter, anything else by J. B. Priestley. I had no information about the production, except that *Time Out* had recommended it as a 'thriller', which is not really what it turned out to be. And yet, as I sat in the stalls of the Olivier Theatre listening to the curtain-opening strains of Bernard Herrmann's *Vertigo* music, I felt the hairs rise on the back of my neck.

In June 1993 I knew nothing about Stephen Daldry. I did not know that he was thirty-three years old, nor that he was the son of a bank manager and a former cabaret *artiste*, nor that he had grown up in a Somerset village, nor that he had learned to fly a plane while on an RAF scholarship, nor that he had joined an Italian circus after taking a degree in English and drama at Sheffield University. Some of these things may turn out to be pertinent to what I have to say in the course of this book about Daldry's directing; none of them were pertinent to my first impression of his work. Sitting there in the theatre, I knew only that I was being spoken to, in and through this play, by a voice I understood. It was a voice that spoke to me about the function of theatre as art, as entertainment, and as political exhortation; it spoke about the relationship between the world onstage and the world outside the theatre; and it spoke about how music, language, lighting, sets, and acting could all work together to produce a specific mood. It spoke to me about Hitchcock and

Brecht, naturalism and expressionism, suspenseful identification and instructive alienation. It spoke, most of all, about *my* role as a member of this particular audience, and it made me feel what I have felt only five or six times in my life: that theatre, at its best, can be the most vital and exciting art in the world. The voice that spoke to me was not that of J. B. Priestley (I have heard the voices of playwrights many times before, and they do not, even at their most thrilling, sound like that). I imagined that it was the voice of Stephen Daldry.

Ten months after that first performance of *Inspector* – during which time I had written to Daldry about watching him work, and had received a brief but cordial note of assent – I walked into the Royale Theatre in New York, where he and his collaborators were staging the Broadway version of the same play. Practically the first words I overheard (eavesdropping being the central technique of this book) were part of a conversation between Ian MacNeil, the set designer, and Rick Fisher, the lighting designer; they were talking about the colour of the light on the proscenium arch. 'Less like McDonald's golden arches,' said MacNeil, 'and more like a rundown old theatre.' I began to smile. And when, a moment later, I learned that Daldry's team had constructed not only the proscenium arch itself but the curtain as well, in this and every other theatre where they had performed the play, a huge grin spread across my face. I had guessed right. The signals I had been picking up from that first performance of *An Inspector Calls* – signals about theatre and reality, actors and audiences, art and life – had been sent out intentionally. I hadn't just been making them up. The voice I had imagined was really there.

My successful interpretation was only the last and smallest in a series. Theatre itself hinges on the art of interpretation. The director – and through him the actors, the set and costume designers, the lighting and sound people, and all the other collaborators in a theatre production – must first interpret the script, transforming it from words on a page into a living piece of theatre. Only then can we in the audience in turn interpret what they have given us. This 'interpretation' does not need to be reduced to words; in fact, the beauty of the whole thing is that it *cannot* be so reduced. Like fluently bilingual speakers, we understand the language of the theatre without having to produce a word-for-word translation between its terms and those of purely verbal communication. (One definition of a successful theatre production might be that it is understandable in this way. Wittgenstein, in that respect, could have been talking about theatre when he said there was no such thing as a private language.)

As with language, the fact that theatre is a matter of interpretation does not mean that everything is up for grabs. If it is necessary to interpret, it is also possible to *mis*interpret. The director can make this mistake, and so can we: the work can be there, waiting to be discovered, and one can fail to make that discovery. The director 'creates the object, but the object was there waiting to be created' (as D. W. Winnicott said in a different context, about babies and their transitional objects); and the 'essential feature', as Winnicott also said, is '*the paradox, and the acceptance of the paradox* . . . we all know that we will never challenge the baby to elicit an answer to the question: did you create that or did you find that?'

I had run into this problem long before I began thinking in a sustained way about theatre, and I had even used that Winnicott quote in an earlier book about literature, painting, and film. Much of the argument in literary theory over the past two decades has focused, in one way or another, on the necessity or validity or debatability of interpretation. Theatre seemed to me to offer a clear way out of the theoretical dead-end because it self-evidently required interpretation: you can't, after all, put a written script on a stage and call it theatre. (Well, you can, but it won't *be* theatre; it will be conceptual art.) Harold Clurman was getting at something like this when he wrote in *The Divine Pastime*, 'No matter how explicit the playwright may be, the moment you transpose his text into terms of flesh and blood, to three-dimensional space, to canvas, wood, electricity, sound and movement, problems arise that are no longer simply questions of "understanding the play" in the library sense of the word.' And

Peter Brook, in *The Empty Space*, remarked on the same directorial problem. 'When I hear a director speak glibly of serving the text, of letting the play speak for itself, my suspicions are aroused, because this is the hardest job of all. If you just let a play speak, it may not make a sound,' said Brook. 'If what you want is for a play to be heard, you must conjure its sound from it.'

The director's role as the primary interpreter of a play is relatively recent. As late as 1895, when George Bernard Shaw was reviewing new London productions of scripts by Henry James and Oscar Wilde, he was dealing with the interpretations imposed by an actor-manager, who would often select a play mainly because it had a role that promised to showcase his particular histrionic talents. Only with the turn of the century, in the person of figures like Gordon Craig and Konstantin Stanislavsky, did the idea of a separate, non-acting director become current. I hope I will not seem to be imposing my own interpretations on history unduly if I point out that the director came into being at approximately the same time as three powerful theories which, in themselves, suggested the need for the director's role. These three theories are those of Marx (the director as controller of the means of production), Freud (the director as interpreter of previously unconscious material), and Einstein (the director as purveyor of relative, subjective truth, embodying the idea of a perceiving sensibility which actually shapes the reality it perceives).

The fact that the director is the primary interpreter does not mean he has usurped the role of the playwright. Nor is a playscript just a blueprint for the finished structure, a mere recipe for what will ultimately be an edible feast. One wouldn't want to describe the written versions of *Macbeth*, *King Lear*, *Hamlet*, and *Antony and Cleopatra* as 'incomplete', for instance – they could well be the fullest imaginable versions we will ever get of Shakespeare's plays. But however complete they may be as literary works, they are not theatre until they are 'transposed' to the stage, 'conjured' into living performances. What Clurman's and Brook's remarks point out is the extent to which meanings and connotations other than the literary ones are added to any performance of a play.

If interpretation is necessary in performance, it is also necessarily ambiguous. This is partly because theatre is a collaborative art, and even the most dictatorial director can never singlehandedly control the ultimate shaping of the interpretation; the actors and other collaborators have their own wills, their own interpretations, and these will not be identical to the director's. Moreover, the director is using materials – 'canvas' and 'wood', 'flesh and blood', 'sound and movement', and of course language – that have their own multiple connotations to begin with. We don't all have the same feelings about the colour red, or an empty house, or a loud-voiced woman, or the gesture of holding still, and our responses to a play will inevitably reflect that built-in multiplicity. There's also a tension between the deeply conscious effort brought to bear on a theatre piece by its director (since nothing is there to begin with – everything needs to be thought up and placed on stage for a reason), and the way the most striking theatrical effects will sometimes arrive by chance, through the momentary whim of an actor or the blundering mistake of a props person. And all of this interpretive variability is exacerbated by the fact that a play takes place in real time and disappears into thin air, only to be repeated all over again, but never precisely in the same way, so that the interpretation can never be frozen.

I have been throwing around the word 'interpretation' here as if it had a fixed or certain meaning, whereas its various possible definitions are precisely what I hope to explore, in a practical way, throughout the rest of this book. This is not going to be a highly theoretical work – its focus on the practice of a single director makes most dramaturgical theory either irrelevant or redundant – but a few questions about how drama operates, or is presumed to operate, should probably be raised at the outset. My thinking on this subject has been informed partly by theory-minded practitioners like Brecht and Artaud, partly by philosophers like J. L. Austin and Stanley Cavell, and most recently by a very intelligent doctoral dissertation, *The Reality of the Theater Event: Logical Foundations of Dramatic Performance*, written by David Saltz.

Saltz is concerned with untangling a number of knotty definitional problems which mostly I leave by the wayside, and I highly recommend his book to anyone who finds my treatment of the subject philosophically unsatisfying. He is also bent on interpreting the word 'interpretation' as rigorously as possible, distinguishing it (in its theatrical applications) from 'translation', 'representation', 'commentary', 'guesses', and other possible choices. Saltz is particularly anxious to rid the world of the notion that the staged version of the play is merely an 'interpretation' of some prior, essential version that exists in script form. 'To perceive a performance as an interpretation,' he argues, 'we must see the play as something *other than* or *apart from* the performance.' But his central point is that the two are not separable: 'We do not watch a performance and a play, or a performance surrounding a play, or a performance taking place on the occasion of a play, but the performance of a play. Performance and play, actor and role, both constitute irreducible conjunctions.' Giving a specific example to buttress his point, he remarks, 'When I watch a performance of *Hamlet*, I am not watching merely an imitation, or a reproduction, of the play. Indeed, I am not watching a representation of the play at all, in any meaningful sense of the word "representation". I am watching *the play*. *Hamlet* is *there*, on the stage.' Saltz eloquently argues that plays 'have "material existence" only in performance', and then adds mockingly, 'Does it follow that they have "immaterial existence" elsewhere? Are we confronted with a phantom entity, an ideal Platonic Play?'

I find most of David Saltz's ideas tremendously enlightening and useful. That should be apparent in the kind of theatre criticism I practise in this book, which presumes that the performance, and not the script, is the essential incarnation of the play. My notion of a director's 'interpretation' is as inextricably joined to a performed play as, for Saltz, a play is joined to its performance. They are, as he puts it, 'irreducible conjunctions': the interpretation *is* the production, and not some prior or separate intellectual process that is merely embodied or represented or manifested in the performance. None the less, I find myself hesitant to let go of some version of Saltz's 'phantom entity', that imagined play behind or within the performed one. It is true that there is no single form in which a play should or must be embodied (and, indeed, part of Stephen Daldry's special skill lies in finding alternate forms of performance that make as much sense of the script as the more traditional forms have done). But if my kind of theatre criticism is to have any validity, it must also be true that there are some performances that are so bad, or inappropriate, or just plain inept as to constitute a false interpretation of the play. I can't say exactly what *a priori* version of the play I am appealing to when I make this statement. I am certainly not referring to the bare words on the page of the script, nor the playwright's assertions about those words, nor the director's guesses about the playwright's intentions, for none of those things is transparently accessible; all require further interpretation, and hence a further exercise of judgment. But I do want to retain the right to evaluate a given production for its faithfulness and (what is somewhat different) its truth.

And this is where Saltz and I part company. He has no need for evaluative judgments; what concern him are questions of classification. At one point, he does admit that 'if a performance diverges too far from what I take to be the constitutive properties of the type . . . I will refuse to regard it as a performance of the play and regard it instead as a mutation, an adaptation, a variation, or, in extreme cases, as an altogether different play. But what difference does it make where I draw these lines? What is at stake in my verdict?' Nothing, he suggests. Even if he imagines himself in the position of the offended playwright, 'not much rests on whether I choose to classify the objectionable performance as a bad performance of my play, an incorrectly performed performance of my play, or as a performance of another play that is masquerading as mine'. But it seems to me that *everything* rests on such distinctions – not only for the play-wright, but for the director, the actors, and above all the audience. We go to the theatre in part to have a communal experience, to participate in a one-time-only event with a limited collection of other people; and at the same time we go to have a private, internal experience, an individual response to this public event. But if we think we are seeing *Hamlet*, while the director and actors – and possibly other members of the audience – think we are seeing *Rosencrantz and Guildenstern Are Dead*, we have been short-changed on both the communal and individual fronts. For it is not only the public event that disintegrates if we are all attending separate plays; the whole idea of an individual response, which depends for its definitional richness on the difference between public and private, also disappears in the face of purely solipsistic spectatorship.

Earlier, I said that I considered some performances to be false interpretations of their plays, and what I meant by this has something to do with my sense of theatre as a communal activity. The truth we are seeking in a theatrical performance is not strictly objective or narrowly subjective – or rather, it is not *only* these. It is also, to a large extent, communal. It depends on our agreeing, at least for the moment, that certain things are the way they are in the world – at least, in *this* (theatrical) world, on *this* (performance) night. Our agreement simultaneously reflects a reality and makes a reality (Winnicott's 'did you create that or did you find that?'). At an immediate level, the sense of community involves ourselves and the actors onstage; in a broader sense, it involves all those present (audience, actors) and all those absent but responsible (playwright, director, designer, previous actors in these roles, previous audience members). The communal truth of a performance is partly verifiable – for instance, through the audience's laughter – and partly unverifiable, internal. It can be built on illusions, or dreams, or wishes. It can be based on patent falsehoods, unrealistic portrayals (as the truth of Tony Kushner's *Angels in America* lay partly in a false, invented Roy Cohn – though it was none the less a communal truth, based in part on a shared sense of history). And one of the ways a play can be true is to its own history as a play. Like the Montaignean version of the self, a play is different each time it is performed and yet faithful to some essential version of its own character.

One result of looking at theatre in this way is that you begin to feel the need for a new kind of theatre criticism. If a performed play is not simply a script on the page (as some literature professors might have it), it is also not a single event that takes place once, for two hours, and is then repeated identically over time (as the methods of theatre reviewers might imply). So perhaps something new is required to fill the gap between the professor's scrutiny of a frozen script and the reviewer's response to a frozen performance. This new form of criticism would have the intensity of a literary close-reading but would be focused on an artwork which is in flux over time.

With this in mind, I have gathered much of the material for this book by sitting through the same production many different times and in many different formats, watching scene rehearsals, dress rehearsals, previews, and performances, fragments as well as wholes, discarded versions as well as final ones. I am not exclusively interested in the process whereby Stephen Daldry arrives at his interpretations – the value of his productions as finished works of art matters, in my kind of criticism – but I can use elements of the process to elucidate the final product, just as a biographically or historically informed literary critic does. Compared to a one-time viewer of a play, I take in information at a snail's pace, slowly and repeatedly going over each piece of dialogue, stage action, or design. The *kind* of information I gather is mainly available to a member of the general public, and if a performance is any good it will have on that hypothetical viewer many of the effects it has on me, but those effects will come all at once, from all angles, and their influence will be largely unconscious. My job, as I view it, is to make the unconscious conscious – to render into words the experience that takes place implicitly in the mind of the attentive theatre-goer. The pitfall of such a technique is that one risks losing sight of the instantaneous pleasure and vitality of theatre, so it is important for me to keep reminding myself that the production is *meant* for those who sit through it once, not for its obsessive scrutinizers (who include both myself and the director). I need, that is, to keep hold of the freshness of the original experience of watching the play, even as I settle down to examine the details of craft.

Watching a good director work on a play is like watching private creative thought made manifest and public. In rendering his interpretation of a play, the director converts his own ideas and visions into something external to himself, and finally exclusive of himself. He (or she, but since my particular subject is Daldry, I will use the masculine pronoun) provides the kind of authority that we expect of, say, a good novelist. I, at least, look for novelists who are powerful but invisible presences: I want to feel them in the background of the work, but I don't want their bulky bodies blocking my view of the characters, nor do I want to see their puppeteer hands pulling the strings. I want a novelist – and, by extension, a director – to give me the sense that a coherent individual vision shapes the work of art, and yet I also want to feel that possibilities remain open. Whatever else narrative artworks are about, they are partly about this conflict between free will and determinism, between the individual acts of the characters and the fates laid out for them by their authors. Narrative tension – which includes, among other things, suspense, sympathy, and credibility – depends on our giving full due to both halves of this conflict: we must see the characters' fates as simultaneously open and closed.

Theatre both embodies and resolves that conflict in a way that no other art form seems quite able to. The words have been set down by the playwright and the actors have been rehearsed by their director, but in the events taking place before us onstage, the unexpected is still possible. And this inherent lability does not just govern the actors. We too, in the audience, are free agents. This aspect of theatre is especially noticeable in contrast to film. The film director has our head in a vice: we can only see what she wants us to see, stare in the direction she wants us to stare. But we in the theatre are free to look around. We can focus on details that are not at the centre of the action, glance casually at something out of the corner of our eye. (Film has no 'casual' glances – everything, in that sense, is telegraphed.) The difference between the two kinds of viewing is even more profound than that: it is the difference between absence and presence. Actors in a film will be completely unaffected by our failure to laugh or applaud, even by our tendency to hiss and boo, since their job has long been finished by the time we enter the scene. But in a play the actors' performances can be altered by our collective response. We too are performers, in that sense, affecting the tone of the action if not its structural outline. The audience is part of the play.

Stephen Daldry is not the only theatre director, or even the only British theatre director, who recognizes this. Part of what British theatre has developed, over the past few decades, is the self-conscious capacity to incorporate the audience without violating the content of the play. Perhaps this is due to the presence of pantomimes as standard Christmas fare, so that the average British theatre-goer has been a participating audience member since early childhood. Perhaps it is due to the inheritance of Shakespeare, or the long history of good regional theatre, or the highly attuned manners of an overpopulated island. I don't know how to explain it. But I do know that Daldry is part of a generation of very strong and thoughtful theatre directors.

Why Daldry, then? Because I too must perform an act of interpretation, and a good interpretation depends in part on a sympathy of vision. 'I'm an old lefty,' Stephen Daldry told me during our first conversation, when he was answering my question about how he chose the Priestley play. And I knew exactly what he meant, because I was an old lefty too, with the emphasis on *old* as much as on *left*. As a student at Cambridge University in the early 1970s I had embraced the British Labour Party, which still bore remnants of its 1945 glory. To an American brought up in the Cold War years, the idea of a mass party founded on socialist principles was little short of miraculous, and I imagine it had somewhat the same effect on a young British director coming of age in Margaret Thatcher's England. The socialism that both Daldry and I looked back to was neither the cramped, defensive, whiny sanctimoniousness of the American postwar left nor the business-minded pragmatism of the late-twentieth-century British Labour Party. What we both remembered, though neither of us had really lived through it, was the Labour Party that had shaped the Welfare State – the Labour Party that was overwhelmingly elected just after *An Inspector Calls* first premièred in Britain. 'I remember the excitement of it all very well, as an RAF pilot in the spring of 1945,' wrote Tony Benn, the Labour Party patriarch, in a programme note for Daldry's *Inspector* production. 'Coming home in a troopship . . . we had a big debate, as we sailed through the Mediterranean, which revealed overwhelming support for Labour . . . Under the surface there was a tide of confidence and hope running that produced the landslide we had not expected.' Something of that 'confidence and hope', so rare in left-wing politics today, was evident in Daldry's production of Priestley's play.

But politics weren't the only thing I shared with Daldry (Daldry the imaginary voice, I mean, the director I sensed at that first viewing of the play). We also seemed to have similar feelings about the integrity of authorship. I saw in him what one rarely sees in directors who have a noticeable style: an enormous respect for the playwright's words and intentions. The National Theatre production of *An Inspector Calls* was strikingly original, but it also felt wonderfully true to the play. Of course, Priestley wasn't alive to confirm this impression, but even if he had been, I wouldn't necessarily rely on him as the sole or ultimate explicator of his own intentions. What I mean by 'the playwright's words and intentions' is something that needs to be judged partially from the outside, since even the playwright, once he has finished his play, is no longer the person who conceived and wrote it. Having said exactly what he intended to *in* the play, the playwright may well have nothing more – or less – to say on the subject; he may rightfully feel that what he carefully put into two or three acts can't be reduced to five sentences. And this summary version of intention is irrelevant to the director's work, anyway. His job is not to reduce the play to its verbal meaning, but to expand it, bringing in all the other elements that are necessary to turn a script into a performance. If he is successful in his interpretation – if he is true to the playwright's intentions – we in the audience will feel no discrepancy between the nature of that expansion and the words of the script, however unusual the directorial technique may be.

Of course, that 'we' in the audience is really a bunch of 'I's, and other responses to Stephen Daldry's work have differed from mine. (Part of what makes theatre an interpretive art is what makes *any* art so: the fact that critical judgments vary.) One old Shropshire gentleman who attended Daldry's version of *An Inspector Calls* after it had been transferred to the West End was so exercised by the production that he felt impelled to write to the management of the Aldwych Theatre. 'It is an excellent play and you murdered it,' he alleged. 'Dear J. B. would have turned over in his grave if he had seen your performance.' Several theatre critics had a similar if less heated response to Daldry's production. They felt it was a case of a director glorifying himself at the expense of an author – though these critics, unlike the old gentleman, seemed to feel that it wasn't a very good play to begin with, and that the glory had come from transforming it unrecognizably. Neither of these responses seems remotely accurate to me. Precisely what I liked about the production was that it was true to both 1945 and 1993, to both Priestley's conception of theatre and Daldry's own. He had chosen to do Priestley because he felt a political and theatrical affinity with him, an affinity that was amply borne out by the quotations from Priestley's writing sprinkled through the National Theatre programme. In this first exposure to Daldry's work, it never occurred to me to think of 'director's theatre' versus 'writer's theatre'. On the contrary, he struck me as a director who spoke through and with the writer's voice – not an act of ventriloquism so much as harmonious choral counterpoint.

But I would be doing an injustice to my initial feeling if I allowed it to sound completely highminded. Yes, I agreed with Daldry's politics, and yes, I felt he treated the playwright well, but I also loved the production because it was so much fun. Stephen Daldry seemed to me to have taken in and carried out the wish Brecht expressed when he said that he wanted to have a live horse onstage in the climactic scene of *The Threepenny Opera*. Brecht wanted there to be a circus-like side to theatre even as he wanted it to be morally instructive. I have always liked that side of Brecht's dramaturgical theory, but I have never seen it exemplified in any of his plays, which generally seem – because of either the translations or the productions – to be too serious and admonitory to be much fun. Daldry, however, had managed to take a relatively serious, extremely admonitory play like *An Inspector Calls* and give it the thrill and glamour of spectacle. And for that I was tremendously grateful.

2 An Inspector Calls

As the members of the audience are still chatting noisily, a siren wails in the background. It is nearly inaudible over the conversational hum, unless you are listening for it. But the siren persists, and soon the house lights dim, silencing the audience, so that eventually everyone can hear the whining clangour that has been blaring under the collective noise. Now the first actor appears: a child climbing out of a trap door, as if emerging from an underground shelter after the 'All Clear' has sounded. Occupying the narrow strip of stage in front of the still-lowered curtain, the child stares around him: at the red-and-gold theatrical curtain; at the faded and flaking proscenium arch, which appears to have seen better days; at the oddly unkempt, standard-red British telephone booth to the left and in front of the stage; at the audience itself. He wraps himself playfully in the tassels of the curtain while, in the background, muffled, distant gunfire rumbles. Then the boy runs over to the right side of the stage, where there is a battered-looking old radio of the sort that might have broadcast the war news to anxious Britons in the 1940s. The radio is lit but silent, so the boy, to bring it to life, kicks it twice and then pounds it once with a nearby plank – three blows, like the sound that in pre-modern theatre would traditionally signal the opening of a play. At the end of the third thump, the music starts: a haunting, eerie, melodramatic theme that will be recognizable, at least to some, as Bernard Herrmann's score for *Vertigo*. As the music swells, more children emerge from the trap door, a girl and two boys, all dressed (like the first child) in *Hope and Glory* wartime fashion. And now the curtain begins to rise, causing two of the children to dive simultaneously for the floor, in a gesture that suggests both the fear of sudden bombardment and the desire to see into the slowly widening sliver of theatrical space.

What they see – and what we, increasingly, see, as the curtain gradually draws upwards and disappears – is a largely deserted landscape covered with uneven cobblestones. To the left, a groggily erect lamppost tilts in the opposite direction to the telephone booth, slightly but discernibly awry. On the horizon is the tiny image of a multi-storey dwelling isolated in the stony moor of cobbles, its upper windows glowing. And closer to us, occupying much of the right-hand side of the stage, is another version of the isolated house. Life-sized (at least in comparison to the distant one) and located in the midst of crumbled, distorted, torn-up stones – as if it had somehow erupted through the ground – this house is raised up on stilts, lit from within, and evidently occupied.

Outside the house a hard rain pours down on the whole set; the wartime children, splashing and playing in the rubble, are drenched to the skin. But inside all seems cosy and warm. Some kind of party appears to be in progress – we can catch glimpses of well-coiffed heads and well-dressed bodies through the windows of the house. As the *Vertigo* music drops suddenly, we hear the undifferentiated chatter of a successful dinner party, from which emerges, in resounding female tones, the statement, 'All right, Edna. I'll ring from the drawing room when we want coffee.'

In Stephen Daldry's production of J. B. Priestley's *An Inspector Calls*, these lines are the first element that can be directly attributed to the playwright. (And they are not even the first lines of Priestley's script, which included an additional ten sentences or so of introductory after-dinner chat.) Everything else, from the rain to the children to the wartime sound effects to the distinctly surreal set, has been introduced by Daldry and his creative team: the designer Ian MacNeil, the lighting director Rick Fisher, and the composer Stephen Warbeck.

Yet one cannot imagine a production that would be truer to the playwright's apparent intentions. 'Only an idiot would consider me a naturalistic dramatist,' Priestley wrote in 1946, less than two years after completing *An Inspector Calls*. 'I was a wild one only pretending to be a tame one.' Daldry's vastly inventive production has given the wildness back to what was in danger of becoming a dull old theatrical warhorse – and, in the process, has given a contemporary stylishness and a political currency to Priestley's postwar socialist ideas.

Priestley's play (which is performed so often in England that, according to Daldry, not only has most of the potential audience already seen the play, but 'twenty per cent of the audience has been *in* the play') is about a family of well-to-do Edwardians who live in the north Midlands city of Brumley. On the night in 1912 when the play takes place, the industrialist Arthur Birling and his wife Sybil are celebrating the engagement of their daughter Sheila to Gerald Croft, a scion of the local aristocracy; Sheila's brother Eric is also present at the dinner. Shortly after the self-congratulatory toasts with which the play begins, the party is interrupted by one Inspector Goole, who proceeds to quiz every member of the gathering on his or her involvement in the recent suicide of a poverty-stricken young woman named Eva Smith. Gradually, as Goole puts each person individually through the wringer, we learn that Mr Birling had the girl fired from his factory, Sheila had her dismissed from a dress shop, Gerald kept her as his mistress, Eric impregnated her, and Mrs Birling refused her the charitable aid that would have kept her and her unborn child alive. Having brought the family to a state of complete emotional disintegration, Goole departs, issuing a final warning: 'One Eva Smith has gone – but there are millions and millions of Eva Smiths and John Smiths left with us . . . We are members of one body. We are responsible for each other. And I tell you that the time will soon come when, if men will not learn that lesson, then they will be taught it in fire and blood and anguish. Good night.'

Following a brief period of mutual recrimination, the Birlings and Gerald begin to examine more closely what has happened to them. Who was this Inspector Goole, anyway? Was he even a real inspector? And if (as they soon ascertain) he was *not* a member of the Brumley police force, why should they believe any part of the story he wove? Perhaps, by dealing with each person individually, he trapped them into thinking that they had all injured the same girl; perhaps he showed them five different photographs and pretended it was one. Perhaps there *is* no dead girl at all. (A phone call to the local infirmary verifies this conjecture.) 'The whole story's just a lot of moonshine,' sputters a relieved Arthur Birling. 'Nothing but an elaborate sell!'

At this point, however, Sheila Birling – who has proved to be the most sympathetic figure in the family, a kind of Intelligent Woman Guided to Socialism – points out the flaw in their reasoning. 'But you're forgetting one thing I still can't forget,' she says. 'Everything we said had happened really had happened. If it didn't end tragically, then that's lucky for us. But it might have done.' Everyone but the heartbroken Eric, she charges, is 'pretending everything's just as it was before . . . You began to learn something. And now you've stopped. You're ready to go on in the same old way.' She, on the other hand, can't simply go back to being the smug little rich girl she was before, 'because I remember what he said, how he looked, and what he made me feel. Fire and blood and anguish.' Eric agrees with her ('It frightens me too'), but the other three only laugh at them. And now comes the final twist in the plot: the telephone rings and Mr Birling answers it. In the play's final words, he turns to the others to report dumbfoundedly that a girl has just committed suicide and 'a police inspector is on his way here – to ask some – questions –'.

Another theatre director, Richard Seyd, once told me that whenever he's developing his own interpretation of a play, he asks himself what the play's most glaring problem is. *An Inspector Calls*, as a script on the page, has many apparent shortcomings: its unfolding mystery plot is creaky and predictable; its dialogue veers from cliché to melodrama; its socialist message is crudely delivered; its action is static and talky; and so on. But as a dramaturgical work designed for the stage, it has only one serious practical *problem*, and that is its set. Does the action take place in one enclosed room (as Priestley explicitly suggests) or in a more open, loosely defined space (as he indicates with a variety of entrances and exits)? If it's only one room – the dining room of an Edwardian house – then where is the telephone that rings in the last scene? Priestley himself acknowledged this problem in the notes that precede Act One. 'If a realistic set is used,' he remarked parenthetically, 'then it should be swung back . . . By doing this, you can have the dining table centre downstage during Act One . . . and then for Act Three can show a small table with telephone on it, downstage of fireplace; and by this time the dining table and its chairs have moved well upstage. Producers who wish to avoid this tricky business . . . would be well advised to dispense with an ordinary realistic set, if only because the dining table becomes a nuisance.'

In solving this problem, this 'nuisance', Daldry and MacNeil unlock the whole play. For by placing the Birlings and their dinner guest inside the comfy little house on stilts, which is in turn located in a bombed-out, bizarrely deserted urban landscape, Daldry has freed the play to generate all the various meanings it is capable of conveying. In Daldry's hands, *An Inspector Calls* becomes not only a play about poverty and wealth, chance and responsibility, isolation and community; it also becomes a play about how our world overlaps with and differs from the world of theatrical characters. Do they inhabit a separate time and space, or is their dimension somehow connected to ours? How real are they to us, and (a very different question) how real are the feelings they produce in us? Can they see us while we are busily inspecting them, or do we remain invisible presences in their lives – and, if invisible, then in what way are we present to them at all? How is our connection to a theatrical character like but also different from our connection to other people, including the living and the dead and the not-yet-born, those we know and those we don't know? And what bearing do these questions about empathy and perception, overlap and separation, existence and imagination, have on our social and political relations in the world? All of this is inherent in Priestley's play, and all of it is brought out by Daldry's production.

That Priestley is speaking about theatre as well as socialism can be seen from some of the lines I have mentioned already. Mr Birling's 'a lot of moonshine' and 'nothing but an elaborate sell' are apt descriptions of a play, just as Inspector Goole's interrogation technique ('One line of inquiry at a time. Otherwise we'll all be talking at once and won't know where we are') purposely reflects the artificial orderliness of theatrical dialogue. Each character's motive for wanting to hear the others' confessions bears a striking resemblance to an audience's ghoulish interest: 'Nothing but morbid curiosity,' Mrs Birling calls it at one point, but later admits she couldn't stay away because 'I had to know what's happening.' And, like a standard theatre performance, the whole action of *An Inspector Calls* takes place during one evening after dinner.

The Inspector himself fills a role somewhere between that of a playwright and that of a director. He steers the characters along their predetermined paths, refusing to allow them to wiggle out of their assigned lines ('You have no hope of *not* discussing it, Mrs Birling') and exerting a magnetic pressure on their attention. At a crucial point in Gerald's confession, for instance, when he is attempting to explain to the Inspector the nature of his feelings for the dead girl, Sheila accurately points out, 'Yes, but why are you saying that to him? You ought to be saying it to me.' And when Gerald begins to apologize, she interrupts him with, 'I know. Somehow he makes you.'

Daldry's production emphasizes the Inspector's directorial role in all sorts of ways – to begin with, by having him enter from behind the audience, striding up the left-hand aisle of the orchestra and clambering up on to the stage while the other characters are still immersed in their mannered dialogue. Whereas the Birlings and Gerald speak in a fluty, exaggeratedly stagy fashion, as if they were characters in an Oscar Wilde or Bernard Shaw comedy, Goole speaks in a rapid-fire, oddly uninflected, rhythmically pronounced way, as if he were acting in a modernist piece by Ionesco or Brecht. In the New York production, the sense that the Inspector was setting the pace and pushing the other characters along was fortuitously heightened by the fact that Kenneth Cranham, who played Inspector Goole, had performed that role in all of Daldry's other recent mountings of the play – at the National Theatre in London, on tour in the rest of Britain, and in the West End – whereas everyone else in the cast was new to the play. Cranham was not just the star from the original production who had to be brought overseas on an Equity waiver (his is not, in any case, a recognizable name to American audiences); he was in many ways Daldry's stand-in onstage, the actor who had most fully absorbed the director's ideas and intentions.

This implicit feature of the performance becomes explicit at the moment in the third act when the Inspector interrupts the squabbling Birlings by yelling 'Stop!' – just as Daldry, in dress rehearsals, had stopped the action of the play whenever something particularly displeased him. The analogy is strengthened by the lighting of this scene, for when Goole issues his booming command ('taking charge, masterfully', Priestley says in the stage directions), the stage lights suddenly darken and the house lights seem to go up – an effect produced by a powerful white beam which emanates from the back of the balcony, picking out the people seated in the front rows of the mezzanine and the orchestra. For a moment the relations between stage characters and audience appear to have been reversed: *they* are in relative darkness, silently awaiting the next crucial interaction, whereas *we* are uncomfortably spotlit. And this moment modulates into the Inspector's final speech – the one about millions and millions of Eva Smiths – which he delivers by speaking for the first time directly to the audience, feelingly and emphatically, rather than in the throw-away asides that have been his wont. We have, for that moment, taken the place of the lectured-to Birlings.

The extent to which we, the inspecting audience, are a visible presence in the Birlings' lives is an open question in this production. At times they seem to recognize our existence, as when Sheila, forced bodily by the Inspector to step forward and face the audience, confesses to us her misdeed at the dress shop; or when Mrs Birling suggests that the father of Eva Smith's unborn child (she does not yet know this is her son) should be 'compelled to confess *in public*' – at which she gestures towards the audience with both arms outstretched. At such moments, we are actively called upon to perform the role that theatrical audiences have always taken, implicitly, in the unfolding of a criminal plot, from *The Oresteia* to *Oleanna*: that is, the role of both witness and jury.

But for the most part Gerald Croft and his hosts (and, to a lesser extent, the Inspector himself) act as if they are performing in a normal fourth-wall drama. They are largely oblivious to our presence. But then, they are oblivious to a number of other things as well – the fact, for example, that their cosy little Edwardian house is located in the midst of a bombed-out postwar landscape; or the fact that their house is so tiny, so doll-like, that they literally need to stoop to squeeze out of its front door; or even the fact that the house itself explodes at the beginning of the third act, shooting off fireworks from its roof, lurching forwards at a forty-five-degree angle and toppling all its loose tableware on to the stage. Daldry's actors deal with the destroyed house as if it were merely a naturalistic mess (a room left disturbed by a burglar's intrusion, say, or a porch disarranged by a storm), and this behaviour provides one of the most amusing moments in the play when Gerald, re-entering the stage from the back of the ruined house, coolly negotiates his forty-five-degree scramble as if he were just stepping around a few pieces of broken crockery. He is characteristically oblivious, in a way that is characteristic not only of himself, but of his whole circle and (the play implies) his whole class.

A central form of obliviousness in *An Inspector Calls* is the wealthy characters' inability to perceive the lower orders. In a move that has no precedent in Priestley's script but which none the less fits perfectly into the parameters set by that script, Daldry fills the stage at the play's climactic moment with a crowd of silent townspeople. Like the silent children in the first scene (by whom they are joined at this point), these 'common folk' wear 1940s-style clothing. They include women dressed as secretaries and servants, men in the clothing of soldiers, clerks, shopkeepers, and manual labourers. They are not the homeless or the poor, but they are clearly less privileged than the Birlings – just as the children in the first scene, by virtue of the fact that they are outside, unsupervised, in the rain, seem deprived and excluded compared to the smug Edwardians inside the cosy house. Like the audience, these 1940s children and adults are silently watching the Birlings enact their fate, observing these antique goings-on from the perspective of a future the Edwardians can't see. In that sense, the silent extras are *our* stand-ins onstage. But in another sense, they bear towards the well-to-do Birlings the same relationship that those on our streets outside (the homeless beggars who are always there, whether in Times Square or under Waterloo Bridge) bear towards those of us who comfortably and expensively sit inside the theatre – a well-lit box which, in the original National Theatre production, rested on very much the same kind of stilts that supported the Birlings' doll-house.

Each of the speaking characters in the play has a different relationship to the silent figures, a different degree of obliviousness to their presence. The Inspector is not oblivious at all. At his arrival onstage he hands an orange to one of the little boys, and towards the end he stands with the silent crowd. He is, in fact, dressed in the style of the extras, in a 1945 'demob' suit; the suitcase he carries indicates that he has only recently been demobilized from active service in the war, and the orange (a fruit unavailable in England during wartime and for years afterwards) suggests that he has come directly from North Africa. He has stopped on his way home from the Front, as it were, to arrest these figures from a previous generation – much as Priestley was doing when he chose to focus on Edwardian industrialists in his postwar socialist exhortation.

Among the family members themselves, Sheila seems to be the only one able to see the silent figures. When she first emerges from the little house to admire her engagement ring on the balcony, she exchanges glances with the leading boy, who stands below her on the cobblestones; the lighting, at this point, captures both their faces so that the moment of mutual recognition can be clearly seen. Her parents, on the other hand, seem to be aware of the silent townsfolk only as an adjunct to the fog that blows in on the third act. They are not people, from the perspective of the by-now-miserable older Birlings, but simply an element in the portentously disturbing atmosphere. And Gerald Croft never sees the silent figures at all: he is offstage during the crowd scene and completely unaware of the children in the first act. When I asked the actor playing Gerald in New York (an Englishman named Aden Gillett) whether Daldry had given them any instructions about the significance of the extras, he said, 'Not at all. But I just ignore them. My character just doesn't see them – wouldn't know how to react. *She* sees them – the girl – but that's because she's supposed to be the audience's Everywoman.'

Something in the actor's Geraldish tones implied class invisibility rather than just theatrical invisibility, conveying the attitude of a master who can 'just ignore' his servants. And, indeed, the single servant written into Priestley's play – the Birlings' maid, Edna – is used in this production as a transitional figure between the silent extras and the speaking leads. Priestley gives her a few lines (basically, the introduction of Inspector Goole to the household) and a few other gestures (answering the door and making tea after the cataclysm of exposure); otherwise, she remains offstage throughout most of the script. Daldry, in a strategy that again ignores Priestley's stage directions but fulfils his artistic intentions, keeps her onstage for the whole play. Silent but ever-present, she observes each phase of the downfall of the Birlings. It is no accident that Daldry has chosen to begin the play with the line that invokes her name, Mrs Birling's 'All right, Edna.'

For most of the first scene, when the family is still enclosed within its tiny house, Edna is outdoors in the rain, fetching and carrying bucketfuls of water. She clearly perceives the 1940s ragamuffins and even attempts to shoo them away. She is also the first member of the household to meet the Inspector, politely taking his coat while the family chatters on idly. After she announces him (her first words are 'Please, sir, an inspector's called' – almost an exact echo of the play's title), she initiates one of the most dramatically spectacular moments in the play. In response to Mr Birling's 'Give us more light', Edna raises her arm towards the house, a gesture that seemingly causes the whole building to crack open down a vertical seam in its front, so that the walls swing back to expose the family seated within. This produces additional light and, more importantly, it produces clarity: for the first time, we can fully see and comfortably hear characters whose conversation has thus far come through to us only in fragmented, muffled bits. In this respect, Edna functions in this scene as *our* servant.

Throughout much of the evening she plays the squelched minion to Mrs Birling's *grande dame*: rolling out a carpet for the imperious lady to step on, snuggling a chair up behind the long, elegant train of her mistress's dress, and making numerous similar adjustments to the comfort level of the vastly uncomfortable cobblestoned set. These gestures of Edna's inevitably produce a certain amount of audience laughter – in part because they seem so ineffectual in the face of the gigantically disastrous landscape, and in part because Mrs Birling so readily accepts them as her due. In New York, Mrs Birling's hauteur was brilliantly rendered by the marvellous actress Rosemary Harris, who squeezed every moment for its humorous potential. In guiding her towards this performance, Stephen Daldry suggested during one rehearsal that she ought to be supervising, with an appropriately steely glance, Edna's little gestures of assistance. 'Are you paying her? Is she under your *employ*?' the director urged. The laughter he aimed to provoke through this relationship was produced, in part, by our inherent discomfort with the very idea of household servants – a discomfort not at all lessened by the fact that we of the theatre-going classes may well employ them ourselves.

At the end of the play, Daldry groups Edna with the likeable, comparatively heroic figures, Sheila and Eric Birling, so that these three are in front of the curtain when it falls on the older Birlings and Gerald, who have once again retreated inside their now-restored doll-house. He's reminding us that Edna is like the younger, 'impressionable' generation – capable of seeing the future, of perceiving what's not yet there. In this play, that capacity also implies the ability to see what's no *longer* there, like the pitifully doomed existence of the now-dead Eva Smith. 'If I could help her now, I would –,' Sheila says early in the play, to which the Inspector responds, 'Yes, but you can't. It's too late. She's dead.' Towards the end it is Sheila who recalls the girl's ineradicable death, when the others are busily trying to forget or ignore it.

This ability to remember or foresee the currently non-existent is linked, in Priestley's conception, with the capacity to appreciate theatre. 'Thinking about the Theatre,' Priestley said in 1935, 'I cling to my belief that in its own time, somewhere along the fourth dimension, everything still exists: that lift of the voice, that gesture, that look, they are still there.' He went on to remark that 'when I think about the Theatre, I only wonder when at least some part of our minds will be able to travel in time, to recapture the past that has not really vanished at all, to see the old velvet curtains rising and falling again, to applaud once more the brave players'.

You can see how this image has informed Daldry's whole production, in which the 1912 'past' and the 1945 'present' co-exist side by side onstage; in which silent, ghostly actors represent the 'brave players' of other eras; and in which an 'old velvet curtain' and a faded proscenium arch have been specially manufactured for each theatre where the play has been performed, in order to suggest the performances of an earlier time. And you can also see how Priestley's time-travel idea applies to theatre in general – to the way plays can 'cause relive/The dead again' (as Middleton and Rowley say at the end of *The Changeling*). What Daldry and Priestley are both getting at, in this production of *An Inspector Calls*, is the extent to which theatrical characters are themselves like figures from the past or the future, like people who have died or have not yet been born.

But unlike biological organisms, stage characters do not follow a normal progression from birth to death. Their time is not our time: it is cyclical rather than linear, climactic rather than quotidian, *in medias res* rather than developmental. 'Settle it afterwards,' the Inspector harshly orders Arthur and Eric Birling, to stop them from squabbling; but we know that for theatrical characters there is no private 'afterwards', only the public time when they appear before us, repeating their drama again and again. Where do theatrical characters come from and where do they go when they leave? Is 'offstage' a place in their world or in ours? Acknowledging our curiosity about such matters, Daldry stages the actors' entrances as a kind of birth from another dimension into this one: the child emerging head-first from beneath the stage, the Birlings squeezing with difficulty out of their too-small door. And if theatrical characters are new souls who have been born into this world, they are also old souls who have been borne out, as the Elizabethans implied when they called actors 'shadows', or shades. That aspect of the drama is underlined by this production's *film noir* lighting, which enables even the tiniest actors to cast huge shadows.

We needn't harp on the Inspector's surname – the play, in any case, spells it out for us. (Literally. We are twice told that his name is G-O-O-L-E, as if to assure us by negation that it is really G-H-O-U-L.) The mistake that Gerald, Arthur, and Sybil make is to conclude that if Inspector Goole is indeed a ghost – a fake, a fantasy, a figment of the imagination – then he never existed at all. On this subject, the younger Birlings pointedly contradict their parents. 'He wasn't an inspector,' says Arthur Birling, to which Sheila replies, 'Well, he inspected us, all right,' earning the most enthusiastic laugh of the play. The line is funny, and it's also profoundly stirring, because it suggests not just that some kind of inspection has actually taken place (by us in the audience, if by no one else), but also that if he wasn't a 'real' inspector, Inspector Goole was none the less just as real as the

Birlings. They are all ghosts, equally – the silent ones and the speakers, the masters and the servants, the people from the past and the people from the soon-to-be-outdated present.

'What about seeing ghosts?' said the great British philosopher J. L. Austin in his book *Sense and Sensibilia*. 'Well, if I say that cousin Josephine once saw a ghost, even if I go on to say that I don't "believe in" ghosts, whatever that means, I can't say that ghosts don't exist *in any sense at all*. For there was, in *some* sense, this ghost that Josephine saw. If I do want to insist that ghosts don't exist *in any sense at all*, I can't afford to admit that people ever see them – I shall have to say that they think they do, that they seem to see them, or what not.'

Sense and Sensibilia is based on a series of lectures which Austin began to deliver in 1947, only two years after *An Inspector Calls* was first performed, and it concerns itself with many of the same ideas that obsessed Priestley – ideas about evidence and perception, illusion and disillusionment, communal response and individual belief. (Why the immediate postwar period in Britain should have stimulated such concerns is not a question I plan to take up here, though the answers no doubt go some way towards explaining why Daldry's choice of a 1945 setting is so effective.) When Austin addresses the subject of ghosts, he does so as part of his effort to break down philosophy's false dichotomy between 'material objects' and 'sense data'. Citing a list of things that includes 'people, people's voices, rivers, mountains, flames, rainbows, shadows, pictures on the screen at the cinema, pictures in books or hung on walls, vapours, gases', Austin astutely comments: 'Are these all "material" things? If not, exactly which are not, and exactly why?' What is the difference, he wants to know, between having 'evidence' that something exists and having seen it? He challenges the philosophical notion of 'perceiving indirectly', asking: 'Does it, or should it, cover the telephone, for instance?' And what, he wonders, counts as an 'illusion' as opposed to a normal part of visible reality? 'Is the cinema a case of illusion? . . . One might as well ask whether producing a photograph is producing an illusion – which would plainly be just silly.'

Of course, that is exactly what the Birlings *do* ask about the photograph, or photographs, that Inspector Goole produces as 'evidence' of their crime against Eva Smith. The elder Birlings, in particular, are such fanatical empiricists that they want to divide everything into the solidly demonstrable and the patently dis-cardable. There is no middle ground in their system for the realm of the merely perceivable – a realm in which they, as theatrical characters, happen to reside. Only their children argue that speech and emotion can have their own form of credibility. 'I remember what he said,' Sheila recalls, 'how he looked, and what he made me feel.' Eric points out: 'It's still the same rotten story whether it's been told to a police inspector or to somebody else ... And I still feel the same about it.' Theatre, they imply, is also a part of reality, and what we jointly agree we have seen or heard cannot subsequently be categorized as non-existent. If revela-tions that bear on our lives have been made, we can't efface them by resorting to claims about 'delusions' or 'illusions'.

Such claims are themselves distinct from one another, as Austin points out in his discussion of ghosts. 'Some people think of seeing ghosts as a case of something being conjured up, per-haps by the disordered nervous system of the victim; so in their view seeing ghosts is a case of delusion,' he remarks. 'But other people have the idea that what is called seeing ghosts is a case of being taken in by shadows, perhaps, or reflections, or a trick of the light – that is, they assimilate the case in their minds to illu-sion.' Some people might be tempted to see going to the theatre as 'being taken in by shadows' ('Nothing but an elaborate sell', as Mr Birling says), but more sophisticated thinkers like J. L. Austin and Sheila Birling are likely to view it differently. Theatrical characters, however imaginary, have their own kind of reality, just as the figures in dreams do. 'Does the dreamer see illusions? Does he have delusions?' Austin asks rhetorically. 'Neither; dreams are *dreams*.' The dream is, in fact, a very good analogy for the kind of theatrical production Daldry has created here – a production in which the never-fully-living and the not-yet-born, the silent and the vocal, the claustrophobically cosy interior and the threatening outer world, are all pressed together in a single continuum.

One of the paradoxes of theatre is that, like a dream, it is both pointedly meaningful and open to various interpretations, at once all intention and all chance. Priestley expresses one side of this truth when he says in his 1947 book, *Theatre Outlook*:

> In a good theatrical production we are offered a piece of life so shaped and coloured and contrived that everything in it, down to the smallest detail, is significant. In this tiny world, artfully created by the Theatre, chaos and chance and the meaningless have been abolished. The shape and colour of a room, the way the light falls through the window, the choice of furnishings . . . a startled look, a cough, a turn of the head, none of these is accidental and each has its own significance. For two or three hours everything offered to our eyes and ears is exquisitely contrived to achieve meaning and purpose.

I saw exactly how this operated when I watched Daldry and his team polish the New York production. Each detail, as Priestley suggested, had its own significance. For instance, every visual element onstage, from the creaseless trousers worn by the Edwardian men to the Inspector's 1940s-vintage wrist-watch, had been selected by Ian MacNeil for its period accuracy; even the pictures on the wall *inside* the tiny house, which were mainly invisible to the audience, fitted their era. In a similarly perfectionist mode, Stephen Warbeck timed each note of the live orchestra's music to underlie, counteract, or emphasize the specific moments in the dialogue. (This had the added, and beneficial, effect of forcing the actors to use their voices as if they too were instruments in the musical composition.) The lighting designer, Rick Fisher, would move a silent extra six inches upstage so that the light could catch his face in a certain way. Daldry's associate director, Chris Barton, would repeatedly urge

an actor to emphasize an unusual word – the possessive pronoun, say – in a given speech, so as to give the line fresh meaning.
Daldry himself worked over every tone, look, and gesture of the
actors' delivery, making minute changes from one performance
to the next – changes that, as I could see from the audiences'
response, made all the difference in the world. And yet, when I
went back to see the play some months later, many of these little
details had been changed (some by the actors, others by the
director), and the production was none the less completely
pleasing. The specific details both mattered intensely and didn't
matter at all.

Take the example of the rain. When I first entered the Royale
Theater on the day before previews were to begin, the set was
still in a dramatically incomplete state – mainly because Daldry
had decided that he needed more rain in the first scene, so new
gutters consequently had to be installed to hold the increased
run-off. As it turned out, this was an excellent directorial decision, well worth the additional anxiety and expenditure, since
the initial sight and sound of the downpour are key features in
the opening spectacle. This first, hard rain differs noticeably
from the lighter rain that falls in Act Three, after the house has
exploded, when several members of the distraught Birling family
lie or stand about on the stage, shivering under blankets and
coats. Due in part to the misty, evocative lighting, the later rain
has a benedictory quality that is absent from the more elemental
rain of the first act. Since the Birlings are now outdoors rather
than safely within, the second rain falls on rich and poor alike,
softly breaking down barriers that previously seemed solid and
insuperable. It is a classically British, indeed Dickensian rain,
much like the one described towards the end of *Bleak House*:

> I recollect that it was neither night nor day; that morning was
> dawning, but the street-lamps were not yet put out; that the
> sleet was still falling, and that all the ways were deep with it. I
> recollect a few chilled people passing in the streets. I recollect
> the wet house-tops, the clogged and bursting gutters and

water-spouts, the mounds of blackened ice and snow over
which we passed, the narrowness of the courts by which we
went. At the same time I remember, that the poor girl seemed
to be telling her story audibly and plainly in my hearing; that I
could feel her resting on my arm; that the stained house fronts
put on human shapes and looked at me; that great water-gates
seemed to be opening and closing in my head, or in the air;
and that the unreal things were more substantial than the real.

The rain, by the third act, has earned its keep as a central element
in the drama, giving rise to many of the same feelings that are
produced by the assembled silent crowd or the disassembled
house.

And yet the first time I saw *An Inspector Calls*, at the Olivier
Theatre in London, there was no rain. You would think that
such an important, seemingly essential part of the production
could not be eliminated without ruining the whole effect; but
that initial experience of the play delighted me as much as any of
the later ones, and seemed to possess all of the production's
richer undercurrents. I didn't, of course, know what I was
missing, but I certainly didn't feel any kind of lack. This quality
of almost infinite replaceability seems to be true for all sorts of
things in a given production – up to and including the specific
actors. In fact, it is in the nature of theatre, as opposed to film, to
require that its roles be imaginable with other actors. (Stanley
Cavell expresses this with characteristic insight when he says, in
A Pitch of Philosophy, that 'on film the actor is the subject of the
camera, emphasizing that this actor could (have) become other
characters . . . as opposed to theatre's emphasizing that this character could (will) accept other actors.') No one could safely predict which element of *An Inspector Calls* would have to be
removed to make the play a failure – which single alteration
would render it something less than Daldry's essential production. It is this kind of uncertainty, among others, which led J. B.
Priestley to say, 'The success or failure of theatrical production is
largely determined by chance and accident. Theatre people tend

to be superstitious, and I don't blame them. Once through the stage door, you might as well believe in astrology.'

Part of the strength of *An Inspector Calls*, as a play, lies in the way it incorporates this theatrically significant acknowledgment of chance and accident into its very plot. 'If it didn't end tragically, then that's lucky for us,' Sheila says towards the very end. 'But it might have done.' If, as the Inspector says, we are all responsible for each other, 'members of one body', that is in part because we can never know for sure which of our innumerable actions towards other people will have a significant or insignificant effect. All of our gestures, intended and unintended, become part of a 'chain of events', as the Inspector calls the series of misdemeanours leading up to Eva Smith's suicide. One possible response to the complexity of the modern social fabric is to try to disown any responsibility, as Mr Birling does when he points out to the Inspector, in a tone of reasonable argument: 'If we were all responsible for everything that happened to everybody we'd had anything to do with, it would be very awkward, wouldn't it?'

This paralysing awkwardness is one of the central problems addressed in the theatre work of Bertolt Brecht – implicitly in his stark, didactic, purposely alienating pieces of 'epic theatre', and more explicitly in the theoretical works that accompanied them. Because 'people's mutual relations have become harder to disentangle than ever before', Brecht says in *A Short Organum for the Theatre*, the task of modern theatre should be to enable the spectator to step back from his own life – to view even his own time and his own social type as if from a distance. 'If we ensure that our characters on the stage are moved by social impulses and that these differ according to the period, then we make it harder for our spectator to identify himself with them,' Brecht suggests. 'And if we play works dealing with our own time as though they were historical, then perhaps the circumstances under which he himself acts will strike him as equally odd; and this is where the critical attitude begins.'

As these brief quotations indicate, a strong Brechtian flavour infuses both Priestley's script and Daldry's production. A contemporary political commentary set as if in another era; characters who seem primarily 'moved by social impulses' rather than their own idiosyncratic personalities; an emphatically artificial atmosphere that makes it 'harder for our spectator to identify with' those characters – all of these elements are built into *An Inspector Calls*. To the already Brechtian structure provided by Priestley, Daldry has added other 'alienation effects' – Warbeck's music, for instance, which has a quality similar to the 'gestic music' Brecht called forth in his collaborator Kurt Weill. Played by four instruments (piano, percussion, cello, and trumpet), Warbeck's score is a version of what Brecht described as 'so-called "cheap" music', like 'that of the cabaret and the operetta', which at its best 'would have a more or less exactly foreseeable effect on the spectator' and might at times force the actors to 'play *against* the emotion which the music called forth'. As if following Brecht's instructions to the word, Warbeck's live orchestra swells into action whenever the lines of Priestley's dialogue threaten to become smarmy, forcing the actors to emote broadly on what otherwise might have become quietly sentimental speeches.

Another Brechtian strategy is evident in Daldry's shake-up of normal theatrical convention. Even the final curtain isn't 'final', for it comes down too far, dropping to the stage to reveal yet another interior tableau. By jarring us in this way, the director repeatedly reminds us that we are sitting in a theatre rather than spying on a slice of unshaped life. He is aided in this by the patent surrealism of MacNeil's set, a design that exactly fits Brecht's prescription for a structure 'which leads real conduct to acquire an element of "unnaturalness", thus allowing the real motive forces to be shorn of their naturalness and become capable of manipulation'. It is this 'manipulation', this alteration in the spectators' way of viewing their own world, that Brecht is finally after in his dramatic work. 'We need a type of theatre which not only releases the feelings, insights and impulses pos-

sible within the particular historical field of human relations . . . ,'
Brecht says in *A Short Organum*, 'but employs and encourages
those thoughts and feelings which help transform the field itself.'
Not feeling alone, but feeling transmuted by thought into action,
is the aim of Brecht's theatre.

In this, he may well differ from Priestley and Daldry, at least
as they express themselves in *An Inspector Calls*. For one of the
central points of this play (one hesitates for obvious reasons to
say 'its moral', though the term forcefully offers itself for con-
sideration) is that feelings alone can matter, whatever their
effects or non-effects. 'You see, we have to share something,' the
Inspector admonishes Sheila and Gerald. 'If there's nothing else,
we'll have to share our guilt.' At the end of the play, a feeling of
guilt is all that Sheila and Eric want their parents to admit to.
Once exposure and punishment are no longer threatened, the
question of who will be held responsible for Eva Smith's death is
no longer a practical one, but the younger Birlings want it to
remain an emotional one. And due in part to Daldry's pointedly
theatrical strategies – strategies that repeatedly make us consider
our own relation to the characters onstage – we in the audience
are also invited to share in the emotion of guilt, if not in the
burden of responsibility for an impoverished girl's death. In fact,
it is only by separating the two (the guilt and the death) that
Priestley and Daldry can lure us into feeling guilty. For we can
easily insist, as Gerald does, that 'No girl has died today'. Even if
some fictional Eva Smith had died in the play, we could still issue
our protective denial, since we in the audience cannot kill a theatrical character. After all, how can a character who has never
really been 'alive' now be 'dead'? (As Shakespeare has his
Cleopatra say about her rival: '*Can* Fulvia die?') So to make our
guilt feel justified in any real-world sense, Priestley and Daldry
must separate it from any criminally prosecutable responsibility.
We missed out on the responsibility this time: 'If it didn't end
tragically, then that's lucky for us.' But the emotions the play
drew from us were none the less real for all that.

The mistake Plato made, in his attack on drama in particular and the literary arts in general, was to assume that what is made up or fictional has no truth value for our real-world existence, has no bearing *as* truth on what we believe ethically. (Or perhaps this was no mistake, but a conscious deception practised by Plato for his own political purposes, since he clearly believed that the emotions roused by the theatre do have an effect in the world; it was the nature of the effect – its uncontrollability by the State – that he was worried about.) *An Inspector Calls*, in Daldry's production, makes exactly the opposite point: that events which move us, and which subsequently turn out to be imaginary, are not thereby obviated in ethical terms. We can and indeed ought to be stirred emotionally by the exemplary, the fictional, the imaginatively constructed, and such emotions are not themselves non-existent or ignorable. Daldry, in this version of Priestley's play, draws on art's extremely moving capacity to acknowledge its status as artifice, to transcend itself by pointing out its own artfulness as if from real life's point of view. He emphasizes the paradox inherent in dramatic art – that if it tells us it's lying fiction, it seems more true, more a part of the world that we in the audience inhabit. And because such art appears to see itself in *our* terms, it can possibly make us see ourselves in *its* terms. It may, for at least the duration of the performance, cause us to realize the essentially public nature of even our private emotions.

Coming together in a theatre, we are asking to share something with those around us and those onstage – the real bodies and minds that occupy that space for the same two hours we do. However known or unknown they may be to us, these people – actors and audience members alike – become our community for that period of time. We shudder or marvel or laugh in response to them, in unison with them, in opposition to them. To assert that 'If there's nothing else, we'll have to share our guilt' may not be a radical principle in Brechtian terms; but in drastically individualist times such as ours, the insistence that we have to share *anything* with people we don't know is itself a communitarian move.

3 Looking Backwards

When an *An Inspector Calls* opened on Broadway in April 1994, the *New York Times* critic David Richards praised the production as 'a steadily engrossing drama and, more significantly, one of the more astonishing spectacles on Broadway today'. (He wasn't wild about the play itself, though: headlined 'Transforming 1946 Stale Into 1994 Stunning', Richards's review disparagingly compared Priestley's script to both Euripides and Rodgers & Hammerstein, who were also playing on Broadway at the time.) Vincent Canby followed up the daily *Times* review with an even more enthusiastic article in the Sunday 'Arts and Leisure' section. 'Not since the arrival of *Angels in America*,' wrote Canby, 'has Broadway had a nonmusical event as seriously exhilarating as Stephen Daldry's re-creation of his London hit *An Inspector Calls . . . An Inspector Calls* has a lot of everything, but most of all it has the brilliant, restless imaginations of Mr Daldry, the director, and Ian MacNeil, who's responsible for the hallucinogenic production design.' Such reviews in turn generated ticket sales, so that *Inspector* was still playing to nearly full houses eight months later – indeed, it was the only nonmusical play launched in the spring of 1994 that was still on Broadway by the beginning of 1995.

All the reviews and most of the accompanying publicity singled out the spectacular set, occasionally even at the expense of the rest of the production. 'Daldry's production is glib but not probing: the substance and the style are at odds,' asserted John Lahr of the *New Yorker*, in one of the very few negative reviews. 'The theme may be one of separation of rich from poor, but the production goes to spectacular lengths to stand out.' In fact, said Lahr, while Priestley's initial purpose in writing the play may have been to sell socialism, Daldry's essential purpose in restaging the play had been 'to sell the idea of *himself* to the British public'. But such *ad hominem* animosity was rarer in America than it had been in Britain (what was the point of attacking Daldry, after all, in a country where no one knew who he was?), and most critics seemed to share the viewpoint of Steven Winn, who wrote in the *San Francisco Chronicle*: 'In what may be the most exciting new piece of theatre to reach Broadway this season, British *wunderkind* director Stephen Daldry has transformed a 50-year-old melodramatic thriller into a thoroughly contemporary Expressionist nightmare . . . An astonishing scenic coup gets the production under way and sets the show's dark and desperate tone.' Even *Time* magazine, second-guessing the Tony Awards in the weeks before their 12 June announcement, suggested that 'the front runner for best revival and best set – a category rarely won by a straight play – is the London import *An Inspector Calls*, a drawing-room melo-drama exploded into a streetscape of urban despair'.

In the event, Daldry's production won the Tony for best revival, as well as for best featured actress, best lighting, and best directing, but the set lost out to Bob Crowley's lavish design for *Carousel* (newly staged by another British *wun-derkind*, Nicholas Hytner, at Lincoln Center). When Stephen Daldry – tall, pale, short-haired, tuxedo-clad, and looking even younger than his thirty-four years – got up on the stage of the Gershwin Theater to accept his award for directing, he thanked everyone connected with the production (backers, lead actors, extras, and even the children) and then singled out each of his collaborators. 'I am triply indebted to Ian MacNeil,' he con-cluded, 'who is my designer, my best friend, and, indeed, my lover.' The 'indeed' was pure England, but Daldry's choice of the word 'lover' (in place of the far more generic and less graphic term 'partner', now commonly used in Britain) showed he had his eye on the American public – not just the Broadway professionals in the theatre itself, but the millions presumed to be out there in television-land. As usual, Daldry wanted to engage his viewers in two potentially conflicting ways: he

wanted to draw them in by using language they could understand, and he also wanted to shake them up a bit.

The Tony ceremony, complete with tuxedo and TV, might
serve as a blatant emblem for the distance Stephen Daldry had
travelled since his first London production at the Old Red Lion
pub in Islington only five years earlier. In 1989 Daldry was
working in a restaurant to support himself, having come to
London to seek his theatrical fortune and to live with Ian
MacNeil. A man named Andrew Lucre, founder of an *ad hoc*
theatre operation called Filthy Lucre, enlisted Daldry to direct a
play by Ödön von Horváth, an expressionist Austro-Hungarian
playwright – roughly contemporary with Brecht – who had
recently been imported into Britain through Christopher
Hampton's translation of *Tales from the Vienna Woods*. Most of
von Horváth's work was still untranslated, so Lucre introduced
Daldry (who didn't read German) to Meredith Oakes (who did),
and she helped him select *Judgement Day*. She was planning to
do the translation as well, but then she and Daldry discovered
there was already quite a good one by Renata and Martin Esslin;
so instead she sat in on rehearsals, an open copy of the German
version on her lap, and called attention to places where the translation didn't fully convey the meaning. (As it turned out, Oakes
also had another reason for being present: Daldry ended up
using her daughter Chloë Sutcliffe as an actor in the part of the
Child.) *Judgement Day* opened at the Old Red Lion on 31 May
1989 and ran until 24 June – a brief life, but not unusually so for
the unpaid world of London fringe theatre.

More than one critic instantly compared the newly produced
von Horváth play to Dürrenmatt's *The Visit*, which it predated
by twenty years. This makes sense, since both plays centrally
involve a railway station, both focus on questions of individual
moral guilt and communal responsibility, and both are obviously
allegories for the social events of their times: the Nazi takeover
in von Horváth's case, the postwar 'economic miracle' in
Dürrenmatt's. It's also true that both plays were performed on
the London fringe within a year of each other – *The Visit* had

been revived in 1988 by Théâtre de Complicité – and that coincidence, more than anything else, probably accounts for the
critics' comparisons. (In what follows, I am uncomfortably
aware of the fact that in order to reconstruct the history of
Daldry's work I have had to rely heavily on theatrical reviews. I
didn't see any of Daldry's productions before *An Inspector
Calls*, and since I wish to write about performances rather than
scripts, the written versions of the plays can take me only a short
distance. But given the proven unreliability of the critics, both
collectively and individually, my reliance on reviews is necessarily dubious – inspiring doubt in my readers, I hope, as well as
myself.)

The plot of *Judgement Day* involves a station-master named
Thomas Hudetz who, briefly distracted by his flirtation with a
young girl ('a very young girl', as Daldry described it to me
many years after the production), makes a terrible mistake: he
fails to change the signal when an express train is approaching,
and as a result there is a fatal crash. Hudetz is taken into custody
for four months but is eventually acquitted after the young girl,
Anna, commits perjury to protect him (and herself). The station-
master's wife – variously described by the British critics as 'crab-
bily jealous', 'savagely jealous', 'embittered', 'barren', and
'beastly' – has seen the whole incident and tries to tell the truth,
but no one believes her; Hudetz is released and given a hero's
welcome. Anna, however, cannot tolerate the prickings of her
conscience and eventually arranges for Hudetz to meet her
under the railway viaduct, where he flies into a frenzy and kills
her. The townspeople viciously seize on one blameworthy party
after another – first Hudetz's wife, then the station-master himself – all the while working overtime to suppress their collective
knowledge of their own sin and culpability. At the play's end,
Anna and the engine driver, both victims of Hudetz's actions,
return from the dead to speak to him; Anna urges him not to
commit suicide, while the engineer jokingly praises the ease of
existence in the afterlife.

Part of what one accumulates, when one follows a single

director's career, is a body of dramatic work that is in some ways unwittingly coherent. If the director has good taste – and if, like Daldry, he is particularly interested in unearthing gems no one else has found – the collection is likely to offer a theatrical education in itself. One English critic, comparing Stephen Daldry to a popular TV sleuth, characterized him as 'the Lovejoy of British theatre', 'a canny antiques dealer' who 'picks up other people's disregarded tat for a song and then performs a brilliant restoration job that reveals the work to be far more valuable than anyone previously suspected'. At the root of this metaphor lies the acknowledgment that the trick can only be performed on inherently worthwhile material. But value is relative as well as absolute, the result of connective importance as well as inherent beauty. If you consider as a whole the series of plays Daldry has chosen to direct in the last eight or ten years, you will find a frequent return to certain preoccupations and obsessions that bear directly on his conception of theatre. Over the decade, as these preoccupations have overlapped with and enriched each other, they have become more visible, more accessible, more finely tuned in performance. Many of them, however, were already evident in that early production of *Judgement Day*.

For instance, a number of the questions at the heart of the Broadway production of *An Inspector Calls* – How much should we be blamed for the unexpectedly disastrous effects of our actions, especially when our motives are comparatively innocent or at least ordinary? How does individual guilt become collective responsibility? Who is on trial in any given case, and who are the judges and witnesses? What is the connection between our moment in history and the one onstage, between our geographical setting and the playwright's? How is it that tragic events sometimes lend themselves to wry or humorous treatment? How do theatrical characters resemble ghosts? Are the emotions roused in us by fictional or allegorical plots *real* emotions? How well can we ever know the people around us? And why is theatre uniquely situated to explore questions like these? – are exactly those raised in Daldry's 1989 production of

Judgement Day. The concerns were there in the script, but Daldry emphasized them in performance, just as he was later to do with the Priestley play.

Kate Kellaway, writing in the *Observer* about the Old Red Lion production, noticed something in the directorial manner that was to become characteristic: she saw in 'Stephen Daldry's stunning production' what she described as 'a dark wit'. 'Hudetz's neighbours,' she elaborated, 'believing him innocent, throw a party in which they impersonate a train and come chugging towards him, each carrying a lit candle – like his conscience on the move.' From that single sentence, one can almost reconstruct the whole mood of the production. And along with this mixture of tones, this 'dark wit', goes a mixture of acting styles. As early as 1989, Daldry had already arrived at the disjunctive ensemble technique that marked all his subsequent work. The acting in *Judgement Day*, according to Michael Billington of the *Guardian*, 'veers plausibly between Realism and Expressionism' – or, as Antonia Denford said in *City Limits*, 'Grotesquery merges with bleak realism.' The negative reviews noticed the same thing but read it differently: 'Stephen Daldry seems unsure whether to play for laughs or tragedy,' complained one critic, and hence 'the actors inhabit their own world without ever bringing the play to a cohesive whole'. A few reviewers felt 'assaulted' by the range of striking theatrical effects ('the relentless clang of cowbells, unmodulated shouting from actors standing a hair's breadth away, being blinded by a naked bulb dangled in front of the eye and, to top it all in the last scene, being asphyxiated by billows of dry ice'), whereas others saw this total immersion as part of the point: 'you are close enough to study the perjured faces of Hudetz . . . and Anna', Kate Kellaway commented approvingly.

As with Daldry's later productions, the imaginatively surreal set – a high, diagonally placed screen punctured with peepholes and covered with clocks, wheels, tableware, broken glass, clothing, tools, and other debris of daily life – was integral to the tone of the play. 'Claudia Mayer's design is superb if at first puzzling,' wrote Georgina Brown in the *Independent*. 'All becomes horrifyingly clear as, with a compulsion as unrestrainable as the train itself, the scene moves to a climax in which the express crashes, killing eighteen people. Throughout the play the crazy screen, to which the characters are oblivious, sustains the idea of lives thrown into chaos by the collision.' Even at this early stage of his career, Daldry was able to guide his designer towards a startling set 'to which the characters are oblivious' – a mode which describes their relationship to their own surroundings but also (as in *An Inspector Calls*) to the ultimate significance of their own actions. And, as in his later productions, music was integral to the piece; more than one reviewer of *Judgement Day* commented on the 'throbbing cello' that 'hauntingly evokes the advancing train'. The composer of that cello music was Stephen Warbeck, who had been working with Daldry ever since they collaborated on a production of *The Canterbury Tales* several years earlier.

For Stephen Daldry did not, contrary to the impression conveyed by the London press, spring fullblown as a director from the brow of the Old Red Lion. 'I had done a lot of regional theatre,' Daldry told me of the years between his graduation from Sheffield University in 1982 and his first London production in 1989. 'I was doing all sorts of things – dozens of productions – and we never got any national reviews. And here was something I'd done essentially in my lunch hours, and the *Guardian*, the *Observer*, all that lot were there.'

The enthusiastic reviews of *Judgement Day* were Daldry's springboard to his first real job in London, as the artistic director of the Gate Theatre in Notting Hill. But the skills that enabled him to make something of that job – to convert the Gate into 'potentially the most interesting theatre in London', as Michael Rutherford of the *Financial Times* called it in 1991, less than two years into Daldry's régime – were honed during the years in the hinterlands. And not just the hinterlands of England. After getting his degree in English and drama at Sheffield, and after entering and then dropping out of an acting programme in London, Daldry joined an Italian circus, Il Circo di Nando

Orfei, where he apprenticed himself to the clown Elder Milletti. 'It was the most deeply unfunny period of my life,' he commented to a London journalist about his ten months as a clown. To me, he confessed that he was both painfully lonely and terribly distressed by the personal circumstances of his life in the circus. Milletti and his lover (a pair described by the generally open-minded Daldry as 'sexually very weird') first tried to draw him into their private games and then, when he resisted, treated him as a despised outcast. He remembers walking through small Italian towns and being mocked by children on the streets who, recognizing him as Olive Oyl from the circus routine, would call out, 'Olivia! O-leev-i-a!'

'I spent a lot of that time in Catholic churches,' Daldry told me at our first meeting. 'If you were Catholic, that gave you an excuse to get away from the circus.' But was he, in fact, Catholic? When I later returned to the question of his religious convictions, Daldry said of that period, 'It wasn't so much coming to the Catholic Church as being welcomed into a community of ritual.'

Once back in England, the community of ritual he sought out and found was that of the more conventional theatre. From 1984 to 1986 he was artistic director of a small group called the Metro Theatre Company, which he had co-founded. One of his old friends and eventual colleagues, Stella Hall, still remembers his early production of *The Ragged-Trousered Philanthropist*, a new play by Stephen Lowe. 'There's quite a lot of that kind of theatre around, in pubs and so forth, and most of it isn't very good,' she told me. 'But this was a very grown-up production – really high production values. It was clearly something special. He was being singled out as a director to watch.' Soon he was taken on as an Arts Council trainee director at Sheffield's Crucible Theatre, where he directed such plays as *Camaraderie, Mozart and Salieri*, and, in 1986, *The Canterbury Tales* on which he met Stephen Warbeck. What was Daldry like then, at the age of twenty-six? 'He seemed very sweet,' recalled Warbeck, who is seven years older than Daldry. 'Open to lots of suggestions, asking a lot of questions. Innocent. Not innocent in a naïve way, but open and not cynical.'

'How is he different from that now?' I asked in 1994.

'He's much, much, much more confident now,' Warbeck replied. 'He feels very unawed by the people he works with, or the material. Not that he was awed then, but he was just more youthful.'

Youthful, perhaps, but also very productive. As Associate Artist at the Crucible in 1987 and 1988, he presented a studio season of new plays. During those years he also directed *Cider with Rosie, It's a Bit Lively Outside*, and (for the Liverpool Playhouse) *Rat in the Skull.* Even as a freelance director working on assignment, he could turn routine material into something much more startling. Ian MacNeil, who first met Stephen Daldry in 1988, was struck by this unusual quality in his work. 'I'd seen two shows of his, *Huckleberry Finn* and *Of Mice and Men.* He did them back to back in Manchester' (where MacNeil was living at the time). 'The *Huckleberry Finn* was very strange – it was kind of a bad adaptation that got foisted on him. But the raft was this sheet suspended on four points, so that when it was lifted up it swayed in the air. I thought that was interesting. And the scenes on the raft between the two of them were improvised. You couldn't really say *why* those scenes were unusual when you watched them, but you could feel that they were. It was just a naff musical,' commented MacNeil (who, though American, chose a distinctively British piece of slang to express the production's lack of sophistication), 'and he was irreverent about the form. Mostly, I liked how he messed about with the form. He didn't respect the Christmas-show-for-kids convention of it, and he did it completely unselfconsciously.' About the *Of Mice and Men* production, MacNeil mainly recalls being intrigued by the heroine's entrance. 'He had her entering from way up above, at the proscenium level. With a romantic dress. And there was a crackly radio on. Again, it was irreverent to the form – going against the received ideas of gritty, 1930s, *small* theatricality for a work like that, and making it hugely theatrical.'

Taking the normally small and making it huge became Stephen Daldry's trademark during his years at the Gate Theatre, which lasted from 1989 to 1992. 'If Stephen Daldry were to enter a competition to write the Lord's Prayer on the back of a postage stamp, it's a fair bet he'd carry off first prize,' wrote Michael Arditti in his *Evening Standard* review of Daldry's final production at the Gate; '. . . his current production of Tirso de Molina's masterpiece marshals almost thirty actors on its tiny stage.' A member of the audience who attended Daldry's first Gate production in March 1990 apparently commented to her seatmate that 'Stephen Daldry's production was the best use of a small space she had ever seen', according to Michael Billington's review in the *Guardian*. (Billington agreed with her, but went on to point out that 'his revival of *Judgement Day* at the Old Red Lion runs close'.) 'The stage seems to get bigger with successive productions,' noted Malcolm Rutherford of the *Financial Times*, midway through Daldry's period at the Gate, 'and the room for the audience smaller.'

Part of the reason for this illusion was that the Gate was forced to turn away increasing numbers of disappointed ticket seekers every season. There were only fifty-six seats in the tiny theatre, which was (and still is) located over a pub in Notting Hill Gate, and by the end of Daldry's tenure there were hundreds of people trying to get into every performance. Each production ran for only three or four weeks – the Tirso de Molina masterpiece that Arditti praised, for instance, began on 16 November 1991 and was over by 7 December – in large part because the actors, who all worked for free, could only afford to commit themselves to an eight-week rehearsal-and-production period. Nor were the actors the only unpaid labour: designers, lighting technicians, musicians, and all other freelancers worked entirely without salary. 'I would probably get about fifty quid for expenses – no, more like thirty quid,' recalls Stephen Warbeck, who did the music for all four plays that Daldry directed at the Gate. But though he had to donate his own labour as well as contrive a full evening's music for just £30, Warbeck

remembers the projects at the Gate with enormous fondness.
'The larger the institution,' he pointed out to me, 'the more conventional the framework is, and you have to take everyone's
departments into account – the actors want to act, they don't
want to be shouting over the music. But if you're a tiny little
fringe venue, they'll accept the lunacy of playing so loud you can
barely hear them. At the Gate, it would be very easy for me to
speak directly to the actors and even take over a rehearsal.'

In fact, a chief characteristic of a theatre operation like the
Gate was that everyone got involved in every task. Stephen
Daldry (who, like the other paid staff, received a salary of £100 a
week – not enough to live on, even in 1989) was not only the
artistic director; he was also the chief financial and development
officer, the chief public-relations person, and the chief
handyman. 'One of my great memories of Stephen,' remarked
Gaynor Macfarlane, who arrived at the Gate during Stephen
Daldry's directorship and stayed on as literary manager after he
left, 'is of him at half-past six with a Hoover in his hand,
Hoovering the seats on the night of the first preview. He's very
much the sort of leader that mucks in.'

I was speaking to Macfarlane in the offices of the Gate
Theatre, which still, in October 1994, looked very much as they
had when Daldry left them. (The theatre itself, on the other
hand, had doubled in size, from 56 to 120 seats; the remodelling
was accomplished in 1993 with money brought in by Daldry.)
Perhaps the word 'offices' conveys too exalted an impression.
The space occupied by Macfarlane, her two co-workers, and
their drop-in visitors was really one workroom about the size of
a school classroom; one narrow closet-like room filled with
desks, files, and a couple of telephones; and one minimalist bathroom that seemed to double as a kitchen, dressing room, and
bicycle storage area. This headquarters, across the street from
the pub-theatre, was where Daldry had planned and produced
three seasons of world theatre. The Gate at that time did no
British theatre: 'There was a kind of generalized international
policy before,' Macfarlane told me, 'and Stephen tightened it

up.' Nor were these international plays simply dredged up from an existing but out-of-fashion repertory: the usual practice was for the Gate to commission a new English translation (often of previously untranslated work) and present the play's British première. Daldry's own projects had included Ödön von Horváth's *Figaro Gets Divorced*, two plays by Marieluise Fleisser (*Pioneers in Ingolstadt* and *Purgatory in Ingolstadt*, both co-directed with Annie Castledine), and Tirso de Molina's *Damned for Despair*; and these were each embedded in a full season of four to six plays.

I thought I discerned a pattern whereby Daldry, in his own directing, alternated roughly between plays written by men and plays written by women. Was this, I asked Macfarlane, a conscious choice? She seemed a bit taken aback by the question, and paused a moment before issuing her gentle correction. 'I think he goes with the playwright rather than the gender. As I hope I do too. The work has to come first, artistically. If you're a nonprofit company, the work is foremost.'

The plays Stephen Daldry directed during his years at the Gate all had artistic merit, certainly, but something else distinguished them as well. Every one of them combined the tragic and the comic, the elevated and the mundane; and every one examined the fate of individual characters trapped within the toils of social or historical processes. Most of all, the four plays Daldry chose to do had a kind of wildness in common – something unconventional in their structure, combined with something weird or offbeat in their dialogue – that left room for his directorial sense of play. Except for Tirso de Molina's *Damned for Despair* (which is indeed a masterpiece), none of the plays Daldry directed feels complete on the page: as you read each one, you can only vaguely sense how well it might work on the stage. And even *Damned for Despair*, with its complicated oppositions and dour jokes, cries out for a vital production to bring it fully to life. They are all, that is, extremely stageworthy plays.

They also enabled Daldry to continue exploring some of the preoccupations about politics, character, and theatrical form already evident in *Judgement Day*. From one von Horváth play to another seems an easy step, and by this time one might argue that Daldry had begun to influence von Horváth – at least in his English incarnation – almost as much as von Horváth was influencing Daldry. (The translator of *Figaro Gets Divorced*, Ian Huish, explicitly thanks Stephen Daldry for 'invaluable contributions to the translation'.) But *Figaro Gets Divorced* is a much more comic and digressive play than *Judgement Day*, which, as reviewers noted, moves towards its shocking moments with the velocity of an express train. Borrowing the Beaumarchais characters who had already intrigued Mozart and Rossini, von Horváth takes Figaro and Susanne, Count and Countess Almaviva, to the period just after an anti-aristocratic revolution from which the Count and his dependants have recently fled. They are all impoverished exiles now, and Figaro soon abandons his erstwhile employers to start a barber's shop. After the divorce heralded in the title, Susanne eventually returns to work unpaid for the by-now-widowed Count, whereas Figaro goes back to their native country and joins the by-now-corrupted revolution. In the end they all get back together, but not without a great deal of strain, and the 'happy' ending is overshadowed by an eerie sense that the whole cycle could start all over again at any minute.

Like von Horváth's play, the two Fleisser works with which Daldry followed it up were products of the highly politicized German-language theatre of the 1920s and 1930s – a theatre which, even when it was not written by Brecht himself, seemed heavily influenced by Brecht's principles. Marieluise Fleisser was in fact a protégé of Brecht: it was he who arranged for the first performance of *Purgatory in Ingolstadt* in 1926 and who then encouraged her to write *Pioneers in Ingolstadt*. But if Ödön von Horváth sounds, as a playwright, remarkably close to Bertolt Brecht – especially in terms of his dark humour, his interest in the politics of class, his con-artist male characters, and his often more admirable, smarter, and more practical females – Fleisser is something much stranger. The two Ingolstadt plays are obsessed

with small-town Catholicism and its restrictive effects on individual lives, abetted by the straitjacketing attempts of families
and other groups to control their less conventional members.
Both plays feature disjunctive and cacophonous dialogue;
Purgatory chronicles the futile attempts of rebellious adolescents
to break free of a stifling group morality, while *Pioneers* focuses
on amoral young soldiers and their maid–servant girlfriends. The
mood of both 'comedies' is pessimistic – not in a mature, politically considered sense, but in a manner true to the teenagers who
are their major characters.

Though they seemed a natural continuation of his involvement in expressionist theatre, the Fleisser productions represented something of a departure from Stephen Daldry's usual
directing methods. He may have earned a reputation as a collaborative director, but this was the first (and, to date, the only)
time in his adult career when he actually co-directed a play with
an equal partner. Reflecting back on the experience in 1997,
Annie Castledine recalled how the partnership came about:
'We'd known each other a very long time,' she pointed out;
Daldry had been at Sheffield when she was directing in Derby,
and 'he came to see almost all the work I did'. After he moved to
the Gate, he happened to read the Fleisser plays in an old translation, and then he learned that Castledine had commissioned
new English translations of them. 'He came to me and said,
"Aren't they wonderful? Let us do them, shall we?" And we
decided to co-direct both of them, rather than each directing
one,' Castledine noted, 'because we both wanted to be in the
same rehearsal room for a long, long time.'

The results apparently lived up to expectations. 'The work was
incredibly harmonious and and creative. What was so wonderful
was the lack of paranoia, the trust. You've got to get a picture of
the rehearsal room,' she stressed. 'Two chairs, side by side. He
would walk forward, or I would, and then we would direct for as
long as we had an idea, and then when we had run out of things to
say or were tired, we would walk backward and the other would
come forward. The baton was handed on by osmosis.' She

remembered in particular one moment when Daldry's encouragement had been crucial to her. Having come up with an idea that didn't seem to be working, she was just about to give up on it: 'I was starting to walk backward, and I heard his voice. "Carry on, it's a good idea." So I did, and it was.' Part of the reason the Fleisser productions turned out so well, she felt, was that the cast of fourteen never sensed any discontinuity between one director's ideas and the other's. The dialogue may have been cacophonous, but the directors 'seemed to speak in one voice'.

In addition to providing him with a truly collaborative experience, the Fleisser plays gave Stephen Daldry a chance to explore the double or triple time-scheme that he was to bring to fruition in his production of *An Inspector Calls*. That is, each of those plays actually called into being two separate historical moments: the between-the-wars Europe in which it was written and the 1990s England in which it was performed. Having chosen the plays in part for their political content, Daldry and Castledine made an effort to remind their audiences that the politics displayed in them were neither distant nor dead. For instance, they had the small-town Catholics in the Fleisser plays speak in Irish accents – a touch that struck some reviewers as a sign of narrow-minded prejudice, but which others praised as 'a shrewd way of evoking a closed-off Catholic community' and a means of 'mediating between 20s Germany and a modern British audience'.

As an answer to those who might have accused him of being anti-Catholic in the Fleisser plays, Daldry offered the spiritually and theatrically rich *Damned for Despair*. Performed as part of the Gate's season of Spanish Golden Age drama, along with pieces by Lope de Vega and Calderón de la Barca, this seventeenth-century Tirso de Molina play pits a religious hermit, Paulo, against a Neapolitan criminal, Enrico. The Devil, disguised as an angel, visits Paulo and tells him that if he wants to know whether he's destined to go to heaven or hell, he need only observe Enrico, whose fate he will share in the afterlife. Learning that Enrico is a common criminal, Paulo despairs and decides to give up the religious life: if he's going to hell anyway, he reasons, he might as well enjoy the pleasure of being bad *now*. Enrico, on the other hand, has one soft spot, his ageing father, and eventually his self-sacrificing kindness to the old man brings about his last-minute spiritual salvation. One of the ironies of the play is thus that the Devil has, as usual, lied – Enrico and Paulo were *not* destined to share the same fate after all. Another and larger irony is the fact that this lofty spiritual dilemma is made accessible to us not only through the earthiness of the dialogue (the play features Sancho-Panza-like sidekicks for the two opposing heroes), but also through the analogies between God-given and playwright-driven determinism. As characters in a play which has already been composed by Tirso de Molina, Enrico and Paulo are both stuck with their pre-assigned fates; and yet as figures on the stage before us, they seem to be choosing their respective futures even as we watch.

For Meredith Oakes, who had followed Stephen Daldry's development since his first production in London, Tirso de Molina's play represented a high point in his achievement as a director. 'My favourite, my very favourite, is *Damned for Despair*,' she said in 1994, when asked which of Daldry's productions she had liked best. 'You can always rely with him on getting tremendous darkness and excitement, but that play, because it had a huge moral theme, had resonance beyond the theatrical effects, which were themselves very striking. It used that kind of demonic side to him, but it wasn't limited to that.' Gaynor Macfarlane, who worked on the play with Daldry, felt that *Damned for Despair* had been converted in production into something other than a work about Catholic doctrine. 'They made it a personal drama rather than a religious one,' she said, 'the conflict between the priest and Enrico.' She also described the staged version as 'very funny. Very contemporary in places as well.'

Perhaps no production of Daldry's before or since has received the kind of uniformly positive reviews garnered by *Damned for Despair*. In 'one of the finest productions of the year', Michael Arditti wrote for the *Evening Standard*, Daldry had demonstrated a 'vibrant' directorial style 'in which the archaic and the anachronistic mix'. Stephen Daldry 'has achieved a fiery production', commented the *Independent*; 'the quality of his production is confident, elated and expansive', said the *Observer*; and 'the theatricality is stunning', suggested the *Jewish Chronicle*. Michael Billington – who thought so well of the play (or of his review of the play, or both) that he included his *Damned for Despair* notice in his book *One Night Stands* – called Daldry's production 'another scorcher', urging his readers to 'get thee to the Gate' and praising the director for 'deploying a cast of thirty with military skill' as he 'cunningly mixes histor- ical reference with modern relevance'.

Almost every review of *Damned for Despair* mentioned two unrelated points: the fact that Stephen Daldry had just been named the next artistic director of the Royal Court Theatre ('director-designate', 'heir apparent', and 'young pretender' were some of the terms used); and the fact that the set for this production was spectacular. Billington referred to it as 'an extra- ordinary set: a red, multi-panelled revolving wall that serves as mountain or prison and that spins round to become brothel or torture-chamber'. Praising 'the inventive set', Mark Lawson from the *Independent* noted that 'a revolving steel drum, made of sliding panels, fills the stage, twisting and splitting to alter location or give a glimpse of hanging children or a charging army'. (He went on to add: 'Daldry builds these stage pictures and marshals thirty actors in a space where most people would struggle to park a Mini.') Other critics cited the production's 'lavish visual boldness (especially some splendid tableaux echoing Renaissance paintings)' and variously described the revolving set as 'a giant oildrum' and a '*Theatrum Mundi*'.

In all the other productions Daldry had directed at the Gate, the designer had been Ian MacNeil. But on *Damned for Despair* it was Tim Hatley. (Apparently Ian MacNeil was busy with another assignment at the time – 'a money job', as Gaynor Macfarlane put it.) MacNeil had earned equally strong praise on *his* designs for Daldry. Reviewers of *Figaro Gets Divorced* singled out the flexible set – flaking plaster and a wall of old, chipped mirrors – that served in turn to establish a once-elegant hotel room, a barber's shop, a forest, a nightclub, and a castle; and one critic wrote about the *Ingolstadt* set, 'Designer Ian MacNeil must, you fancy, have a lucrative sideline turning box-rooms into adventure playgrounds.' But the point was that, forced to do without MacNeil, Daldry could evoke similarly imaginative and startling work from another designer.

I got some sense of how and why the design elements meshed so fully with Daldry's conception of each play when I talked to Ian MacNeil about the development of *An Inspector Calls*. The set designs for the von Horváth and Fleisser plays at the Gate were not the first work MacNeil had done for Daldry; they had begun their theatrical partnership with a first attempt at the Priestley play – a kind of proto-*Inspector* – done as a freelance job in York. (This was in 1989, shortly after the two had begun living together: 'We started a relationship before we worked together,' MacNeil noted.) Daldry himself had already mentioned this production to me, referring to a 1947 version of *Inspector* that had apparently been performed by British troops in North Africa. It was this version that got him thinking about the dual time frame he eventually inserted into the play.

'I remember Stephen reading the play every day for about three months,' MacNeil told me. 'He was unemployed at the time. And he was reading everything he could get his hands on *about* the play.' He was also reading everything he could find by J. B. Priestley: novels, plays, radio talks. 'But mainly he just read the play over and over. And then in one flash he got the whole idea: the idea of the house. Well, he got the initial idea, but it took about a month of me bullying him for him to say what would *happen* in the house.' So the incredible set, the 'hallucinogenic' design praised by all the New York critics, was really Daldry's as much as MacNeil's? 'The look was mine, but the idea was his,' said MacNeil. 'The idea of being inside and outside a house, and the idea of the house tipping up, were his. I thought it was vulgar at first, but it works.'

The York production contained many of the elements that would ultimately appear in the London *Inspector*, but neither Daldry nor MacNeil viewed it as a completely successful rendering. Still, they filed it away in their minds as a respectable attempt. Then, in 1992, Stephen Daldry suddenly found himself with time on his hands and an offer to direct a play at the National Theatre. He had been named director-designate of the Royal Court, but Max Stafford-Clark, the outgoing artistic director, was not scheduled to leave until 1993; meanwhile, though he shared responsibility for both daily operations and theatrical productions, Daldry was less than fully occupied. It was during this period that he turned back to Priestley's play.

Daldry's *Inspector Calls* may have been embryonically present in the earlier production, but it wasn't until he brought it to the National that it really came to life. What kinds of change, I wondered, took place between York and London? 'This one was much more fully realized,' said Rick Fisher, who did the lighting for both versions. 'It had rain. It had other new details, lots of little things. And I think the leading actors were better: Barbara Leigh-Hunt, Richard Pascoe, Kenneth Cranham. I don't even remember the guy who played the Inspector in York.' But the younger actors at the National – those who played Sheila and Eric Birling – were the same people who had performed those roles in Daldry's York production three years earlier. 'It's very typical of Stephen,' Fisher commented, 'to be loyal to the people he works with.'

An Inspector Calls, which had its première at the National Theatre in late 1992, went on to become the kind of success most directors only dream of; and Daldry followed it up a year later with another prizewinning production, this time of Sophie Treadwell's *Machinal*. 'Stephen was supposed to be director-designate and watch Max for eighteen months,' one Royal Court employee told me. But even as he was producing and directing at the Royal Court, 'he went off and did *Inspector* and *Machinal*, and in the process became world famous and changed the course of his own life and that of the Royal Court. And it was all due to that chance arrangement. It's like that Robert Frost poem – do you know it? – about the two roads in a yellow wood.'

The road taken, at any rate, led Stephen Daldry from one triumph to another. When his *Inspector Calls* opened on the National's Lyttelton stage in 1992, he was a struggling fringe director whose work at the Gate had only been seen by a few hundred theatre fanatics each season; by the time *Machinal* had its première in October 1993, Daldry had received the coveted Olivier Prize for *Inspector*, had negotiated that play's lucrative transfer to the West End, and had become the sole artistic director of the venerable Royal Court. *Machinal* thus marked Stephen Daldry's début as a confirmed *wunderkind* who now needed to beat his own previous record. His collaborators felt he *did* beat it. 'We all talk about it very fondly,' Ian MacNeil said of *Machinal*. 'We consider it a more mature work than *Inspector*.' 'The company line on it,' Rick Fisher told me, 'is that *Inspector* was a hit single and *Machinal* was the concept album.' Stephen Warbeck agreed, selecting *Machinal* as his favourite among all the productions he had done with Daldry between 1986 and 1994. 'We had a lot of time in rehearsal, improvising with musicians. About a third of the play is underscored,' Warbeck explained, focusing on his own department at first. Then he broadened the basis of his praise: '*Machinal* is a fantastic vehicle. You can *make* the world that was crushing the central character.'

Sophie Treadwell's *Machinal*, which was first performed in 1928, is one of the lost and intermittently found classics of American expressionism. Based loosely on the true story of Ruth Snyder, who was executed for murdering her lover, the play follows the career of a 'Young Woman' (all the characters are designated by generic titles) through work, marriage, motherhood, adultery, murder, and finally execution. Treadwell's sympathies and intentions are made clear in the notes preceding the play. 'The woman is essentially soft and tender,' she writes, 'and the life around her is essentially hard, mechanized.' Her expressionist technique is also laid out:

> In the dialogue . . . there is the attempt to catch the rhythm of our common city speech, its brassy sound, its tricks of repetition, etc. Then there is, also, the use of many different sounds chosen primarily for their inherent emotional effect (steel riveting, a priest chanting, a Negro singing, jazz band, etc.), but contributing also to the creation of a background, an atmosphere. The hope is to create a stage production that has 'style' . . .

And style is what Daldry and Company gave her. They took the Lyttelton stage at the National Theatre – a space known for its cavernous coldness and its array of technological contraptions – and made it even colder and more mechanical. Eliminating all the standard stage apparatus (back and side walls, curtain, and so on) and using rust-coloured paint to 'distress' the visible parts of the theatre that remained, they installed a huge steel set that did everything but cook supper for the audience. All the technological wizardry employed in the course of the production resulted in a fascinating irony, whereby this 'damning expressionist vision of the metropolis can't help but impress itself on you as an uplifting *celebration* of the vast mechanical resources of the Lyttelton', as Paul Taylor noted in his *Independent* review. He went on to cite the details, 'from the stunning moments near the start when the revolving cubicles of a packed cacophonous office loom in from the back of the stage, like some bureaucratic circle of hell that Dante had overlooked, all the way through to the stark electric chair scene when the steely intestines of the Lyttelton's nether regions are bleakly exposed'. Another critic, Charles Spencer of the *Daily Telegraph*, observed that 'the whole production is dominated by a massive ceiling of steel girders and wire mesh that is raised, lowered and tilted on chains to suggest the harsh, machine-like world of Treadwell's city of night. Throughout,' he added, 'the play is accompanied by an extraordinary musical score (composer: Stephen Warbeck) in which dissonant notes compete with the pulsing thumps of machinery.'

Of all the plays Daldry has selected for production since 1989, *Machinal* is the only script I actively disliked when I read it. Despite the flashy expressionist mannerisms, I sensed a poisonous sentimentality underneath – the kind of sentimentality that, by virtue of its special pleading, ultimately makes us turn against the pathetic wrongdoer defended in the play. Why, I wondered, should the Young Woman be seen as merely the soft, sensitive victim of the mechanical age, when all the other characters – her greedy mother, her oblivious husband, her faithless lover – were held accountable for their actions? Why didn't they qualify as victims too? 'But that's all right,' Stephen Warbeck assured me after I broached the subject of *Machinal*'s essential unfairness, because 'the play happens in her head, as it were.'

That would certainly be one way to interpret the script, and it would be a way that saved the play from its own illogical preachiness. But it is not the way Stephen Daldry chose. He took great pains – not only in the programme notes, but also in the casting of the powerful, charismatic actress Fiona Shaw as the heroine – to suggest that the Young Woman's view of the world had some validity. For this he received a substantial amount of critical flak. 'Should wives be empowered to kill their husbands? Not at random, of course; I don't think anyone is proposing that,' mused John Gross in the *Sunday Telegraph*. 'But for specific offences – having fat hands, perhaps, or telling off-colour jokes, or boasting about their successes in business.' Daldry had opened himself up to this kind of criticism by sticking to the author's view of the play: 'The woman is essentially soft and tender . . .' (as opposed to, say, a selfish neurotic who can't tolerate the normal pressures of existence). In his loyalty to authorial intention as well as to expressionist form, Daldry demonstrated that he was something other than 'a flashy director with a talent for choreography' who had mastered a 'very minor' play by giving it 'a breathtaking new staging', as Sheridan Morley backhandedly enthused in the *Spectator*. He was, instead, a director who was willing to listen to the playwright's own voice – even when the suppression of that voice would have made him look better as a director.

From *Machinal*, Daldry went straight to his first major production at the Royal Court. (About a year earlier, in April 1993, he had done a small staging of Howard Korder's *Search and Destroy* for the seventy-seat Theatre Upstairs, the workshop space at the Royal Court. None of the Warbeck/MacNeil/Fisher team had been involved in this British première of a 1990 American play about money, drugs, violence, and alienation; instead, Daldry had designed his own set – a circular steel contraption that rose and fell – and had executed it with the help of a group of Royal Court employees who jokingly referred to themselvers as the Inhouse Design Team. 'Actually, it was a bit naughty of him,' one member of the inhouse team later told me. 'You pay a designer to see that these technical things are achieved.' *Search and Destroy* had a modest critical success and sold out its run – but then, almost all plays produced in the Theatre Upstairs tended to sell out.)

In taking over the artistic directorship of the Royal Court Theatre at the age of thirty-three, Stephen Daldry was necessarily intensifying the critical spotlight that already shone on him. Located in the fashionable Chelsea neighbourhood of Sloane Square, the Royal Court had premièred the work of a long line of major British playwrights running from George Bernard Shaw to John Osborne and beyond. Daldry's immediate predecessor, Max Stafford-Clark, had nurtured Caryl Churchill and Timberlake Wertenbaker, both of whom went on to commercial and international success. Although the Royal Court had recently fallen on financial hard times (due to insufficient funds, the Theatre Upstairs had to be closed down for a couple of years in the early 1990s), it was still considered one of the three most important non-commercial theatres in London – the other two being the far larger and more heavily subsidized Royal National Theatre and Royal Shakespeare Company. Of the three, the Royal Court was the only one to focus primarily on new British theatre.

For a director who had made his London reputation resuscitating seventeenth-century Spanish dramas and German

expressionist plays, this was considered something of a challenge. Daldry always countered the insinuations about his relative inexperience by pointing out that he had directed several
seasons of new British plays in Sheffield, mainly at the Metro
Theatre Company, but London journalists persisted in viewing
him as a 'canny antiques dealer'. At any rate, he met the challenge of his first mainstage production at the Court by going
back to the future: that is, by giving Arnold Wesker's *The
Kitchen* its first full staging since the play's première, which had
taken place thirty-three years earlier at the Royal Court. *The
Kitchen* was one of Wesker's earliest plays; he was twenty-four
when he wrote it, and the stage directions with which he filled
the script's opening pages – endless instructions on how each of
the twenty-eight characters is to chop, cook, and serve the
imaginary food – seem characteristic of a young playwright's
belief in total authorial control.

Both the details of Wesker's wishes and his broader intentions
('The world might have been a stage for Shakespeare but to me it
is a kitchen . . . Each person has his own particular job') were
extravagantly carried out in Stephen Daldry's production, which
opened at the Royal Court on 22 February 1994. If the *Machinal*
set could do everything but cook a meal, this set rectified that
omission: 'Mark Thompson's design of the kitchen itself is so
solid and realistic that you feel the cast would be capable of
serving the entire audience with hot dinners during the course of
the show,' commented the *Telegraph*'s Charles Spencer. Ripping
120 seats out of the stalls, Daldry and his designer built a full-
scale kitchen-in-the-round on which the audience could look
down, watching the cast at work. 'The cast of *The Kitchen* performs wonders for him,' said the *TLS* review of Daldry's
achievement, 'using every cooking utensil, but no food, and one
soon forgets its absence . . . Stephen Daldry does not so much
direct *The Kitchen* as orchestrate it.' Though the production
received a few of the standard complaints incited by Daldry's
work (mainly to the effect that the plodding play was not up to
the glorious staging), the reviews tended towards the wildly

enthusiastic: 'a masterpiece of drilled ensemble', 'a piece of triumphant theatricality', 'a teeming portrait of workplace discontent', and 'the superbly choreographed horror of the lunch-time rush' were a few of the superlatives critics employed. Even John Lahr, no fan of Daldry's other work, acknowledged in his *New Yorker* review that 'Stephen Daldry's current exciting revival of *The Kitchen* . . . pays proper honor to the innovations of the play, and brilliantly illustrates the conundrum of English political theatre, which, while paying vehement lip service to the workers, rarely shows them at work'. Indeed, part of the director's brilliance was to have chosen a play in which the work displayed – that of restaurant employee – represented a job that many theatre people, including Daldry, had at one time or another taken to support themselves.

But Daldry's mainstage début, though it displayed his ability to work within and simultaneously invigorate the Royal Court tradition, did not assuage the concerns of those who worried that he couldn't develop new plays. That, then, became his next task, and he turned his mind to it as soon as he got back to London after the Broadway première of *An Inspector Calls*. Perhaps it should not be surprising that the script he eventually selected, though it was certainly the work of a new playwright (her one previous play had been performed two years earlier in a National Theatre workshop production), was by someone whose judgment and theatrical taste he had already come to know and trust.

4 *The Editing Process*

Theatre reviewing, which routinely requires a critic to deliver an instantaneous judgment after seeing a play only once, is an inherently self-defeating task. It is difficult enough when the reviewer is judging a new production of a well-known play, in which case details of staging that took weeks or months to construct, acting nuances that can alter the meaning of previously hackneyed lines, and minor cuts and alterations to the text must all be grasped on the fly. But when the play itself is new, the theatre reviewer's job is essentially impossible. What makes it impossible is not just the unfamiliarity of the text (though that is indeed a problem), but also the lack of distance between the critic and the object of her criticism. A play written long ago, however unfamiliar to us, has already been absorbed to a certain extent into our history: if we know its temporal and geographical context, we already have some perspective on it, even the first time we see it. But a play that has just been written, if it is any good at all, is bound to take us by surprise. Because it is in part about us, we are self-protectively blinded to its subject matter. And because it borrows its dramatic strategies from the world we take for granted (our own visible world, expressed in our own contemporary language), we are destined to remain oblivious to its sharpest points.

Meredith Oakes's *The Editing Process*, in a production directed by Stephen Daldry and designed by Ian MacNeil, had its première on 2 November 1994 at the Royal Court Theatre. I attended five performances, one full dress rehearsal, and numerous scene-by-scene working sessions; I watched the play from the stalls, the dress circle, and the upper circle, from the right side of the house and from the left. Each time I saw something new and different (for that is in part what this production was about – how what you see is affected by where you stand, or sit). And yet I cannot say I grasped the play completely.

I *can* say that the critics who responded to the play in the week after its first performance largely failed to comprehend it. Whatever else it is, *The Editing Process* is an elusive and difficult play. If it is unlovable, that is by choice; if it remains sealed off from attempts to convert it into either enjoyable comedy or laudable social commentary, that too is by intention. Daldry and the rest of the Royal Court staff did their best to allow the play to be judged on its merits alone: a publicity blackout ensured that no pre-emptive author profiles or advance discussions of set design would muddy the critical waters, and printed copies of the text were, as usual, given to reviewers on the opening night. Yet the members of the press remained wedded to their precon-ceptions. Informed by ads and press releases that they would be seeing a 'scathing comedy' about 'the battle for the editorship of *Footnotes in History*', the newspaper critics mainly viewed *The Editing Process* as a straightforward if not entirely successful drama about the opposition between the good old days of British publishing and the bad new ones. Jack Tinker of the *Daily Mail*, invoking Royal Court predecessors like Joe Orton and Edward Bond, described Oakes's play as being 'set in the fast-disappearing world of the small literary magazine, a symbol, surely, of that eccentric English enterprise and national identity which has been all but crushed under the accountants' jackboot of the market economy'. Benedict Nightingale of *The Times* felt that the play chronicled the 'inevitable destruction' of a 'cosy little journal . . . by the opportunists and philistines', though he complained that as a drama it was 'marooned somewhere between highly mannered satire and the humane comedy' of plays by Michael Frayn and Simon Gray, with 'not sufficient wit for the first category nor reality enough for the second'. Such critics, since they presumed that we were meant to side with the editor of the antiquated journal, deplored the character's lack of appeal: 'There can be no indignation where there is no sym-pathy,' admonished Paul Taylor of the *Independent*. Even the

Guardian's Michael Billington, who seemed willing to grant the play some doubleness of vision ('To her credit, Oakes shows that the old world is full of torpor and mendacity'), none the less faulted the author for failing to ask 'the big, awkward questions'. Billington went on to offer several of his own: 'How do you reconcile the integrity of small magazines with the demands of the corporate balance-sheet? Can you even apply big-business methods to small publishers? And does capitalism in the end diminish rather than promote diversity and choice?', as if these near-rhetorical questions, had they been expressed in the script, would have allowed *The Editing Process* to 'achieve the big, over-arching statement' which the play otherwise lacked.

To view *The Editing Process* as being essentially about the problems of small publishers in relation to big business is rather like describing *The Cherry Orchard* and *Uncle Vanya* as plays about the ownership and sale of land or the unequal distribution of labour and reward. These social problems are indeed present as central plot elements in Chekhov's plays; but had he attempted to propose solutions to them, or even to address them explicitly, he would have crushed his own dramatic works, which depend for their peculiar tone on a kind of free-floating, timeless, if none the less historically located anxiety. Like Chekhov's 'comedies', Oakes's play does not seek to make us chortle with superior delight. The laugh that occasionally escapes us at *The Editing Process* has a sharp, bitter, somewhat painful edge, the sign of a humour that has to be delicately handled, for it cuts both ways.

I am not saying that *The Editing Process* is as good as Chekhov. Very little is, after all. What I *am* saying is that Oakes shares with Chekhov an interest in subtly blurring the standard boundaries of theatrical genre – a formal concern that itself seems to spring from an obsessive interest in disintegrating structures as subject matter. Voices like theirs emerge when things fall apart, and at first we are likely to mishear them because we ourselves do not yet perceive the extent of the disintegration. Against rising evidence, we go on acting as if the abstractions of our daily life – 'corporate balance-sheets', 'big-business methods', 'capitalism' – have some visible, identifiable reality, whereas they are (and perhaps have always been) utterly intangible. 'This company's not for real,' says one of the very few sympathetic characters in *The Editing Process* – and the line, spoken towards the end, echoes with the sense of all the man-made, invisible, non-existent things that have been invoked throughout the play.

The first invisible element becomes apparent as soon as the safety curtain rises on Act One. A handyman, singing softly to himself in Polish, leans out of a high window built over the right-hand stage entrance and paints on the wall next to him. Later in this scene, a character who dislikes the smell of fresh paint says to him: 'Can't you go and do that somewhere else? It's a beautiful colour; there are so many places it could go.' If you are sitting on the right-hand side of the theatre, with only the painter's head and brush visible to you, the remark will seem amusing enough. But if you are sitting on the left side, in full view of the painted surface, the line will gain an added twist from the fact that the paint has no colour at all. The man is painting on a black surface with a bare brush, and what he leaves behind is simply more black.

As anyone who has ever worked in an office knows, where you sit and at whose invitation is a crucial element of the office hier-archy. Things look different from the typing pool and from the inner sanctum, and a secretary called into her boss's office will stand to receive instructions whereas an important visitor will be seated instantly. In his production of this play about office man-ners and office barbarism, Daldry spread the seating problem around: it afflicted not only all the characters, but the audience as well. The 'problem' was not, as at most plays, that we were likely to see too little from the wrong seat; rather, we were likely to see too much. For beneath and behind the tall, circular, partially transparent set – a set which was visible to us, in the opening scene, as simply a curve of green-tinted plexiglass, or Perspex – lay a vast, stripped-down, opened-out, all-white theatre space.

From the front rows of the stalls you could look far up into the area above the set, to where the lights would normally hang shielded by a false stage ceiling; you could also look deep into the wings, where the actors (always in character, even when they were 'offstage') would enter and exit. From higher up, in the dress circle and especially the upper circle, you had an excellent view of the structures at the back of the stage: the old brick wall of the Royal Court, the metal railings and pipes, and even a delicately curved spiral staircase leading downwards to the bowels of the theatre on the far left side. At first you were likely to view all this white space as simply a bare, untouched stage. But then, if you thought about it, you would realize that enormous effort had had to be made to create this look of bareness. Conventional side walls and back walls had been deleted, the light fixtures had been raised high or else hidden beneath the stage, and the whole of the Royal Court's backstage area, brown or black in its normal state, had been painted a glaring white. Like Ian MacNeil's revolving set, which achieved a look of smooth transparency at great technological effort and expense, the wider stage was itself evidence of just how costly it can be to produce the invisible.

When I asked Meredith Oakes, who was sitting in on all the rehearsals and previews, what she felt Daldry was doing with that big, bare, white stage, she answered, 'Well, it opens out psychologically as well as physically. It puts the characters on another planet, and that's how I wanted it. The way I wrote it, the play opens in a completely empty space with just a telephone, because I wanted it to be just a blank page, just *air*, that it comes out of. So the white set is a sort of correlative of that.'

The first character to walk out on to this empty stage is an unsuccessfully importunate writer (played by Julian Rhind-Tutt), who is crumpling a sandwich bag and closing up his Thermos as if to terminate a long and impatient wait. 'Sorry,' he says in his melodiously nasal, kazoo-like voice – a voice in which any apparent apology is really a complaint. 'Sorry, I can't wait any longer,' he continues, addressing the completely unresponsive painter. 'Could you please give this to the editor. Please.' He slams down a computer diskette on a table that appears to be in the middle of nowhere, and then disappears. The stage remains empty as the telephone, perched on that singular table, begins to ring. While it is ringing, we watch a tweedy gentleman in late middle age, wearing a brown fedora and carrying a furled umbrella, emerge from the far-left corner backstage. (If we were attending closely from the upper seats, we might even have seen him trudge up the spiral staircase.) He reaches centre-stage and languidly picks up the phone. '*Footnotes in History*,' he drawls, to audible titters on the part of the audience. The name of his magazine says it all: the academic stuffiness, the marginality, the flirtation with oblivion.

William, the editor of *Footnotes in History* – which has recently been relocated from its charming old Russell Mews offices to this glass-and-metal highrise in the outlying region of characterless Poplar – is a man who carefully observes the hierarchies. 'My secretary Peggy,' he says, introducing the new 'girl', Eleanor, to a middle-aged woman who is rushing around looking for misplaced tea-chests. Peggy's major function, throughout the first few scenes, is to bring William his chair: he is apparently too delicate, or too important, to fetch it himself. (Prunella Scales, a veteran stage actress best known to British audiences for her role opposite John Cleese in television's *Fawlty Towers*, played the part with a prim exactitude that made Alan Howard's William seem even more histrionic by comparison.) 'In addition there is Ted . . . ,' the editor says to Eleanor, and proceeds to elaborate the subtleties of rank: 'Ted is the assistant editor. You are the editorial assistant.' William is disdainful about Ted – 'Ted's not very good,' he sniffs – but he's also somewhat frightened of his youthful ambitiousness, especially when he learns that Ted has already come in the day before to learn about 'the systems'. 'He picked it up quite quickly,' Eleanor remarks innocently, to which William responds darkly, 'Yes. Ted. We're surrounded by this magnificent technology, aren't we, whose powerful rays may soon mutate us into superbeings as well as facilitating the editing process.' So the very title of the play, delivered to us in ironic quotation marks, turns out to be a piece of futuristic gobbledegook, Siamese twin to a despised neologism like 'facilitating'. If we thought *The Editing Process* was going to be about verbal meaning, this remark gives us an early clue that it may instead be about meaninglessness.

The line also, in its compact and casual way, suggests several other strands of thought that interweave throughout the play. One of these is the idea of man-made things that possess a kind of ghoulish life. 'I like to feel that with the advantage of maturity in this modern company we can be a sort of old head on young shoulders,' William chortles into the telephone receiver at the beginning of Act Two, '. . . ha, ha, very good, Frankenstein's monster, very good.' He is the only one to specify this myth of the technologically created life-in-death, but towards the end of the play another character, Tamara, seems to borrow from it when she complains, 'I've been trying for some years to create a man that would match me. I've assembled them a hundred different ways but I've never yet managed to invent one that would stand up on its own, and the reason is, the modern ingredients are rubbish.' And then Peggy, in the last scene, borrows from both William's Frankenstein speech and Tamara's echo of it when she attacks William and, by extension, herself: 'One shouldn't have cosseted you, and hated you, and kept you foolish, and doted on a cheap, vain, man-made substitute for life where I have dwindled away till I'm numb.' We have seen Peggy cosseting William throughout the play – hauling his chair from one side of the stage to another in her weak, mousy arms, plugging in the kettle for his instant coffee, reminding him of the subject of a recent article when he momentarily forgets the name – and we have also watched their relationship, finally, change. For when Peggy goes to look for him at the end, after they've both been fired, she tells the slimy representative of the new corporate owners, who has been lolling about on a steel banquette while she stands waiting, 'I'm going to find William. At least he'll offer me a chair.' Which he does, for probably the first time in their lives.

Transformation – of character, of setting, of relationships, of work – is another of the play's underlying and recurrent themes. But, as William's early speech suggests ('the powerful rays may soon mutate us into superbeings'), change is not necessarily something to be blithely welcomed. Ted, in the course of the drama, mutates from William's lowly and rather unattractive minion into his co-editor and eventually his replacement, now tricked out in a snazzy new pink sweater and adorned with the sexual glamour bestowed on him by Tamara and Lionel, the two representatives of the new corporate order. These two are themselves so outlandishly up-to-date that they seem to be from another universe: 'they're so innovative, they're practically mutants', as Tamara says in praise of a graphic design team. When they first bustle onstage into William's old-fashioned, box-bedecked office, Lionel is wearing a suit, a ponytail, a baseball cap, and dark glasses, whereas Tamara's get-up features black-and-red spandex, a bare midriff, a truly remarkable quantity of make-up, and a hairstyle (complete with lacquered vertical topknot and oiled spitcurl) that makes her look like an extra from some 1950s movie about Venusians. Indeed, the impression they create is so inhuman that in Lionel's next scene, which he opens by announcing commandingly, 'Unwind me!,' I fleetingly thought he was referring to his robotic mechanism; it took me a moment to realize he was only making a sexual play for Ted.

If Lionel and Tamara are the agents of mechanically driven, futuristic change, they are also seen as something organic and evolutionary. 'I don't like new people who've been carried in on the latest tide and start behaving as if they were there all along,' Peggy tells Lionel in the nearest thing she ever comes to an attack on him. During the previous scene, William has said to him, 'People like you swim in the polluted waters of this company all oblivious, opening and shutting your mouths with the idiot complacency of dying fish.' The dying or dead fish theme has in fact been around throughout the play: in the smoked oysters that Ted erroneously supplies for Tamara's sex games ('I'm not doing it with preservatives!' she flounces); in the 'good fish restaurant' that William misses from Russell Mews, and in the tuna-fish sandwich he brings to work as its replacement; even in Lionel's own speech about the survival course he attended – 'Twenty-four middle management hay-fever sufferers . . . holding a rope in one hand, clutching an inhaler in the other one. Gasping like fish.' As in Lionel's speech, the fish metaphor often seems linked to a survival-of-the-fittest, Spencerian view of evolutionary history and business economics. 'I'm the only survivor now,' Lionel concludes, 'I've sacked the rest.'

Responding to the linguistic texture of the play as well as to its larger themes, Daldry and MacNeil designed the set around the idea of fish. As the stage first revolved in the break between Scene One and Scene Two, we could see that the tall Perspex wall which had previously blocked our view was actually a semi-circular cylinder diagonally sliced across its top edge, so that it seemed to spiral upwards. Clear plastic above and green-tinted below (sea green, but also corporate-bureaucracy green), the Perspex shell cupped the office in its curve, creating an interior that, because it was open on one side, was continuous with but also opposite to its exterior, as in a Möbius strip or a spiral seashell. The set, like a fish-bowl, was transparent and round, and it was placed on a revolve, around the edge of which the characters occasionally moved, floating more than walking, like fish swimming around the outside rim of their bowl. The roundness of the revolve was picked up in Johanna Town's lighting, which featured circular spotlights for the characters' monologues, tiny round inset lights marking the semi-circular edge of the office space, and fluorescent inner tubes of white light under the surreal Act Two computers. The fish-bowl idea was also there in Stephen Warbeck's music and Paul Arditti's sound effects: in the whale noises that accompanied the opening moments and several important scenes, for instance, or in the throbbing, flickering variations on a theme, composed of bubble-like notes from a marimba, which sounded in the background every time the revolve moved.

In Act One, mellow, golden light played across a set that was essentially the old packed within the new – wooden and card-board boxes piled high against the Perspex, wood desks, old-style office chairs, a coat rack, a wheeled tea trolley, wicker trash bas-kets, a multitude of books and folders and old magazines, piles and scraps and pads of paper, and only a couple of standard-issue computers to indicate that this editing process was taking place in the late twentieth century. When the harsh, white lights of Act Two came up, they shone on a scene that had been utterly trans-formed. The boxes and files had all been banished; plastic-topped tables and moulded chairs had replaced the old office furniture (except for William's chair, his sign of authority, his throne); the wicker baskets had turned into transparent, plastic wastepaper bins; and on the desks were three outlandishly post-modern computers, consisting of water-filled transparent monitors in which real goldfish gently swam among fronds of green seaweed. Set into the green Perspex wall (now fully visible, with the boxes cleared away) was yet another fish tank. Large, rectangular, glam-orously lit, it constituted a 'window' between the interior office and the exterior hallway, at once a barrier and a connecting space; but it was also the standard, decorative, green-tinted office aquarium. The metaphor had become reality. The characters who occupied this set, however, didn't seem to notice the extravagance of the change: they continued to tap at their keyboards and examine their fish-filled monitors as if they were really editing words. Only in the very last scene of the play, as the lights died down and the revolve went around for the last time, did we see the triumphant Ted feeding the fish in his computer – a gesture implying that if he has finally seen through the illusion, he has accepted it none the less.

The Act Two set was stark and technological and eerily inhuman, but it was also breathtakingly beautiful. It suggested the attractions of extinction, the lure of sterile emptiness, the possible pleasures inherent in banishing the human. 'I've termi-nated three publications this afternoon,' Lionel tells Ted early in their acquaintance. 'Wanton destruction. It's wonderful, isn't it, getting paid for being wanton.' At this point in the play, cosily ensconced in the gentlemanly format of Act One, we don't really see his point: he's just a boorish carnivore, out to destroy what he can't consume. But by the time we get to Act Two, the aesthetic beauty of 'the editing process', whereby things are stripped down to their essence, has become a bit clearer, and we can almost imagine choosing the active, vital death-dealing of Lionel and Tamara over the wasting, deadly passivity of William and Peggy. 'I mean, I do think this is more to the point than colour schemes, don't you?' says William to Lionel, defending his plan to disseminate *Footnotes in History* via television and simultaneously taking a crack at Tamara's 'image consulting'. But in a strikingly visual production like this one, colour schemes *were* the point: the whole office, down to the paper napkins, was colour co-ordinated in shades of green, and characters wore matching or complementary colours when their fates were linked, switching to clashing hues as they started to diverge. (At one point I noticed that Peggy, who gratuitously criticized Ted's yellow-brown pullover in the play's second scene, was wearing a sweater of very much the same colour at her next appearance.) So William, when he attacks 'colour schemes', is struggling futilely not only against his own corporate environment, but also against our theatrical pleasures and perceptions.

However attached we may be to history and little magazines and old English ways, something in us wants to see stick-in-the-mud William gobbled up, sent into limbo, dismissed from his position – in short, 'made redundant'. 'Redundancy . . . to be declared redundant. After a lifetime spent trying to silence the inner voice that said one always was,' William muses to himself, absentmindedly stepping into the clear plastic wastepaper bin, one foot after the other. The pun is typical of the play's linguistic amusements, but it also has a richer undercurrent of self-reference. For redundance, in the sense of repetition, is one of Meredith Oakes's primary dramatic techniques. Phrases and images appear early on and then resurface over and over again, like familiar goldfish reappearing at the front of the bowl after swimming around the back. The same information about

impending lay-offs gets presented to us several times, by different people and at differing levels of explicitness, until eventually it reaches its intended victims – so that we are like office
workers who receive generalized memos about imminent cut-
backs, each one more specific and more ominous than the last,
until finally we see the actual memo of dismissal delivered to the
cubicle next door. The structure of Act Two is especially redundant, with pairs of people meeting to talk and then giving way to
other pairs, all discussing essentially the same subject matter and
using essentially the same terms. ('Sorry'/'*I'm* sorry' becomes
like an operatic motif in the second act, with all the possible
British meanings rung on the phrase, from a conventional
'Excuse me, can I get by?' or a request for more audible speech to
shocked disbelief, sincere regret, and suppressed anger.) Almost
all of these Act Two conversations are, in one way or another,
about termination, disappearance, extinction. Transformation
may be death, but the failure to transform is also death. 'You
haven't changed a bit,' Peggy tells William after a month's absence,
and then adds, 'They tell me you're disappearing.' To which he
responds: 'You know who's replacing me, don't you? In this
building sheep become wolves, frogs become princes.
Unfortunately I remained the same. So I'm coming to join you in
the afterlife.'

But if transformation is death, death is also transformation,
and therein lies its dramatic appeal. In the face of eternal dead-
lock, death can be viewed as release and salvation; it is, at any
rate, a change. This, I think, accounts in part for the emotional
power of a little scene that takes place midway through Act Two.
It is technically part of a longer scene – the very long, continuous, final Scene Five, which is subdivided by personnel, so that
different pairs or trios of characters are onstage at any given
time, with one or two exiting as another comes on. In the little
segment I'm referring to, William has just interrupted a desperate verbal duel between Lionel and Tamara. Poking his head
in the door just as Tamara has screeched, 'Why don't you fuck
me?' William politely but bumblingly asks, 'Are you in a

The Editing Process 75

meeting?' She leaves, he enters, and in the wordless interlude that follows this speech, the stage begins to darken and the revolve starts to turn. For once we are extremely aware of the marimba music in the background, in large part because Lionel and William are walking, turning, and sitting down in unison, as if performing a little dance. And it is indeed a little dance – a dance of death, as things turn out, because Lionel is about to sack William. As the two men sit side by side, facing forward on the metal banquette, with the lit aquarium to the left and behind them on the convex wall, we notice that the lighting has suddenly turned deep red. For the first time in the entire play, that everlasting green has been banished; even the Perspex sheets which we *know* to be green look red in this light. And the feeling conveyed is not purely one of ominousness, but also one of emotional richness and promise. Something is about to change. The endless circle is about to be broken.

It's very much like the moment in Samuel Beckett's *The Lost Ones* when, after sixty pages of unremitting sameness, after an infinity of tedious life, these nameless, identity-less 'lost bodies' are at last allowed to die. 'So much roughly speaking for the last state of the cylinder and of this little people of searchers one first of whom if a man in some unthinkable past for the first time bowed his head if this notion is to be maintained,' Beckett ends the little book. In fact, the similarities between Beckett's fictional text and Daldry's production of Oakes's play extend to a number of the details. Much like the characters in *The Editing Process*, the creatures in *The Lost Ones* inhabit 'a flattened cylinder fifty metres round and eighteen high for the sake of harmony. The light. Its dimness. Its yellowness. Its omnipresence . . .'. Like the actors in Act One of Daldry's production, who are forever going up and down ladders, stepladders, and stools, Beckett's lost bodies are constantly climbing ladders: 'For the need to climb is widespread . . . The purpose of the ladders is to convey the searchers to the niches. Those whom these entice no longer climb simply to get clear of the ground.' Like the stage figures moving in time to Stephen Warbeck's marimba music, the

Beckett people are accompanied in all their actions by a 'faint stridulence'. And like Ian MacNeil's set – divided up into the front of the stage, the circular pathlike revolve, and the interior of the Perspex cylinder – Beckett's cylinder

> comprises three distinct zones separated by clearcut mental or imaginary frontiers invisible to the eye of flesh. First an outer belt roughly one metre wide reserved for the climbers and strange to say favoured by most of the sedentary and vanquished. Next a slightly narrower inner belt where those weary of searching in mid-cylinder slowly revolve in Indian file intent on the periphery. Finally the arena proper . . .

The resemblance is uncanny, and it almost makes you feel as if this stage production of *The Editing Process* were some kind of mutant version of *The Lost Ones*, made concrete and visible through plastic and transparency.

Stephen Daldry did full justice to the death-embracing side of Meredith Oakes's play. He staged it in such a way that we could hear the connections between obsolescence and oblivion, as in the exchange about Peggy's redundancy:

> **Lionel** The fact is, Peggy, you'd been gravitating towards retirement age and with things as they are, very often in that sort of situation there's a tendency to fast-forward.
>
> **Tamara** Fast-forward to the grave, I think you mean, don't you, Lionel, with your usual sensitivity.

As Peggy herself accurately perceives, what we really want from life is to be *used*, and it is the loss of such usefulness that makes retirement death-like. 'I do imagine, do you see, that I'm of use to you,' she says to William in Act One, unaware that Lionel has already insisted she be fired. At the very end of *The Editing Process*, when William kneels beside her, holds her hand, and laments, 'I'm really, *really* sorry' (with feeling, for perhaps the first time in the play), Peggy responds, after a series of disjunctive comments, 'One does like to make oneself useful. Doesn't one. William. We did enjoy making ourselves useful. Didn't we.' And the very last lines of the play, just after these words of Peggy's, are Ted's comments about the writer who left off the diskette in the opening scene: 'Isn't that the chap who says he'll write for nothing? I think we should use him.'

Ted himself has already expressed both the fears and the pleasures of being used when he complains to Lionel in Act One, 'I feel I've been used,' and then modifies that to 'If someone's going to use me, the least they can do is use me up.' According to the psychoanalyst D. W. Winnicott, the inability to use people (or, in some cases, to let oneself be used) is a problem which stems from the fear that use entails destruction – the fear that the object of use will indeed be 'used up'. In a famous essay entitled 'The Use of an Object', Winnicott says:

> As analysts, we know what it is like to be used . . . Many of our patients come to us with this problem already solved – they can use objects and they can use us and can use analysis, just as they have used their parents and their siblings and their homes. However, there are many patients who need us to be able to give them a capacity to use us . . . In meeting the needs of such patients, we shall need to know what I am saying here about our survival of their destructiveness.

Winnicott's theory was based mainly on his work with infants and small children, whose healthy psychological development depended, he felt, on their coming to recognize the difference between themselves and other objects (including other people). 'Should the philosopher come out of his chair and sit on the floor with his patient,' Winnicott wrote, '. . . he will find that after "subject relates to object" comes "subject destroys object" (as it becomes external); and then may come "*object survives* destruction by the subject". The subject says to the object: "I destroyed you," and the object is there to receive the communication.'

Lionel, whose 'wanton destruction' somewhat resembles that of an infant, makes exactly this kind of discovery in the last scene of *The Editing Process*, when he realizes that his victims have survived, that he is not in fact 'the only survivor'. 'Didn't I sack you?' he says to Chris, the ever-present but often silent handyman, who avoids giving an answer by offering Lionel a joint. The two of them are still sitting on the banquette together, smoking, laughing, and enjoying life, when Peggy unexpectedly appears and asks where she can find William. 'William's about,' says Lionel (though he has just sacked him too). 'Everyone's about. Even you.' Though Lionel seems not to view his *own* behaviour as particularly babyish ('William's an infant!' he screams in his last long speech. 'The building's full of them. Infants with big wide mouths and grabbing little hands . . . How am I supposed to look after them?'), he none the less chooses as his retreat that most characteristic infantile behaviour: sleep. 'I need a good night's sleep,' he announces in his final lines. 'I'm resigning.' Even in this line he is demonstrating an affinity with his erstwhile victims, for it is Peggy who, throughout the first act, has met every major obstacle with the threat 'I resign.' Lionel, however, appears not to be bluffing. As delivered by the extremely persuasive Nicholas Woodeson, these lines seemed to signal Lionel's voluntary self-destruction, his welcoming of the oblivion of 'the afterlife'.

Death comes to *The Editing Process* early and often, and Daldry directed the play in such a way as to pinpoint those moments. He gave a lovely resonance to William's first, startling monologue about death, when he had the actor step out of the frame, move to the front of the stage, and begin: 'Death first visits us as children hiding in our beds from the night. At that time Death is to us a huge, fantastic shadow, like the shadow of a monster on a wall . . .'. And by this time we may notice that the scene is lit in such a way as to cast huge, fantastic shadows on the back wall of the white stage. William goes on, 'But Death passes us by and leaves us less fearful' – and here he pauses for a moment, moving from one spot of light through the intervening darkness to another lit-up circle, where his face reappears, speaking the rest of the line – 'and the next time he visits, we find that we have been growing while he has diminished, and so he keeps diminishing and fading.' Alan Howard may have tended to stint on the character's psychological side, but he could play his voice like a Schubertian clarinet. ('If you listen to him, he more or less sings,' commented Stephen Warbeck about Howard's performance. 'I can actually write down in note form what he says.') So this speech about death, inherently moving in any case, attained a kind of riveting, aria-like splendour through its lighting and delivery.

Still, however attentive he was towards it, Stephen Daldry could not bring himself fully to share the play's bleak vision. This was the director, after all, who had triumphantly staged Tirso de Molina's *Damned for Despair*, a funny, powerful drama about the necessity of keeping up hope, even on the brink of death and damnation. Daldry is no sentimentalist, but he *is* a romantic. He is drawn to dark emotions, but not for their own sake; he seems to want them to lead somewhere, to have some galvanizing effect. In a conversation with me the night before *The Editing Process* opened, he admitted to feeling stumped by the play's essentially passive irony. 'I thought it would be Ostrovsky,' he said, referring to a satiric nineteenth-century Russian playwright, 'and instead it turned out to be Flaubert.'

The play offered one possible escape hatch from terminal pessimism, and Daldry made the most of it. In the characters of Eleanor, the editorial assistant, and Chris, the handyman, Oakes has given us two people who are not actually paid by the giant corporation that has swallowed up *Footnotes in History;* therefore, they cannot be fired by it. They work in the building for their own personal reasons – Eleanor because she wants to 'find' herself in a way that will 'lead to a position', Chris because 'I want to make something of myself. Each different place I go to, like a building site or a hospital or an advertising agency, I walk in off the street and make something different of myself.' The way they express these apparently similar intentions shows how different the two of them are from each other. Eleanor is young, lost, and rather inert; Chris is an active maker of his own fate, always vigorously playing a role. He tries to transfer some of his vitality to her ('Smile!' he urges in one of their brief meetings, and 'Don't you ever stop apologizing?' he says in another), and in the end he succeeds. Eleanor, who has a neurotic habit of washing and wiping her hands thoughout the play, finally drops her crumpled green napkin when she admits to Chris, 'I hate it here.' He has just revealed to her (and to us) that he is not a paid handyman, as everyone assumed him to be, but a self-designated volunteer. Eleanor laughs for the first time when she hears his story; then she bursts into tears. Chris dries her tears, kisses her, and says, 'We'll go then . . . This company's not for real.'

For many of the people working on *The Editing Process*, these two characters were the source of appeal, the life-force of the play. 'I love Eleanor and Chris,' said Jo Town, the lighting designer. 'I can't bear the other characters – I think they need shooting.' Stephen Warbeck also felt that these two possessed a warmth the others lacked, and he wished the play had more of it: 'For instance, their kiss, and his wiping her tears away – if that could be expanded, it would be a big help.' Ian MacNeil, who liked the play and its portrayals ('I love that about the anachronism between a figure like Peggy and a figure like Tamara,' he said), none the less admitted that as a *person* Eleanor was by far the most likeable. 'Eleanor is massively sympathetic,' he commented, praising both the character and the actress who played her. 'She's really well written and she does it very well.' MacNeil spoke about the usual tendency for that kind of uppercrust, superficial 'Sloane Ranger' to be treated with satiric mockery: 'That character is an English archetype of femininity, but she gives the vulnerability inside that. Usually onstage one would write off a Sloane, but one doesn't with her.' And even Meredith Oakes confessed to some authorial partiality: 'I wanted to be evenhanded about it, but I *have* got rather fond of Eleanor, I'm afraid. The second time I saw it read – that's when it really started to happen.'

What makes Eleanor appealing is not, I think, her victimiza-
tion (Peggy has that, and it only annoys us); it is her combination of empathy and lunacy. 'That's unfair,' she says when
William blames Peggy for the fact that 'electronic circuitry has
been damaged' by 'allowing organic matter to find its way into
the systems' (translation: somebody has spilled smoked-oyster
oil on to the computer, causing a major blow-out). *We* happen to
know that the fault is mainly Ted's and partly Peggy's, but none
of the characters know the full story. Peggy herself is unfairly
trying to blame Eleanor. Yet Eleanor, instead of defending herself, defends Peggy. She also tries to comfort William when he
gets fired: 'I'm sorry,' she says gently, touching his hand, which
causes him to cling to her until she has to scrape him off.

But niceness alone would not be enough. It takes Eleanor's
slight craziness to make her really engaging – to make us see her
as the 'organic matter' that has somehow found its way into 'the
systems'. The first sign of this note in her character occurs
during an early encounter with William, when he wants to have a
heart-to-heart with her. In his typical lordly fashion, he motions
her towards a footstool next to his desk; while he is waiting for
her to sit down on this very low and uncomfortable seat, he
glances away at some paperwork on his desk. But when he
swings his head around at a lowered level, to meet what ought to
be her eyes, he encounters instead her knees. For Eleanor, misin-
terpreting his gesture, has climbed up on to the footstool instead
of sitting, and now stands towering above him. She does this
partly out of inexperience (she doesn't know office etiquette),
partly out of disconnectedness (she fails to ask herself what *possible* office etiquette could require her to be standing on a footstool), and partly out of the kind of inherent searchingness that
causes Beckett's lost ones to 'climb simply to get clear of the
ground'. The comic effect of this scene can be credited almost
entirely to the play's director, for the Oakes script contains no
stage directions at this point, and it is the physical movement,
introduced by Daldry, which makes the episode funny.

The audience giggles when Eleanor climbs on to the footstool, but it laughs out loud when she has her next big scene, in which she flies into a rage at the thought of how her uncle stole 'Granny's corner cupboard . . . the only thing in my grandparents' house that Mummy really wanted'. (Later in the play she is to say of this uncle, a corporate board member whom the other characters are always trying to get her to call on their behalf: 'I don't know why people keep drawing attention to my uncle as if he were some part of my body that everyone can see except me. If I could see where it was I'd cut it off.') Eleanor's rant about the corner cupboard rises to a melodramatic shriek, and William is so taken aback at her outburst that he can only murmur, 'Did you have a *normal* childhood?' at which the audience roars even more loudly. The episode became such a success that, midway through previews, Daldry decided to focus more attention on it and asked Jo Town to bring up the lights for that scene. 'Since it's now the biggest laugh in the show,' he said, 'we may as well help her out a bit.'

Caroline Harker, the young actress playing Eleanor, felt that Stephen Daldry had been helping her out all along. 'He pushes you a bit bigger than what you do normally,' she told me. 'It was good for me, who normally does acting that can't be detected. I loved being pushed to be bolder.' When I asked her how much guidance Daldry had given her about the character of Eleanor, she first said, 'I think he let me work it out from the script,' and then added, 'No, he gave me the handwashing thing. He suggested I read a book about complexes – a psychology book, you know – and that was very useful.' She also described a day in rehearsal 'when I came in and he'd completely changed the way I'd done something. He'd suddenly turned his interest on me, the way I'd seen him do with each of the other actors . . . He seems to see *everything*. I've asked him questions and he doesn't say, "Hang on, I'll have a look at that next time." He always seems able to answer because he's already noticed it.'

If Daldry pushed Eleanor to be wilder, he created Chris's wildness out of whole cloth. In the published script, Chris is described as a twenty-six-year-old man of no particular nation-ality – therefore, presumably, English. Into this role, Daldry cast Christopher Rozycki, a forty-something Polish actor who, after training at the Lodz School of Theatre and Film, emigrated to England in 1978. Since then he has performed in a number of British productions, including Daldry's *Machinal*, but his English remains heavily accented and not fully grammatical. (The English – and in some scenes Polish – that he used onstage in *The Editing Process* was identical to his offstage speech.) What Rozycki introduced into this play was a breath of fresh air, a whiff of a warmer, looser, non-Perspex, non-air-conditioned outside world. From his first appearance as the painting handyman singing to himself in Polish, through his confrontation with Ted over a Xerox machine (in which he spoke his lines in Polish, with Ted answering in English), to his argument with Eleanor over the meaning of the British 'Sorry', this actor brought to the part a sense of a more flexible, liberating code of behaviour than the one governing the English middle classes. When Chris announces that 'Each different place I go to . . . I walk in off the street and make something different of myself,' we believe him because we can see him doing it before our very eyes. As played by this actor, he *is* something different.

According to Meredith Oakes, Stephen Daldry heavily shaped the dramatic function of Chris's role, to the point of actually altering the development of the script. 'The character of Chris showed his hand early,' Oakes said of her original version, in which one knew from nearly the beginning of the play that Chris wasn't an employee. 'Stephen showed me that if I kept his actions consistent with that, but held back his revelation until the end, it would work better.' How did she feel, I asked, about having her twenty-six-year-old British Chris turned into a much older Pole? 'It's quite a surprise,' she admitted. 'But what it adds is the same thing Stephen adds when he puts children in a play – the wild factor, something that even *he* isn't in control of. I've seen him do that frequently: introduce something that even he can't control. It energizes him.'

Once previews began, Daldry realized exactly how much

energy this wild card added to the scenes he was in. And so he began adding him to others. We would see Chris silently painting the side of the toilet cubicle during Ted and Lionel's conversation in the Gents; seated cross-legged on the floor beneath the aquarium, looking back and forth at Lionel and Tamara as they attacked each other across him; quietly enjoying a smoke with Lionel after confessing – in a way that sounded like an evasive lie but was really the truth – that he was working for 'No one'. (Lionel's mordant response to that was, 'Of course. So no one's sent you to check on me . . . Could you please remind no one that without my organizational skills he never could have succeeded in creating this mess!') In adding a silent Rozycki to these places in the play, Daldry was following a pattern that had already been set in the script, where Oakes has Chris present but unspeaking in more than one scene. It is an obvious aspect of the handyman role – 'I'm so much a part of the scenery in this building, people don't see me at all,' Chris points out to Eleanor in his final confession – but sometimes, as that line itself suggests, the obvious is the easiest thing to overlook.

Chris was also useful because he offered the best possible channel for Daldry's characteristic games with theatricality. For Stephen Daldry, theatre is never simply a pageant taking place in front of viewers, like a warm-blooded movie with life-sized, three-dimensional dolls. Not for him the transparent fourth wall of boxed-in, realistic drama. He wants the performance to reach out and pull the audience in; he wants the audience to acknowledge *its* role in the events onstage. At the Gate Theatre, this involvement was practically inherent in the theatre's tiny size: the audience members had to walk across the stage to get to their seats. With *An Inspector Calls*, he converted the audience into a counterpart of the assembled townspeople – or, at times, a mirror for the guilty Birlings. *Machinal* made all its viewers into witnesses at an execution. Because of its airless, self-enclosed, circular quality (built into the play's subject and reflected in its set), *The Editing Process* did not lend itself to such theatrical devices. But Rozycki's character, as a self-described performer who took on one role after another, seemed to offer a way in. For example, when Chris announced at the end, 'what they've done is, they've made me a security guard', Daldry had him pop a guard's hat on to his head – as if to say, in clownish fashion: the costume makes the role. And when Eleanor laughed at this moment, she was echoing *our* appreciation of the purposely clownlike performance.

We cannot, however, enter the play sufficiently through the characters of Chris and Eleanor, especially since their primary characteristic, their primary appeal, is that they somehow remain *outside* the play. Daldry's problem was to get us to acknowledge ourselves as part of the hateful little world depicted in *The Editing Process*, to make us put ourselves exactly where we did not want to be: inside that sealed-off, inhuman building. He therefore introduced certain gestures designed specifically to pull in the audience. When William, for instance, complains in the first scene about the air-conditioning in the building and compares it to the mummification process in Guanajuato, Mexico, where there are 'rows of desiccated corpses leaning up against the wall like so many dried umbrellas', the actor illustrates his lines by pointing his furled umbrella back and forth along the rows of seats in the stalls. When Tamara, the corporate image consultant who, according to Lionel, 'can put a Rubik's cube in order by the action of her eyes alone', first sets foot on the stage, she begins by looking outwards at the audience, surveying the theatre as if to say: Now what could be done with this old dump? And when, in conversation with Eleanor, she unleashes a string of bureaucratic clichés ('crisis of identity', 'no such thing as a bad company', 'confused company', 'new corporate image'), Tamara's key words appear in boldfaced letters on placards that she casually, almost involuntarily displays. This is a potentially marvellous moment, merging as it does Brecht's signboard technique with advertising's graphic exhibits; but the audience repeatedly failed to be struck by it.

It does no good to blame the audience in such cases. If theatre doesn't generate a response, it hasn't succeeded as theatre, however intelligent the ideas behind it. One of the hallmarks of Daldry's work, up to *The Editing Process*, had been his capacity to bring abstract theatrical principles into vivid, exciting stage form. But something in this play was partially defeating his ability to do that. Something was keeping him, and therefore keeping *us*, from fully entering the play – and it was not just the enclosed, circular subject matter, for Daldry had previously shown himself capable of cracking harder nuts than that.

As a play about the dangers of technology which took place on an entrancingly high-tech set, a parable about the superficiality of mere 'colour schemes' which was itself colour-co-ordinated and strikingly visual, this production embodied the Daldry group's mixed attitudes towards technology. Stephen Daldry, Ian MacNeil, and Stephen Warbeck (as well as their usual fourth collaborator, Rick Fisher, who happened not to be working on *The Editing Process*) had already tested out some of their ambivalences when they staged Sophie Treadwell's *Machinal,* another play by a woman writer about the evil effects of mechanical progress on overly sensitive souls. 'Of course, it was a load of men doing it,' Ian MacNeil remarked about *Machinal*. A load of men who loved machines, I pointed out. 'Yes, exactly,' said MacNeil. He went on to tell me that in preparation for *Machinal* they had all watched *Modern Times*, *Metropolis*, and other productions of the period. 'That was a time with a lot of mixed feelings about machines,' he observed. 'You were allowed to be ambivalent about them.'

Some of that bifurcation crept into MacNeil's design for *The Editing Process.* 'I love all this,' he said, gesturing at the old furniture and mellow lighting of Act One, 'and I love the other as well' – meaning the sleek, futuristic look of Act Two. MacNeil felt that one of Daldry's special strengths as a director, particularly visible in *Inspector* but present in much of his other work as well, was to bring together past and present. 'That's a very English skill, that fusion,' he said. I suggested that *The Editing Process,* set entirely in our own period, didn't offer much scope for such doubleness of vision, but MacNeil disagreed. 'It *does* put two things onstage simultaneously – the old Britain and the new Britain,' he said.

'Unfortunately, it's a world we have very little to do with,' explained Jo Town, using 'unfortunately' to suggest her own incapacity, as a theatre person, to comprehend the 'new Britain' of office labour. 'My neighbour works in a place something like that, but it's not a world we know anything about.' Town felt that the play was about 'values in the nineties being pretty appalling', something she had been protected from by spending the early 1990s as chief electrician at the Royal Court – two years under the artistic directorship of Max Stafford-Clark, and two years under Stephen Daldry. When I asked her to compare Stafford-Clark to Daldry, she said, 'I admire them both as directors. But they're complete opposites. Max didn't *hate* lighting, but he didn't like lighting and sets to take over from the play. Stephen's just the opposite – very visual.'

But being 'visual' can have its costs. In the text of *The Editing Process* itself, there is much discussion about the enormous expense entailed in Tamara's makeovers of the corporate image. 'She's embarked on a massive overspend which cannot be condoned,' Lionel repeatedly chants to Ted. At one point Tamara gaspingly rejects some hyacinths brought in by Chris ('Get rid of these floral dildos!') and instead requests 'aerodynamic plants that make your eyes move faster. I want plants that make me think I've hallucinated them.' When Ian MacNeil, after the second preview, talked about wanting to buy or construct something that fit Tamara's description exactly, the production manager put her foot down. 'There is *no* more money for props,' she said emphatically. Elsewhere around the Royal Court, people had suggested to me that Stephen Daldry would 'make our fortune, if he doesn't bankrupt us first'. I asked Jo Town if *The Editing Process* had a higher-than-average production budget. 'Not originally, no,' she said. But it grew? 'Yeah.'

When I hinted to Ian MacNeil that perhaps there had been a massive overspend *on* the play as well as in it, he denied going over budget at all. He did acknowledge, however, that the eventual price tag of £100,000 on the original *Inspector Calls* set had struck the National Theatre management as excessive, and that as a result Daldry and his collaborators had been forced to submit three separate designs for *Machinal* to keep the total costs under £80,000. The high price of visual splendour had been even more evident in New York, where the Broadway *Inspector* had cost about two-and-a-half times the British version. 'That's just because New York is absurd,' MacNeil pointed out.

But price is not a peripheral issue. One of the appealing things about Daldry's version of theatre is that it marries the dramaturgical techniques of 'poor' theatre (such as Brecht's or Grotowski's or Peter Brook's) with the magnificence of operatic display. His work is visually exciting partly because we can perceive just how much has been spent on it. And the awareness of that expenditure, however subconscious, contributes to our privileged sense of conspicuous consumption.

To produce the kind of theatrical fireworks that Stephen Daldry favours requires more than just money; it also requires a detailed knowledge of how stage mechanisms work – the sort of technical preoccupation that, according to Jo Town, Stafford-Clark didn't have but Daldry does. Such knowledge is in part generational. Speaking about Ted in the first scene of *The Editing Process*, Eleanor strikes fear into William's soul with the lines, 'I was showing him the systems . . . He picked it up quite quickly.' As we can see from their earliest scene together, in which William is working with sheets of paper while Ted fiddles happily with the computer, Ted is much more comfortable with the new technology than William is. About the furthest William can pull himself into the twentieth century is the use of photocopies, and even then he has Eleanor make them. Ted is rather supercilious about this already obsolescent technology, an attitude he makes clear when he says to William at the beginning of Act Two, 'Up to you, William. Photocopying is unnecessary, but it's up to you.' Ted is the adaptive organism in office evolution, able to function under either technology. As Ian MacNeil said about the character, 'Ted is the pivotal figure, malleable in either direction. He straddles.'

If Ted 'straddles', that is in part because, like Daldry and MacNeil, he feels an allegiance to both the old and the new. '*Footnotes in History* has existed for a hundred and fifteen years,' he protests when Lionel mentions the possibility of axing it. 'That's why it doesn't have much sex appeal,' Lionel answers. Ted, who is just approaching thirty, begins at this point to realize that his youthfulness itself is sexy – sexy in personal terms (to Lionel and Tamara, who both pursue him) and sexy in business terms. 'Congratulations, Ted,' Lionel says to him midway through Act Two. 'The owner's impressed by your handling of the Board. He's making you co-editor.' To which Ted, in one of the most brutal moments of the play, responds: 'But won't people think the change is just cosmetic? I'm trying to envisage the masthead. I think my name will have to be first.' As delivered by Tom Hollander, a talented and mercurial actor, this line was simultaneously menacing and oblivious.

By a strange coincidence, Stephen Daldry (who himself came to power at the Royal Court Theatre at the behest of a 'Board') had originally been obliged to share the 'masthead' with his predecessor. In 1991 the Royal Court management was looking for new blood to reinvigorate the 100-year-old theatre and, according to the *Observer*, the youthful Daldry 'charmed the pants off the selection committee'. But Max Stafford-Clark, who had headed the Royal Court since 1979, was not willing to go gently into that good night of retirement and freelance directing. As the *Guardian* reported the situation in November 1991:

> The trouble started in 1988 when Stafford-Clark . . . was reappointed to the job. Some felt he had done it for quite long enough and Stafford-Clark himself said that after another three years it would be time to move on. When his three years were up, he changed his mind and reapplied, throwing the theatre's board into a state of confusion which has, after a little faffing around, resulted in a compromise-cum-dream-ticket whereby

Max stays as artistic director for 18 months, with Stephen under his wing. Then Max moves on to be associate director for another 18 months, while Stephen finally gets the hot seat.

The *Evening Standard*'s report in January of 1993 was a bit more brutal:

> They were ringing out the old – or should have been – at the Royal Court last night as departing director Max Stafford-Clark offered the unlikely choice of *King Lear* as his farewell production to Sloane Square, but where precisely stands the new man in the confused machinations of life at the Court?
>
> It is more than a year since a little-known theatre director called Stephen Daldry was appointed the new artistic director of the Royal Court . . . in a bizarre deal which included a year in joint harness with his predecessor and indications that limpet-like Max will never go away at all.

Even the fish imagery seems to mark this story's affinity with the fictional ouster in *The Editing Process*.

I am not suggesting that Daldry behaved like any of the ruthless characters in the play. His position was, and remained, as friendly and straightforward towards Max Stafford-Clark as Ted's was underhanded and oily in relation to William. But structurally the two situations had much in common, with Daldry perceived as the new broom coming in to sweep away the old cobwebs. He did not help matters when he gave interviews to the press along the lines of the one reported in that same *Evening Standard* article. 'Why is our audience so f****** middle-aged?' Daldry was primly quoted as saying. 'We are not telling the right stories . . . We have to listen to the kids. A younger audience – that's vital.' One employee of the Royal Court who lived through the transition told me, 'When he took over here, everyone was afraid he would get rid of all the old people, especially those over forty.' But her fears were soon allayed. No one was made redundant – 'quite the opposite, he's been wonderful to us', she said. In fact, Daldry seemed to go out of his way to be friendly to the old-guard staff; and when, for instance, he eventually hired a new personal assistant, he chose Marieke Spencer, a woman in her mid-forties who had started her career as Lindsay Anderson's assistant at the Royal Court twenty years earlier.

All the kindness and goodwill in the world, however, cannot erase the fact that both Max Stafford-Clark and *The Editing Process*'s William were fearful of the 'afterlife' that would greet their termination. Nor did the parallels end there. For both Meredith Oakes's play and the Royal Court's recent history were in part about the relationship between labour costs and the production of art. Daldry, who had not paid actors at all at the Gate Theatre (and had thereby managed to produce elaborate shows with huge casts on a shoestring), instituted some of the same budget-redistribution measures in his first major show at the Royal Court. When he decided to direct Arnold Wesker's *The Kitchen* in early 1994, he was, according to the *Guardian*, 'flouting the financial problems that have beset the theatre over the last decade' by selecting a play that demanded twenty-eight actors. He chose, however, to devote a large part of his budget to the stunning kitchen-in-the-round (which, because it took up a large part of the stalls section of the theatre, actually *reduced* ticket revenues), and therefore had to economize on actor payments. 'Brazening his way through union principles,' the *Guardian* reported, 'he persuaded the actors' union, Equity, to allow him to take on 15 amateurs.'

Had Daldry used his production of *The Editing Process* to stress the connection between an uncommercial publishing venture like *Footnotes in History* and a non-profit theatre like the Royal Court, he might have been able to make the audience perceive its own complicity in the events onstage. It is for *our* benefit, after all, that the twenty-eight actors are brought in, the extravagant sets designed at astronomic costs, the technical details made as up-to-date as possible. We who love the theatre do not wish to support a moribund, nearly extinct, sanctimoniously preserved relic, nor ought we to. The theatre at its best is an entrancing, vital, immediate spectacle, and we are within our rights to demand that of it. But there are costs involved – in terms of actors' wages, playwrights' fees, directors' and technicians' salaries, design and staging expenses – and if we aren't willing to pay enormous sums for tickets, we must be willing to allow for some cuts. *Someone* must pay, and if it's not ourselves, it will be those who produce the art. So if we desire the thrill and dash of the circus, we learn to tolerate the mistreated performers; and if we want the visual delight that technical wizardry can bring, we accept certain economies on the human side.

In that sense, there is a direct analogy between an operation like Ted's *Footnotes* ('Isn't that the chap who says he'll write for nothing? I think we should use him') and Daldry's Equity-compromised theatre. I suspect that on some level Daldry recognized the parallel when he chose to direct *The Editing Process*. I imagine that some part of him knew, 'not consciously, Lionel, not consciously' (as Ted says), but knew none the less that this play had an autobiographical lure for him. Had he brought that knowledge to the surface, Daldry might have been able to inject into the play his usual theatrical intensity, might have drawn us more fully into the otherwise repellent circle of the play's life. On the other hand, I have the feeling that if he had consciously recognized his own personal stake in the subject matter of the play, Stephen Daldry might never have been able to stage *The Editing Process* at all.

5 Managing a Career

By the summer of 1995, nine months after the opening of *The Editing Process*, Stephen Daldry had not yet directed another production. In part, this could be attributed to the normal pacing of an increasingly successful career. When he started out, as a trainee and then associate director at the Sheffield Crucible, he was routinely staging three or four plays a year; but the higher he rose in his profession, the more administrative responsibilities began to edge out purely artistic ones. This was true even at the Gate, where Daldry had directed an average of only two plays a year, leaving the other seasonal offerings to guest directors while he handled fundraising, script selection, scheduling, publicity, and all the other managerial tasks. And by comparison to the tiny Gate, the Royal Court was a huge operation: a historic building containing two theatres (the 400-seat main stage and the 70-seat Theatre Upstairs), with over 30 full-time employees and as many more part-time. Daldry had taken on a hard job, as the artistic director of an underfunded, understaffed, but none the less extremely prominent British theatre, the only one of the three major non-profit-making theatres devoted primarily to developing new plays; and he had made it even harder by expanding the number and range of the Court's activities. 'Last year we did nineteen premières,' he told a *Vanity Fair* reporter who came over from New York in June 1995 to interview important figures in the British theatre scene. 'We are experiencing record-breaking years at the box office.' And, he noted, the Royal Court was continuing to get a hefty chunk of funding from the Arts Council – 'about a million pounds a year, which accounts for 36 per cent of our income. I'm pleased to say it was 53 per cent when I arrived,' Daldry added, calling attention to all the new sources of support he had obtained for the theatre.

By all reports, he was good at the business side of the job –
charming corporate sponsorships out of W. H. Smith and the
Evening Standard, garnering play-development funds from a
Californian organization called the Audrey Skirball-Kenis
Foundation, urging Barclays Bank to continue underwriting an
annual summer festival of experimental theatre work from all
over the United Kingdom. And in cases where the experimental
became the controversial, he knew how to smooth ruffled
feathers. For instance, when *Blasted* (a notoriously violent play
by Sarah Kane) was premièred at the Theatre Upstairs in January
1995, scathing media attacks and full-page ripostes in the
Guardian made it the *cause célèbre* of the month. But the con-
troversy didn't rattle the people at the Jerwood Foundation,
which was sponsoring the Theatre Upstairs season: Stephen
Daldry had alerted them in advance that there might be a bit of
bother, and they were prepared to sit tight. Daldry had a way of
making financial sponsorship seem like an adventure, an exciting
risk, a brave gamble – and this free-fall attitude had its payoff in
terms of artistic freedom. 'If there are strings attached to a
cheque, we return it,' he said in one press interview. That went
for the government as well as private sponsors: 'I told the Arts
Council, if they want to have a discussion with me about the
artistic policy of the theatre as a minority funder, then I have to
let Barclays Bank or Sky TV have a say too.'

Part of Daldry's spit-in-your-eye sense of independence no
doubt came from a feeling that the board of directors at the
Royal Court backed his spirit of adventurousness. Stephen
Evans, a film producer serving on the Court's board, told me
about his first meeting with Stephen Daldry. 'I was on the selection committee at the Royal Court,' he said. 'We interviewed a
lot of the bright young things in the British theatre. It's a presti-
gious job, and Max Stafford-Clark had had it for twelve years,
and it was time for him to leave (and I say this though I'm a
friend of Max Stafford-Clark's, and helped him set up his own
theatre company). Stephen, in the interview he gave, had so
many fresh, exciting ideas. After the interview we were practi-

cally unanimous in wanting Stephen – not quite all of us, but most of us wanted him. We thought if we chose him we'd have an interesting time of it. And we *have* had an interesting time of it.'

Daldry, in turn, responded to this confidence in him by praising the board for its willingness to take risks. 'The National has predetermined artistic goals, and we do not,' he explained to one interviewer, distinguishing between the Royal Court and its larger, better-endowed sibling on the South Bank. 'I'm in the enviable position of being able to determine the direction myself. And we don't have to be audience-led. There's still a delight on my board when we have a flop. We're in the unique position of being able to fail.'

As the Royal Court's leader, the spokesman for its collective 'we', Daldry may indeed have felt that way about flops, but as an individual he apparently found them somewhat more difficult to tolerate. One of the explanations some people gave for the long gap between *The Editing Process* and Daldry's next play was that he was still recovering from the unaccustomed failure. 'He really lost his confidence with *The Editing Process*,' said someone who worked at the Royal Court (and who chose, in giving this assessment, to remain anonymous). 'He hasn't directed anything since then, and it's been months.' Even Stephen Warbeck, Daldry's staunch supporter and long-time collaborator, had observed during rehearsals that he seemed less confident with *The Editing Process* than he had with any previous production. Warbeck attributed that to flaws in the play itself, especially compared with the other scripts they had worked on together. 'The texts had more in them that you could hang more on, theatrically,' he said of their earlier plays, whereas *The Editing Process* 'exists on an English comedy level – everything you try on it seems to stretch it'. Speaking two days before *The Editing Process*'s première, Warbeck felt that Daldry was frustrated and foiled by the play's polite limitations: 'I think he wanted it to be madder.' According to another old friend of Daldry's, he himself was explicit about the production's failures. 'I remember Stephen coming in to me and saying, "I'm not a comedy director",' said

Stella Hall, who had known Stephen Daldry since 1983 and was now running the Barclays New Stages Festival for the Royal Court. Though she had seen and loved many of Daldry's productions, from *The Ragged-Trousered Philanthropist* in 1984 to *The Kitchen* in 1994, she didn't see *The Editing Process* because 'everybody said don't bother. He put me off it himself. The feeling in the building was: this isn't quite right.' The feeling outside the building was even more emphatic. 'Lousy,' said Stephen Evans, when I asked him what he thought of *The Editing Process.*

It wasn't, in fact, as bad as all that, but the expectations surrounding Daldry's 'new writing' début were insurmountably high. Perhaps, as some suggested, he should have waited for a more suitable play. 'I think it was a timing thing,' Stella Hall guessed. 'It was time for him to do a mainstage production. Or maybe it was something else: he might have got along well with Meredith and wanted to do something with her.' If timing influenced Daldry's choice of play, it may also have affected the critical response. 'It was time for Stephen to have a flop, so they called it a flop,' said Ian MacNeil, one of the few people who was willing to defend the production even after it had failed at the box office.

Everyone who works in the theatre has had failures. They are the bitter herb that lends seasoning to even the most triumphant career (as Moss Hart's beautifully composed autobiography, *Act One*, illustrates with great skill). But Stephen Daldry was singularly accustomed to success. 'Stephen was always lucky. He had the golden touch,' remarked Julian Webber, an old English friend of Daldry's who now directs the SoHo Repertory Theatre in New York. 'The thing is, you can be very talented and very good and still not succeed. So much in life is a matter of luck. And Stephen is very, very lucky. If you follow him around for a while, you'll see. Five-dollar bills will drop into your path.' In other words, one adjunct of Daldry's extraordinary luck was that it tended to rub off on those around him. 'Stephen's recognition of other talent is *extremely* good,' Webber said. 'To make sure the other shows at the Gate, and not just the one he was directing, were equally good: that was very important. He was the flagship, but the others had to be good too. Again, it's about generosity.'

Stella Hall used the same word, generosity, in describing Daldry's attitude towards his associate directors at the Royal Court, Ian Rickson and James Macdonald. She felt that Daldry had recognized their talents as being other than his own and had drawn them into the Royal Court for that reason. 'Ian is very sensitive, very considered, very intense, very interior. James brings a real theoretical, academic rigour – he's brilliant with text.' Even Max Stafford-Clark, Stephen Daldry's predecessor, had been brought back to the Court as an occasional visiting director, complete with his own touring company, so that, as Stella Hall put it, 'Max is adding something to the tapestry.' It was her opinion that Daldry would give up a good play to another director if he thought that made sense. 'He may well have wanted to do it,' she said of a planned revival of David Storey's *The Changing Room*, 'and someone else may have demonstrated a passion or a desire to do it, and he may have passed on it. I don't think of him as a possessive director.'

James Macdonald, who was scheduled to direct *The Changing Room* in the Court's 1995–6 season, confirmed that Daldry had originally planned to do it himself. But 'he decided not to do it. And that's a play we've both been interested in for quite a while – at one point we even talked about doing it together.' About the whole process of choosing who directed which plays at the Royal Court, Macdonald commented, 'It's an odd thing about plays. I don't recall, since I've been here, any kind of dogfight about who's going to do what. It seems to work out quite organically.' Ian Rickson concurred: 'We all work together . . . there's no competition. Plays get assigned between us with real harmony.'

With this in mind, one could read in various ways Daldry's decision to keep a low directorial profile in the months succeeding *The Editing Process*. It's possible that he was afraid of another failure, fearful that his good luck had temporarily turned bad. But it's equally (or even simultaneously) possible that he was exercising to the full his characteristic generosity, allowing other directors to take on the flashy, exciting plays. In the season that followed Daldry's 'flop', James Macdonald directed Sarah Kane's *Blasted* (her agent had sent him the play, which he loved from the beginning) and he was also given Sam Shepard's *Simpatico*, the Court's biggest financial success of the year. Meanwhile, Ian Rickson – a newer and younger associate director who had previ- ousy worked only in the Theatre Upstairs – was assigned the mainstage production of *Mojo*, a first play by twenty-six-year- old Jez Butterworth. Because Butterworth was the first novice playwright to have a première at the Court's downstairs theatre since John Osborne's *Look Back in Anger* opened there in 1956, his main-stage début (and therefore Rickson's) was likely to make a splash. And if Macdonald's and Rickson's productions turned out to be the hottest plays in the Royal Court's 1994–5 season, that was in part because Daldry used all his charm, connections, and theatrical clout to make them hot.

For if *The Editing Process* had been a setback for him person- ally, it had in no way damaged his prospects as the up-and- coming director to watch. 'He may have balls of brass, and the skills of Rumpelstiltskin, but even Stephen Daldry must be sweating about putting a first-time playwright on the main stage of the Royal Court' was how *Time Out* began its lead 'Theatre Preview' article just before *Mojo*'s opening. When the Royal Court brought in Eddie Izzard (who, long before he became a well-known comedian, had been a Sheffield University friend of Daldry's) for a few weeks of midsummer 'improv', the show was billed by the *Independent* as 'evidence of artistic director Stephen Daldry's desire to keep the Royal Court unpredictable'. Even bad publicity became good publicity in Daldry's hands. 'Does the controversial play *Blasted* show that Daldry is unsuit- able to be, as widely suggested, the National Theatre's director?' trumpeted the *Sunday Times* in the subhead to a January 1995 profile by Tom Morris. The question was by no means rhetor- ical, for the article proceeded to delve into Stephen Daldry's background and achievements with the attention normally reserved for likely winners. 'Daldry's popular image, meanwhile, remains untarnished,' Morris commented. 'Even when his fellow professionals grumble at his hands-off managerial style or his bulging eye for the main chance, the press invariable tumbles into his embrace.' As did Morris, who, after praising Daldry's selection of James Macdonald and Ian Rickson as associate directors and commenting on the fact that 'the profile and finances of the theatre could not be in better hands', concluded his article with the line, 'If I were on a boat in a storm with somebody with that kind of luck, I'd give him the rudder.'

Whether Stephen Daldry would indeed be offered the rudder of the National Theatre when Richard Eyre stepped down in 1997 was still an open question in the summer of 1995. As the *Vanity Fair* interviewer put it, 'You're supposed to be a candidate, aren't you, for the National Theatre? Are you or aren't you?'

'One doesn't declare one's candidacy,' Daldry replied rather icily.

But *Vanity Fair*, which – in the person of John Heilpern – had sought Daldry out precisely because of this career possibility, was not to be squelched so easily. 'If you were offered it, would you take it? Yes or no?'

'One never knows what one will do,' Daldry answered. 'My inclination would be no. But things change from one year to another. I've never had a career structure all mapped out. I never planned to be at the Royal Court. I just do what comes next . . . I'm very happy where I am,' he concluded.

'But you didn't say no, did you? You'll keep your options open, will you?' Heilpern persisted.

'I will,' said Daldry, in a tone that mixed faint resignation with a clear desire to be done with the subject.

Though he had no reason to be particularly honest with *Vanity Fair*, his expressed reservations about the job at the National were consistent with other aspects of Stephen Daldry's behaviour that summer. Early in June he told me he had an appointment to meet Richard Eyre, who wanted him to direct another play at the National Theatre, where *An Inspector Calls* and *Machinal* had both been huge critical successes. 'He's going to try to get me to do something before he leaves,' Daldry said. 'But I'm afraid I'll have to say no.'

'Why?' I asked, thinking this was odd behaviour for an ambitious heir-apparent.

'Too busy.'

It seemed unlikely that he could really be too busy, for two whole years, to carve out a few months' space for the kind of work that had made his international reputation. I wondered if this was indeed fear of failure, as a few people had suggested in the aftermath of *The Editing Process*. But perhaps it was something more complicated than that: a sign of Daldry's recognition that if he was to create new productions on the scale of *Inspector* and *Machinal*, he needed the leisure of a freelance life, untrammelled by the obligations of running a building.

He was indeed remarkably busy, as the unfolding summer was to demonstrate. The week of his appointment with Richard Eyre, he had just returned from three weeks away from the Court: one week cementing ties with a theatre in Berlin, one developing connections with Israeli and Palestinian playwrights in Jerusalem, and one putting the finishing touches to a version of *An Inspector Calls* for a festival in Vienna. (In the year since it had won a Tony on Broadway, Daldry's *Inspector* had also opened in Australia and Japan, and a new British production was scheduled to start touring in September, after which it would settle into the West End for an unlimited run.) After two days back in the office attempting to catch up, Daldry had an important initial meeeting with Edward Beckett – Samuel Beckett's nephew and literary executor – about his long-range plan to put on a Beckett radio play, *All That Fall,* as a stage production starring Joan Plowright. That evening Daldry was himself onstage at the Royal Court, as part of the Barclays New Stages Festival, interviewing the Welsh playwright Ed Thomas about his own work and Welsh theatre in general. On the Friday of that week, after meeting Richard Eyre in the morning, he attended the

George Devine Award ceremony, at which Jez Butterworth received the prize for his soon-to-be-produced *Mojo*. The playwright David Storey eloquently and wittily spoke for the whole prize committee (which also included Jocelyn Herbert, Dominic Drumgoole, Sara Daniels, Graham Whybrow, and Daldry himself) when he praised the originality and power of the script. 'Thank you so much, David. I didn't recognize the play in your description,' said the dark-haired, wide-eyed, still-wet-behind-the-ears young playwright as he got up to accept the award – to which the white-haired Storey replied, 'You will.'

And this was all in addition to Daldry's normal weekly workload, which included the regular two-hour Monday morning script meetings, attended by the three directors, the two members of the literary staff, the director of the Young People's Theatre Programme, and the current writer-in-residence; the evening workshops with the thirty-eight writers being 'developed' by the Royal Court; irregular but frequent meetings with the associate directors and the literary manager; weekly lunches with the theatre's patrons at the Garrick Club, hosted by author John Mortimer; intermittent publicity interviews with representatives of all forms of media, set up by the Court's press officer; conferences with architects about a proposed remodelling of the Royal Court; regular business meetings with the theatre's general manager and members of the board; special meetings with corporate and foundation sponsors; incessant phone calls, both business and social; and, in the spaces in between, solitary script reading. Permanently perched on Stephen Daldry's desk was a never-diminishing pile of unread scripts, about thirty inches in height. When Edward Beckett commented on the stack during their meeting about the radio play, Daldry answered him with a little metaphor. 'I like to compare it to the air traffic controllers' booth at Heathrow, where the object is to keep as many planes circling in the air as you can. That way you have a chance to land some of them, divert others to other airports, and perhaps convince some never to come back to your airport again.'

Even without the excess manuscripts, Daldry's was a punishing schedule. For years he had traded on and benefited from his seemingly unlimited supply of energy. 'He was always ready to say yes,' Julian Webber observed. 'If someone wanted to go out somewhere at five o'clock in the morning, I'd be likely to say, "No, thanks, I'm going home to bed," but Stephen would always say yes. And that's part of his luck, too – being in the right place at the right time.' But now, at thirty-five years of age, with the entire Royal Court and a number of other burdens on his back, it seemed possible that Stephen Daldry had said yes to too many things. By the middle of the summer, just before *Mojo*'s decisive opening night, it was clear that he was on overload.

There was, first of all, the normal autumn season to organize, with more new plays opening than ever before, in both the Theatre Upstairs and the main theatre. 'This theatre's doing twice as many plays as it was four years ago,' James Macdonald told me; and even the 1991 level of production was an increase over the rate fifteen years before, when the Court premièred fewer than five plays a year. In typical fashion, Daldry had left many of the crucial decisions about the upcoming season to the last possible moment, so that he was now having to scramble to make everything work. But in addition to the regular autumn season, he had also decided to run a special revival season at a theatre in the West End – a new series of 'Royal Court Classics', featuring David Storey's *The Changing Room*, Ron Hutchinson's *Rat in the Skull*, and Terry Johnson's *Hysteria*, each with a seven-week limited run. This in turn involved the selection of a theatre (Daldry picked the Duke of York's, a large, old, attractive space on St Martin's Lane), protracted negotiations with commercial co-producers, and all the numerous other time-consuming tasks associated with setting up a new season in a new place. The entire revival season was to be sponsored by the *Evening Standard*, and that too involved delicate negotiations. (In one business meeting I sat in on, the Court's general manager, Vikki Heywood, was urging the need to pin down the exact terms of the *Standard*'s request for 'sole sponsorship', whereas Stephen Daldry preferred to leave the arrangement vague, suggesting that the major funder could be described as the season's 'sponsor' and any smaller donors credited as 'supporters' of individual plays.)

Daldry himself was scheduled to direct *Rat in the Skull*, a play about Northern Ireland that had had its première at the Royal Court in September 1984 in a production directed by Max Stafford-Clark. Why, I asked James Macdonald, had Daldry chosen this play with which to break his directorial silence? 'He's very interested in Ireland, and in theatre about Ireland,' Macdonald answered. 'He's always loved the play.' He paused. 'It's been talked about quite a bit over the last couple of years. It's something he's been trying to do for a while.' This shed a whole new light on the issue of timing; that is, the long or short gaps between plays might be attributed not, or not only, to a director's desires and fears, but also to the external factors that made a play castable, or available, or otherwise appropriate for production at any given time. If it could take years to arrange to do a specific play, then it became more difficult to draw any conclusions about the order of its appearance in a director's *œuvre*. (On the other hand, there were always plays available. Macdonald himself, for instance, had directed four plays for the Royal Court in the preceding twelve months, during which Daldry had only done *The Editing Process*. So if directing wasn't completely a matter of choice, *not* directing certainly seemed to be.)

Because the Irish situation had changed in recent months due to a negotiated ceasefire and the subsequent, still fragile 'peace process', Daldry had asked Ron Hutchinson to rewrite the play slightly. He was also meeting fortnightly and sometimes weekly with William Dudley, the designer he had chosen for this production. (Ian MacNeil was occupied during this period with the design of an opera, *Tristan und Isolde*, and in any case Daldry had already decided not to use him for *Rat*.) The director–designer discussions included everything from the structure of the set to the specifics of casting, with detailed reference to the atmosphere and content of the dialogue. Daldry at this point had an ambitious plan for using projections in the design, and the projector he wanted was so expensive that he was searching for additional subsidies; that too took time. Finally, he had to cast the play in time to begin rehearsals in early September, so throughout the summer he was calling agents, sending out Xeroxed copies of the script, and meeting with actors who had, or could do, the requisite Irish and English accents.

At the same time, he was making all the preparations for the next (and possibly last) production of his *Inspector Calls* in Britain. Ever since transferring from the National Theatre to the West End, *Inspector* had been Stephen Daldry's primary means of support. 'He's obviously establishing independent means through *Inspector Calls*, financially,' said Stephen Evans, who, as a stockbroker-turned-producer, had a healthy respect for money's relationship to art. Julian Webber estimated that by early 1995, Daldry's profits on *Inspector* had been sufficient either to secure him a reasonable income for life or to buy a large house in London; he chose home ownership. (Actually, the house was a joint purchase on the part of Stephen Daldry and Ian MacNeil, who were together remodelling their new Notting Hill Gate home – in 'a bizarre combination of Shaker and high-tech', as MacNeil wryly observed, assigning the high-tech tastes to his partner – during the summer of 1995.) So Daldry's reasons for agreeing to do *Inspector* again were financial as well as artistic – in which category I should include messianic, since he explicitly wanted as many people as possible to hear J. B. Priestley's still timely exhortation. By getting Julian Webber over from New York to help direct this British production, he would also be training Webber to handle the American touring production on his own.

Daldry's commercial partners wanted to bring *Inspector* back because they felt they had taken it out of the Aldwych prematurely, when it was still drawing crowds; in retrospect, they figured it had at least six more months' life in it. They also saw this as a kind of best-and-final version of *An Inspector Calls*, with all the kinks ironed out of the production and a top-rank cast. By the beginning of the summer Daldry had half the parts filled, including the Inspector (Nicholas Woodeson, who had taken over Kenneth Cranham's Broadway role after finishing his brief run in *The Editing Process*), but he was still searching for Sheila, Eric, and Mrs Birling. After auditioning nearly two dozen young actors and actresses, he chose Helen Schlesinger as Sheila and a newcomer named Tom Goodman-Hill as Eric. By mid-July, however, he had still not found a senior British actress willing to take on the role of Sybil Birling, and rehearsals were scheduled to begin in August: 'My personal nightmare' is how he described the situation to his producer. (He did eventually come up with an excellent 'Mrs B' in the person of Susan Engel, but by that time there were only two weeks to go before rehearsal – a close call, even for Daldry.)

In addition, Daldry was making long-term arrangements for other special projects. One, the Beckett play starring Joan Plowright, would be done at the Royal Court sometime in 1996, if he could secure the rights from the Beckett estate. But the other project had nothing to do with the Royal Court, except that it drew on one of the contacts he had made during the selection interview. Stephen Evans, whose company, Renaissance Films, had already backed films directed by Kenneth Branagh (*Much Ado About Nothing*) and Nicholas Hytner (*The Madness of King George*), had proposed to Stephen Daldry that he too make a film, and Daldry, excited by the idea, suggested a movie version of Iain Banks's first novel, *The Wasp Factory*. By the summer of 1995, the project had passed beyond the discussion stage into the specifics of scheduling, with Daldry's own availability being the major determining factor. In mid-June he attended a meeting at the Waldorf's Palm Court with Stephen Evans and his development director, the team of two screenwriters who had been hired to write the script, and Iain Banks. By the end of that meeting, they had arranged for the script to be written over the summer and polished in the autumn; for the option on the book to be purchased in January (after an earlier option had expired); and for the film to be shot in Scotland during eight weeks in the late spring and early summer of 1996.

So this was another task for Daldry to keep in the back of his mind, another artistic responsibility looming on the near horizon. I wondered, given the vagaries of the film industry, how likely it was that the movie would really be made; how certain, I asked Stephen Evans, was the financing? 'It's 100 per cent,' he assured me.

Though they may have occupied him mentally, Daldry's own special projects took up a relatively small percentage of his time. The vast majority of each day was spent on activities that would increase the stature of the Royal Court – or, in some cases, the stature of non-commercial theatre in Britain as a whole. His schedule was littered with public meetings, parliamentary testimony about the arts, and appointments with figures from the Arts Council and the government. And the Royal Court frequently acted as a high-profile site for events that served the entire theatre community. For instance, a special press conference featuring playwright David Edgar as its primary speaker took place in the Royal Court's Circle Bar on the last Friday in June. Its purpose was to publicize a recently developed proposal for a New Writing Fund which would subsidize new plays by imposing a so-called 'royalty' on *all* plays, even those long out of copyright; the funds collected by this means would then be redistributed to non-commercial theatres to support the extra costs of producing new drama.

'The problem that new work faces,' said Edgar, 'is that it is the most expensive kind to present. It takes longer to develop, it takes longer to rehearse, and it costs more to promote – because, unlike *Hamlet*, it is not already a known quantity . . . We are attracted by the idea that William Shakespeare should, from beyond the grave, as it were, aid and abet his successors.' Edgar more than once called attention to the appropriateness of making this announcement on the premises of the Royal Court, for many decades the acknowledged leader in staging new British drama. He pointed out to the assembled reporters that he was facing them 'not only from in front of the sign for the Gents, but the poster of the play which I regard as having launched the most vibrant period of contemporary British theatre' – and he gestured over his shoulder at a large, black-framed advertisement for *Look Back in Anger*. Stephen Daldry sat through the press conference in silent collegiality, his presence (as well as his role as nominal host) suggesting support for the flat-royalty idea. But when, after the formal presentation, he was asked by reporters from the *Daily Telegraph* and *Time Out* what he thought of the proposal, he impishly responded that it would all become irrelevant in September or October, when the floodgates of the National Lottery charity grants would open and millions of pounds would come pouring into the non-profit theatres.

Daldry's own plans for the National Lottery money, dictated by the capital-improvements rules of its distribution, involved a major remodelling of the Royal Court building. The feasibility study alone cost £20,000, and the actual reconstruction – which was budgeted at twenty-one million pounds – would require the theatre company to move elsewhere for a two-year period. The architectural plans, which had been arrived at after consultation with every member of the staff (and also with non-staff freelancers like Stephen Warbeck and Bill Dudley), included expanded office space, a technically improved auditorium, and an underground entrance leading from the theatre to the middle of Sloane Square.

Perhaps no Daldry project was more controversial than the proposal to rebuild the Royal Court. The outsized grant application caused raised eyebrows and ideological disputes even among his oldest friends. 'The grant is massive,' said Kate Rowland, a close friend of Daldry's since 1987. 'He wants it to be big. He wants to leave a memorial to Daldry,' she continued, using his surname – as she habitually does – to indicate a combination of affectionate irony and wry respect. 'And when I was arguing with him about that, he said, "You shouldn't knock this, Kate. It's important. Leaving something for the next century." And in a way he's right.' Rowland, herself a theatre director and radio-drama producer, understood exactly the extent to which the permanence of bricks and mortar held a special appeal for someone who normally worked in the ephemeral medium of performance. Acknowledging that Daldry's grandiose plans didn't in any way signal a departure from his basic political convictions – 'He doesn't sell out,' she noted – Rowland went on to praise him for 'putting an enormous amount of energy into the building. It's impressive, and it needed to happen.'

Others, however, were less understanding – particularly when, in September 1995, the lottery money came through at a record-breaking sixteen million pounds, by far the largest grant awarded to any theatre. On the afternoon of the grant announcement I was in a taxi with Stephen Daldry, heading towards a celebratory party at the Royal Court, and when Daldry asked the driver to pull over at the theatre in Sloane Square I heard the cabbie mutter, 'Oh, the place that just got that bloody huge chunk of money.'

'Yes, what do you think of that?' responded Daldry, always ready to engage.

'I think it's bloody awful,' said the cabbie. 'The money should be going to cancer research instead.'

'But those charities are going to have their chance later . . . ,' Daldry began, and when I got out of the taxi he was still explaining to the driver, in excruciating detail, the business and politics of lottery-grant funding.

The cabbie's pounds-and-pence objection, which had its corollary in the undisguised envy of less fortunate administrators of non-profit arts organizations, was not the only reason to criticize the remodelling plan. To many in the world of British theatre, the Royal Court building was a venerated landmark, not to be tinkered with lightly. The brick-fronted, four-storey edifice had originally been constructed as a theatre in 1888, and it bore its Victorian ancestry in the lineaments of its façade – in the purely decorative gables, the symmetry of its window placements, the slightly italic lettering in which 'The Royal Court' was spelled out at the top level. Just after the turn of the century it had housed Harley Granville Barker's acting company, which premièred eleven plays by George Bernard Shaw as well as other new dramas by Galsworthy, Ibsen, and Maeterlinck. As a schoolboy, Laurence Olivier saw his first theatrical production at the Royal Court and, somewhat later, his first Shakespeare play. After being dark for a number of years, the theatre was converted into a cinema in the early 1930s; then it was bombed in the Second World War and left abandoned until its reconstruction in 1952.

Its most noteworthy phase began in 1956, when George Devine and his colleagues – initially Tony Richardson, eventually John Dexter and Lindsay Anderson – founded the English Stage Company. Among the first season's offerings were Angus Wilson's first (and last) play, Arthur Miller's *The Crucible*, and John Osborne's *Look Back in Anger*, which was to give the theatre its lasting reputation as a home for 'Angry Young Men'. Under Devine, the Royal Court became the primary British outlet for new plays by Beckett, Brecht, and Ionesco. It also developed home-grown talents in playwriting (not only Osborne, but Arnold Wesker, Ann Jellicoe, David Storey), set design (Jocelyn Herbert), and acting (Alan Bates, Joan Plowright, Michael Gambon, Alan Howard, Bob Hoskins, and innumerable other names which still dominate the stage and screen). Devine relinquished his leadership of the Court in 1965 and died soon after, at the age of fifty-five; and though the theatre he left behind kept the name of the English Stage Company and continued to occupy the old building, its history in the subsequent quarter-century mainly lacked the lustre and excitement of that first decade.

No one was more interested in the historical associations of this old building than Stephen Daldry. After accepting the job of artistic director, he plunged himself into reading about the place, researching George Devine as he had once researched J. B. Priestley. On the wall of his tiny office (in which three desks, belonging to Daldry, Macdonald, and Rickson, occupied a space taller than it was wide) hung an array of eighteen posters, simply and identically designed in black, white, yellow, and orange, announcing the seasonal offerings of the English Stage

Company's first few years. Directly above Daldry's own desk was a black-and-white photograph of George Devine. Books, articles, and clippings about the history of the Royal Court were stuffed into various nooks and crannies of the overcrowded room. 'I think some people have been surprised that Stephen has so thoroughly immersed himself in the organization and its history,' Stella Hall said to me. 'The last two Christmases he's organized treasure hunts that show a remarkable knowledge of the building and everything that's taken place in all its little corners.'

Yet it was Daldry who was proposing to introduce drastic changes to the interior of the historic building. He had even suggested redesigning the stage area of the main auditorium, a jewel-box of a theatre which put the audience intimately in touch with the performers. These remodelling suggestions had the strong support of designer Bill Dudley, who had worked frequently at the Royal Court in the 1960s and had found its stage annoyingly inflexible. But they were deemed unnecessary and, indeed, highly objectionable by most of the playwrights associated with theatre's past. In this respect as in others, Daldry was like the Ted figure in *The Editing Process*, who (as Ian MacNeil put it) 'straddles' the two worlds. He was drawn to both the old and the new, and though he treasured history, he was also able and willing to adapt to change, even if it meant altering a building he loved.

To make the situation still more contradictory and ambiguous, there was a historical precedent for Daldry's radical remodelling, in the form of an architectural renovation plan developed by George Devine himself. According to Richard Findlater's summary in the 1981 anthology *At the Royal Court*:

> Devine's biggest managerial headaches concerned the reconstruction of the Sloane Square building . . . He planned to eliminate the proscenium arch, replace the hierarchical three-level auditorium with a one-tier showplace, and build an experimental studio behind (or on top of) the Court. These changes were linked with hopes of establishing a new local identity by opening the building through the day for exhibi-

tions, discussions and film shows (like some of the new civic theatres now appearing on the horizon); of developing training and educational work; of acquiring a second, larger house (perhaps the Chelsea Palace?) and even of setting up a second company, with a permanent base in the West End.

But 'the visionary plan collapsed under the weight of a budget at least double the original estimate', as a result of which 'Devine knuckled under and produced a modest compromise programme at a tenth of the cost (about £22,500)'. Ironically, if George Devine had been allowed to go ahead with his 1960s remodel, the Royal Court might now be saving millions of pounds in 1990s construction costs. Still, it's probably just as well that his plans were thwarted, since Devine's radical redesign would have destroyed the perfectly proportioned auditorium so treasured by the Court's playwrights.

It's also true that by the summer of 1995 the various activities taking place at the Royal Court far exceeded the building's capacity to contain them. The old Victorian structure on Sloane Square was like the house on stilts in Stephen Daldry's production of *An Inspector Calls*: a tiny, vastly overcrowded building just waiting to explode. Each small office space, designed to hold one person comfortably, was packed with three and sometimes four over-worked, stress-ridden staff members. The network of narrow hallways leading between the offices was routinely described by Daldry as 'a warren', and no one who had been there fewer than five times could hope to find her way out unassisted. Arrangements were so *ad hoc* that in order to get from the directors' office to the publicity department, it was necessary to go through the theatre itself. The only public gathering place in the building was the Circle Bar. With its tall windows overlooking Sloane Square, its elegantly curved counters and banquettes, its red-plush stools, and its idiosyncratically sloping ceiling (against which tall people sometimes bumped their heads, just like careless actors emerging from the too-small door in *Inspector*), the Circle Bar was a pleasant enough space when nearly empty. But it was ragged with over-use, with morning meetings giving way to lunches for the International Summer School participants and then to crowded afternoons, during which auditioning actors mingled with aspiring playwrights, resident technicians, and people waiting for appointments with Stephen Daldry. The building was so packed that a number of its peripheral activities – lunches for theatre critics and arts editors, workshops for the development of children's theatre programmes, rehearsals of forthcoming plays – had to be farmed out to neighbouring sites in Chelsea, an arrangement that in turn required the Royal Court staff to rush in and out all day. The place felt like a madhouse, and in many ways it was one.

That there was method behind this madness came through in an interview Stephen Daldry gave to the novelist Margaret Drabble, who dropped by the theatre one evening towards the end of June. Drabble was there in her capacity as a 1995 judge for the Prudential Awards for non-profit theatres (one of which Daldry had won for the Gate when he was there in 1992), and she was particularly interested in hearing about all the Court's development activities, from writers in residence to theatre in the schools. From everything Daldry said to her, it became clear that he was intentionally following the principles laid down by the original founder of the English Stage Company – intentionally, but also characteristically, because it suited his own temperament as a leader to govern as loosely as George Devine had. What the *Sunday Times* had darkly referred to as 'his hands-off managerial style' was Daldry's way of restoring Devine's 'plurality of tastes' to the theatre – 'as opposed to the Stalinist mode that prevailed under my predecessor', he told Drabble. He felt strongly that a theatre of new writing should spring from many tastes, not just one, and he quoted Arnold Wesker's line to the effect that George Devine had always hated his work but was willing to do it because John Dexter liked it. (Wesker's actual words, as printed in *At the Royal Court*, were: 'They didn't like or understand what I wrote, but they took the risk. I'd like to think they trusted the writer. Perhaps they only trusted the directors – Anderson and Dexter. But whoever and however, they gave this writer self-confidence and to them I owe an unreturnable debt.')

Ian Rickson, who had worked as a freelance director at the Royal Court under Max Stafford-Clark and had then been appointed associate director under Daldry, was able to compare the so-called 'Stalinist mode' to the current 'plurality of tastes' strategy. 'Max has wonderful rigour,' Rickson said (choosing exactly the same word with which Stella Hall had described Max Stafford-Clark). 'Rigour, focus, and detail. What I learnt off Max was, look after the detail and the whole will look after itself. Sometimes that attention to detail and focus could be a weakness as well as a strength, in so far as he was less able to let go of control. But I don't really want to slag off Max, because I really respect him. And the opposite, in Stephen, is that he's more permissive, more open . . . That's a very positive thing about Stephen – he's extremely permissive and trusting.' James Macdonald seconded this view when he commented, 'What's extraordinary about Stephen is the amount of space he gives to other people to run with their own ideas and tastes.'

Daldry's permissiveness was especially apparent in the way he allowed Ian Rickson, a young director with no mainstage experience, to handle the important première of *Mojo*. 'He never manifested any anxiety about that choice; he was just very encouraging,' Rickson told me. 'He likes that phrase – is it George Devine? – "Policy is the people you work with."' (Actually, it was William Gaskill, or so Gaskill claims in his autobiographical book *A Sense of Direction*.) Rickson and I were seated in the office Rickson normally shared with Daldry, and at this point he glanced at the photo that hung over Daldry's desk. 'He seems to be turning into George Devine, have you noticed? He's even getting to look like him.'

I *had* noticed. It was Daldry's method, in taking on a new play, to enter, chameleonlike, into the persona of its author. For *Machinal*, he had immersed himself in contemplation of machine-age artefacts of the 1920s. When he did *An Inspector*

Calls, he had absorbed all of J. B. Priestley's theatrical, philosophical, and political opinions. 'Those aren't his politics – he
just adopted them for *Inspector*,' Julian Webber had at one point
commented about Daldry's old-leftism. 'He has a tendency to
take on whatever is in a given play.' This perhaps overstates the
case, for the plays Stephen Daldry chose to direct already had
something of his opinions in them. He was not so much trading
one personality for another as unearthing a different side of his
own character. Still, Webber's analysis was pertinent to Daldry's
career at the Royal Court. He was approaching the administra-
tion of the theatre much as he would approach a script, by sub-
merging himself in its author's views – with the result that he was
indeed, as Ian Rickson said, 'turning into George Devine'. My
sense of this was confirmed when I read John Osborne's tribute
to Devine, which closely echoed what Daldry's associates had
said about him. 'He could contain and comprehend many different things: that was one of his strengths,' Osborne wrote. 'It
wasn't that he was weak or compromising; he could be brutal or
dismissive, and he went for what he wanted. But he had a special
kind of tolerance. He suffered talent gladly.'

The Devine connection explained, in part, why *Mojo* was such
an important play for Daldry. Three years into his appointment
at the Royal Court and two years into his solo reign, it indicated
that he was capable of finding his own version of *Look Back in
Anger* – that he too, like George Devine, was in the business of
discovering and developing talented young playwrights. 'That
was talismanic for us,' Ian Rickson said of *Mojo*'s success. 'There
were more safe bets we could have filled the summer with, more
starry things, but this felt like the sort of dare we should go for. I
mean, the very act of theatre is an act of faith, isn't it?' The play
had landed on Rickson's desk, sent by an agent, and he and
Daldry were especially enthusiastic about it. They secured the
rights to it and scheduled it for a performance date only two
months away – a huge risk, given the rough state of the script
and the normal difficulties of putting on a new play. When, a
week or two into rehearsals, Jez Butterworth won the George

Devine Award (a prize given independently of the Royal Court management, and open to scripts from all over), it must have seemed to Daldry like a ghostly confirmation of his act of faith.

I saw *Mojo* twice – once with Stephen Daldry, at the dress rehearsal, and once on press night, with what appeared to be half of theatrical London in attendance. Between the dress rehearsal and the opening performance, *Mojo* had lost fifteen minutes of dialogue and gained an audience. It was the second factor that made the difference. In rehearsal, the writing had seemed snappy and musical and clever, but somehow dead, like a symphony played in a concert hall with horrible, flattening acoustics. With an audience laughing excitedly in response to the black humour and falling silent at the moments of greatest tension, the play came to life: its rhythms finally made sense. The first act, I thought, was stronger than the second, and the script as a whole had its limitations: it would be easy to argue that *Mojo* was not really the best new play to première at the Royal Court that year. (My own vote, in fact, would have gone to Sebastian Barry's *The Steward of Christendom*, which – in a production directed by Max Stafford-Clark – opened at the Theatre Upstairs in spring 1995 and initiated the mainstage season in the autumn.) Butterworth's début was not, in that sense, exactly comparable to John Osborne's in 1956. But *Mojo* undeniably represented the discovery and cultivation of a major new playwriting talent.

I knew that Daldry had gone backstage after the *Mojo* dress rehearsal to give his 'notes', and Ian Rickson later told me that this was the first and last direct advice he had given. 'He wanted me to put in as much sex as possible,' Rickson said when I asked him about Daldry's suggestions. 'When they come downstairs right at the end of the play, he wanted them all naked. But I'd tried that, and it just looked farcical, like a Joe Orton comedy.' Rickson did, however, end up taking other parts of Daldry's advice. 'I knew I had to make some cuts; he suggested areas where they could be.' Mostly, he felt, 'Stephen was just supportive and encouraging'. James Macdonald confirmed the fact that Daldry only gave his associate directors as much advice as they needed. 'He'll come in . . . I will get notes off him at some point,' Macdonald said. 'He's very good at being helpful at a point when you need help.'

However little he may have influenced the actual production, Daldry stood to gain or lose a great deal from the success or failure of *Mojo*. It may have been Jez Butterworth's première and Ian Rickson's mainstage début, but for Daldry it was the first real proof (or disproof) of his effectiveness as leader of the Royal Court. And in that respect the play turned out to be an enormous success. 'Jez Butterworth's *Mojo* marks the Royal Court's most dazzling main-stage début in years,' Michael Billington said in the first sentence of his *Guardian* review, and these words were echoed almost exactly in *Time Out*'s rave notice. Shaun Usher of the *Daily Mail* called it 'the most striking first play in my experience'; Charles Spencer announced in the *Daily Telegraph* that 'the Royal Court had discovered a won-derful new writer. Everyone knew they were at the birth of something special'; and even critics who were doubtful about the play, like Benedict Nightingale, admitted that Jez Butterworth was 'a British dramatist of obvious talent and terrific promise' whose first work made you 'long to see his next play'. That this all redounded to Stephen Daldry's credit was made explicit in a small item in *The Times*. 'Stephen took over the junior common room at Royal Court Comprehensive so young – was he 11 or 12? – that some had their doubts,' it began coyly. 'After two years, these are mostly answered . . . he has an unprejudiced eye, an instinct for quality and a willingness to take a chance: Sam Shepard's *Simpatico* and, especially, Jez Butterworth's new *Mojo*.' The plays cited may have been directed by Macdonald and Rickson, but it was Daldry who received the media laurels.

His Devine impersonation was complete. He had successfully masterminded the careers of both a startling new playwright and a sensitive new director; and, working with the lightest of touches, he had brought forth this and other premières in a way that elicited praise for his generosity, trust, and openness. But Stephen Daldry was not, finally, George Devine, and the forces that had attracted his talented colleagues to the Royal Court were other than those that had brought in Tony Richardson, John Dexter, and Lindsay Anderson. George Devine was an actor as much as a director; he was known for spotting stage-worthy plays and for cultivating talent in others, but he was not famous for the quality of his own productions. Stephen Daldry, on the other hand, was. What had brought people like James Macdonald, Ian Rickson, and Stella Hall to the Court was not just Daldry's charismatic personality or exciting ideas, but the chance to work with someone whose own directing they deeply admired. 'What I've liked about all his work,' explained Stella Hall, 'is the painting glorious pictures, the choreographic sense, the musicality, the rhythm. None of that is to downgrade any other aspect of it – it's not style over substance. Those things all contribute to reveal the writer's intentions, but they also create a very satisfying theatrical whole. What I like is the seamless marriage of words, sound, image.' Ian Rickson was equally admiring, though he spoke of slightly different qualities. 'What's special about him is that he has an extremely potent inner world,' he said of Daldry as director. 'So he's able to create a world that has a wonderful sense of play, but is rooted in very primal social and psychological realities. So something like *Inspector Calls*, what's so exciting about that production is the way he's made the kind of myth of the play really vivid and accessible and exciting – and theatrical, of course.' James Macdonald, when I asked him what he thought of Daldry's own directing, simply answered, 'I love it. I think it's extraordinary. I think he's fantastically good at telling a story in the most theatrical way possible, so that it really touches you on every level.'

Even the board of the Royal Court had chosen Stephen Daldry in large part because of his artistic achievements. They may have been pleased with his ability to imitate George Devine's managerial accomplishments, but they also expected from him what they would have expected from Deborah Warner, Sam Mendes, Declan Donnellan, or any other first-rank director of that talented generation: they expected him to direct stunning plays. And they were still waiting for that. 'Of course, the jury is out,' Stephen Evans had told me. 'The work he's known for is not at the Court, but at the National – both with amazing sets. The jury's still out on how he can do with more conventional plays, how he can work with actors.' *The Editing Process* didn't count – most people were willing to write it off as a random, idiosyncratic failure – but this meant that it had been a full eighteen months since Daldry had directed one of his characteristically extraordinary productions. That earlier success, in February 1994, had been a revival of an old Royal Court classic, Arnold Wesker's *The Kitchen*; and perhaps with this in mind, Daldry now selected another Royal Court revival with which to prove his powers. It was also a revival for him personally, since *Rat in the Skull* was one of the plays Stephen Daldry had done as a freelance regional director in the late 1980s. As with *An Inspector Calls*, which he had to do twice (first in York, and then, triumphantly, in London) before he finally got it right, he was planning to revisit a play he had already directed in an attempt to improve on his own work.

6 *Rat in the Skull*

'He does like to restage things,' said Daldry's old friend Kate Rowland. She was speaking to me in September 1995, by which time she had been following Stephen Daldry's career closely for over eight years. They'd met, in fact, during his original production of *Rat in the Skull*, which opened on 3 June 1987 at the Liverpool Playhouse Studio; as associate producer in charge of the Studio theatre, Rowland had been responsible for bringing the twenty-seven-year-old Daldry over from Sheffield, where he was then an associate director, to stage something in Liverpool. The choice of *Rat in the Skull*, she remembered, had been his.

'It was stunning,' she said of that production. 'I suppose I'd use the word "startling". He used the studio completely in the round, with a metal walkway all the way around and an area of peat in the middle. So you had these two conflicting images. And you were totally surrounding it, and it was very claustrophobic . . . What it had – which was rare, knowing his subsequent work – was a cleanness. Stephen can sometimes overdo. That one, because of its simplicity, was so good. It's not often you can remember the exact details of a production, and even the full cast, this many years later.'

Part of the reason the production needed to be so 'clean' was that *Rat in the Skull* is itself such a complex play, both structurally and politically. 'Be careful,' warned a reviewer for the Liverpool newspaper, giving Daldry's production an otherwise glowing review. 'If you are not familiar with the Irish Question it could be heavy going.' The play's structure seems, at first, deceptively simple: it has only four characters, and it takes place mainly during one afternoon and evening in the Paddington Green police station in London. But this apparent simplicity masks a host of complications. The four characters – Michael

Patrick de Valera 'Demon Bomber' Roche, an IRA terrorist who
has been captured by the London police; Detective-Inspector
Nelson, a member of the Northern Irish, Protestant-run Royal
Ulster Constabulary, who has been called to London to 'turn'
Roche and convert him into an informant; Superintendent
Harris, the English officer in charge of the station where Roche
is being held; and Police Constable Naylor, the young English
policeman assigned to supervise Nelson's interrogation of Roche
– are each made to represent a full range of attitudes about the
so-called Irish Question. Through their soliloquies and interactions, we are exposed to the proprietary English sense of empire,
and the duties attendant on such powers; the countervailing
English distaste for the problems of 'aliens', accompanied by the
desire to be rid of Ireland politically and militarily; the mutual
hatred between Irish Protestants and Irish Catholics, dating
back centuries before the 1921 treaty split off the six Northern
counties from the Southern republic; and, coupled with and perhaps mitigating this hatred, the strange sense of kinship between
the two kinds of Irishmen in the face of English prejudice and
control.

The plot, which jumps about in time, involves the RUC
officer's inexplicable beating of the IRA prisoner (a beating
which invalidates the arrest and thereby frees the prisoner) and
the English superintendent's subsequent effort to unravel the
motive behind the fight. Consisting largely of loquacious monologues designed to be spoken in rapid-fire Belfast accents, *Rat in
the Skull* is a harsh, prickly, verbally aggressive, quick-witted,
and extremely masculine play. It was its masculinity which,
among other things, caused it to stick in Kate Rowland's mind as
an example of the way Daldry 'combines his own personal politics
with the text – not imposed, but organically. In that piece,' she
recalled about the 1987 production, 'it was the maleness, the sexuality, the attraction – that highly charged atmosphere – that made
it Stephen's. Somebody else would just do cops and robbers.'

As she spoke, the London revival of *Rat in the Skull*, which
Stephen Daldry was directing for the 1995–6 Royal Court

Classics season, was in the midst of its third week of rehearsals. Two weeks later, the cast of four men – Rufus Sewell as Roche, Tony Doyle as Nelson, John Castle as Harris, and Pearce Quigley as Naylor – would move into the Duke of York's for technical rehearsal, dress rehearsal, and previews. Though they had been shown a model box of the set at an early rehearsal, the 'tech' was the first time the four actors would actually try out the theatre space William Dudley had devised for them, a completely restructured auditorium in which the Victorian endstage of the old Duke of York's had been transformed into a theatre-in-the-round. The stage itself – which rested on top of the newly constructed stalls, at shoulder height to the lowest level of the audience, while tiers of seats rose above it on all sides – consisted of a rectangular metal walkway and, within it, a separated-off diamond of compressed, garden-variety dirt. Bill Dudley had never seen Stephen Daldry's 1987 version of the play; until the third night of previews for the 1995 production, he had never even heard of it. Yet Daldry had managed to get his designer essentially to recreate the stage on which he had first presented *Rat in the Skull*.

How this was accomplished says something about the play itself as well as about Stephen Daldry. For, like his original interpretation of *Rat in the Skull*, the set design was 'not imposed, but organically' arrived at, with the full collusion if not the full foreknowledge of Bill Dudley. When Max Stafford-Clark directed *Rat in the Skull*'s première at the Royal Court in 1984, it had been set on a bare grey stage which virtually all the reviewers described as 'a police station' or 'a police cell' or 'a cell in Paddington Green police station'. Daldry wanted to get away from that image – from that 'cops and robbers' look, as Kate Rowland put it. 'I want to do it again because I think it's really a poem, not a play,' Daldry told Rufus Sewell when he came to audition for the part of Roche on 19 June 1995, 'and I want to do it as a poem, with all its metaphorical aspects. Not in a police station, the way it was done the first time. I want there to be two territories on the stage, and the Irish don't go into the English section, and the English don't

go into the Irish. And I want them to be in mud,' he said, referring to the Irishmen. It would be a literal patch of earth which, by
the end of the play, would come to represent the beloved land
over which these characters were struggling.

By 26 June, when Stephen Daldry and Bill Dudley met at the
Duke of York's to look over the theatre for the first time, Dudley
had already come up with a rough sketch. At this point they
were talking about an endstage production with a series of complicated projections – visual images that would include the pris-
tine Irish landscape, news footage of IRA bombings and Ulster
reprisals, photographs of beaten-up prisoners, and so forth. Still,
the essential division of territories was already built into the
design. In Dudley's Macintosh-produced sketch (with a pair of
scanned-in Francis Bacon nudes representing the two Irishmen
and the figure of a formally dressed English gentleman standing
in for the London police officers), two men struggled together in
a peat-textured circular pit, while above them four metal cat-
walks radiated outwards from a round, hollow core. Holding the
sketch in his hand and examining it closely, Daldry mused, 'I'm
having an anxiety about the practicalities of where people are at
each point. The body of the play, in the interrogation, I'm not
worried about at all. The problem is Naylor, fucking Naylor,
when he's in the cell – he can't be in on their ground, but where
is he? He can't be in the middle,' said Daldry, gesturing towards
the empty core, 'but –'.

'Can't be marginalized,' interrupted Dudley, finishing the sentence with typical intuitive accuracy.

'Right,' said Daldry. 'So that's a problem. The next problem is,
the position for Harris and Naylor at the beginning and end of
the play, the first twenty minutes and the last ten. What would
be useful to do – and it's fucking boring – is actually to plot
through where the bastards are. I want to avoid a two-shot;
they've got to be able to move. Maybe the structure itself –
what's over Ireland – actually moves.'

'There's a penalty for movements, on a piece like this,' Dudley
warned.

'There is a penalty,' Daldry agreed. 'The great danger is that we overproduce.'

Bill Dudley thought a moment. 'This thing of the England and Ireland separate –'

'That's got to hold,' insisted Daldry. 'It's just the mechanics. This is the world that's difficult,' he said, his finger circling over the raised walkways, and then, pointing to the pit, 'not this world. What I quite like about this is it's abstracted from literal old Strangeways.'

'Exactly,' answered Dudley.

The metal walkways, the patch of dirt, and the abstraction from a literal prison were still there in the final design, but everything else had changed. About two weeks before the first day of rehearsal, Dudley and Daldry decided to switch the design to an in-the-round structure, with a square, shallow box of dirt set diagonally on the middle of a larger structure consisting of metal walkways. Each of them told me later that they had made this decision jointly – in part to pick up on all the 'Oriental' elements they had 'quite independently' noticed in Bill Dudley's sketches. 'We've used a kind of Kabuki theatre shape, where you have a walkway area that is roughly at shoulder height to the stalls,' Dudley explained in his presentation of the model box. 'The raised area to simulate Irish peat is a bit like a sumo wrestling area. In a way it's an English detective's perception of Ireland, and in another way it's a wrestling ground.' And at this point, with the action set in the round, the projections automatically dropped away. They were replaced in part by posters that fluttered from the tiers of seats at every level – sheets of newsprint showing the before-and-after condition of the beaten Irishman's face, charts and statistics about Irish terrorism, photographs of evidence rooms and demonstrations and sites of terrorist bombings, a composite portrait of the suspected bomber, and so on. 'These banners – again, it's very Chinese – represent the incident room,' said Dudley, 'where all the police's case against Roche, the bomber, is blown up and stylized.'

When the play was actually performed, part of the atmosphere that would have been created by the projections was produced by Rick Fisher's lighting, Stephen Warbeck's music, and Paul Arditti's sound effects. But the new design was not concerned primarily with replacing what had been lost with the projections. Mainly, what the in-the-round structure did was to substitute the audience's own imagination for something more pictorial. Discussing the set in front of a group of foreign theatre professionals on the night after the play opened, Stephen Daldry commented, 'I think the idea was to focus it, to try to release the play, and to find a poetic language rather than a literal language. If it's end-on, you have to be physically looking at something. Part of the idea of getting rid of that was that a physical manifestation of where they were could only be "decor" . . . It was a matter of trying to unclutter the play, and the main danger was that it would look like *Prime Suspect*, with all these realistic coppers going about their police business.'

Among other things, the newly devised set solved some of the problems Daldry had raised during his 26 June meeting with Bill Dudley. The danger of 'overproducing' had disappeared with the projections. Like *The Editing Process*'s clean-lined, nearly transparent set, the design for *Rat in the Skull* was a triumph of negative capability, managing to achieve, through great expense and effort, a look of complete bareness. The still, stark image was an unusual one for Daldry: there were no revolves, no raising and lowering of heavy machinery, no exploding houses, no fully operating kitchens. The only things that moved in this set were the actors. And Bill Dudley had designed the four-sided metal walkway and the internal patch of dirt so that the actors really *could* move: rushing on to the stage at the play's opening to the clang and bustle of alarms, ringing phones, and feet pounding against metal; circling clockwise and counter-clockwise around the central dirt square, and even coming right up to its slightly raised edge; chasing each other, following each other, facing each other down. The set that was finally constructed in the Duke of York's became a place where the choreography of the actors' movements could match the velocity of their words, and where each character's relation to the other three could be played out physically. Even the problem of Constable Naylor's location had been solved. As witness and transcriber of the central interrogation, he had been given a small fold-up chair along one side of the metal walkway, just in front of and next to a stage-level box in which paying playgoers were seated – so that Naylor, as the naïve Englishman watching the incomprehensible Irishmen play out their rough game, sat pretty much with the rest of the Duke of York's audience.

And if Naylor sat on the sidelines with us, then we in turn were dragged into the action with him. Part of what *Rat in the Skull* had to tell us, in this particular production, was what Superintendent Harris told PC Naylor in their final scene together. 'You're in the ring,' Harris avuncularly if rather sharply advises the younger man, 'and no one cares that you couldn't be less dead uninterested in the hows and the whys and the back in the mists of bleeding time.' We were *all* in the ring, in this staging – especially those of us who sat in the inner stalls seats, between the outer walkway and the central box of peat, with the action taking place all around us and the harsh words flying over our heads. But even those of us in the upper tiers which ringed the stage were part of the action, for we were simultaneously the avid observers of the wrestling match and the captive audience of the play. Trapped behind wire-mesh barriers in our high-tech imitation of a prison, silenced for the duration of an intermissionless two-hour play, we were one of the necessary circles in the concentric rings that made up *Rat in the Skull*'s structure.

One sign that Ron Hutchinson had, in constructing his play, exchanged linearity for something more like circularity lay in its odd use of time. The play begins with Roche talking to an audience of unseen listeners about his arrest and interrogation in London. The moment is confusing, and it is never explicitly clarified, but by the end of the play we have enough information to guess that this half-joking, half-defensive initial 'confession' is taking place in front of Roche's IRA chums, perhaps a few months after he's been released. We can't know this when we first hear it, however; and immediately after meeting Roche (who is seated centre-stage, lounging and smoking in a swivel chair planted exactly in the middle of the dirt square), we are introduced to Superintendent Harris, who strolls around the outer walkway issuing orders in response to 'what happened to the Irishman this afternoon'. If we are exceedingly quick – and if we have focused on the medallions of rosy light that flashed briefly on the blown-up photos of Roche's beaten face, just before his first speech – we *may* be able to deduce that Roche's ironic line about 'the holiday snaps' and Harris's reference to finding 'Paddy in that condition' allude to the same beating incident. But even if we have made it this far, we'll be very unlikely to understand that the subsequent scene between Roche and Harris is actually played out in two very different places at two very different moments in time. Roche only seems to be speaking to Harris; he is actually in Ireland, responding to questions posed by his IRA controllers some months later. And Harris only seems to be answering Roche's smart remarks, for *he* is actually back at the police station with his sidekick Naylor, trying to puzzle out what has happened to explain the fact that 'this morning they had one Hibernian in here in mint condition', and, 'Now that man looks like he's had major roadworks on his face and ribs.'

From Harris's first attempt to deal with the crisis, which takes place just after the beating has occurred, we then move back in time to the arrival of DI Nelson, the RUC 'specialist' who has been 'pulled back from leave' to 'turn' Roche. Most of the play consists of Nelson's interrogation of an alternately silent and shouting Roche. However, even this chronologically sequential section is crucially interrupted not only by Nelson's own explosively imaginative tales – he invokes a whole mythical Irish-Catholic family history for Roche, and then another equally implausible Protestant one for himself – but also by a strange monologue from PC Naylor which has no apparent location in real time. ('Naylor's Dream' is how Pearce Quigley, the actor playing Naylor, jokingly referred to this hilarious but heartfelt speech, in which Naylor, stepping off the 'English' walkway into the 'Irish' dirt, complains, 'I'm in there with them. They'd signed me up. I'm part of their Holy Fucking War and leave me out, I'd said.') Harris reappears briefly – he yanks the action into the near future by questioning Naylor about what occurred in the cell, as if it has all happened already – and then disappears again, leaving the interrogation between Nelson and Roche to take its course. Immediately after Nelson has turned Roche, he beats him up before he has the chance to name any names – though we don't, in this production, actually see the beating. During the few seconds of darkness and noise that represent the moment of violence, the scene shifts again, to another interrogation room. This time it is Nelson who sits in the central swivel chair, partially silent under the barrage of language, while Harris tries to find out why he did what he did. Nelson gives no satisfaction, and Harris abandons him in disgust: his parting line is 'Paddies? I can smell them. Animals, they are.' He leaves Nelson alone onstage, accompanied only by the inert body of the beaten Roche – which, in the actual time and place represented by that theatrical moment, isn't really there.

Roche then rises slowly from the dirt in which he's lying, and we get the end of the play, a brief, powerful, and utterly mysterious scene between Nelson and Roche. The flickering green-and-white lighting, the vague smell of peat, and the background music (an Irish-sounding theme combining accordion, bodhrán, and tin whistle) all suggest that they are back in Belfast together, months or even years after their London encounter. As in the initial Harris–Roche scene, they at first speak at cross-purposes to each other, seeming to address their lines to different, invisible listeners. Eventually, though, they engage in a real exchange – until, at the very end, Roche suddenly describes Nelson as if setting up a target for an IRA assassination ('That's him. The blue Sierra with the roof rack . . .'). After a brief but fraught pause, Nelson responds with an Irish joke: 'Pat and Mike are ordered to bump off this RUC man . . . The RUC man doesn't show. "Dear

God," says Pat to Mike. "He's late. I hope nothing's happened to him."' And on that line, in that non-existent territory – an Ireland created by music and lighting, where an assassination is countered with a joke – the play ends.

This imagined, perhaps imaginary piece of land lies at the heart of Ron Hutchinson's play, just as its physical embodiment lay at the centre of Stephen Daldry's production. Though it widens out to encompass a number of surrounding themes, *Rat in the Skull* is first and finally about the place that some call Northern Ireland – that patch of ground where (as Nelson says in the play) 'we can't even agree on a name for what we're fighting about. Ulster? The Six Counties? The North East? The bloody North?' The place is imaginary in part because some of its inhabitants flatly refuse to acknowledge it, as Nelson also points out when he says that Roche 'denies the existence – note – the existence, not just the right to exist but the established fact, the stub your toe on the concrete reality that there is such a place'. And it isn't only the IRA supporters who have trouble perceiving Ulster as a 'concrete reality'. Even its Protestant inhabitants may have a sense of their country's illusory nature, and for some it is only by leaving Northern Ireland that they can make it real to themselves. So it was for Ron Hutchinson, at any rate, who never wrote about his homeland 'in an Irish accent' until after he'd left it for England.

When Stephen Daldry first announced to his colleagues at the Royal Court that he wanted to revive *Rat in the Skull*, they were doubtful about its topicality. The play had been written in the early 1980s, in the context of IRA bombings and counter-terrorist acts; things had changed since then, and by the early 1990s that period seemed like ancient history. But Daldry's instincts proved correct once again. In the weeks before his production of *Rat in the Skull* opened in the West End, Northern Ireland was increasingly in the news. The first anniversary of the ceasefire fell on 31 August 1995, just five days before rehearsals started. The subsequent election of a new Ulster leader, the continuing refusal of the IRA to disarm before peace talks began, and the unexpected anti-

England verdict in a European Court case (which had involved the killing of IRA members in Gibraltar) all brought Northern Ireland to the front pages and the *News at Ten*. As part of its coverage of the evolving peace process, the *Independent* ran an excerpt from Seamus Heaney's essay 'The Frontiers of Writing' in its 12 September issue. A Catholic from Northern Ireland who was shortly to win the Nobel Prize for Poetry, Heaney – who now lives in Dublin – commented eloquently on his birthplace in words that echoed the sentiments behind *Rat in the Skull*. 'The whole population is adept in the mystery of living in two places at one time,' Heaney wrote:

> they make do with a constructed destination, an interim place whose foundations straddle the areas of self-division, a place of resolved contradiction, beyond confusion. A place, slightly to misquote Yeats, that does not exist, a place that is but a dream, since this promised land of durable coherence and perpetual homecoming is not somewhere that is ultimately obtainable by constitutional reform or territorial integration. Or perhaps one could say that it exists as a state of unresolved crisis which Ulster people don't quite admit as an immediate realistic expectation but don't quite deny as a deferred possibility.

What seems most uncanny about this passage is the way it reflects not only Hutchinson's play but also Daldry's and Dudley's self-divided set – a literal rendering, in metal and dirt, of the 'constructed destination' Heaney refers to.

But if *Rat in the Skull* is a political play about two nations located in one place, it is also very much a personal play about the connections between particular men. The political conflicts are personal, and vice versa: there is a sense of kinship behind the apparent hatred, and a sense of hatred even in acknowledged kinship. This intensity is clearest in the relationship between Nelson, the Protestant Irishman, and Roche, the IRA man; and it is precisely the odd nature of the bond between them that the play, through Harris's inquiry, seeks to explore. The closest we ever get to a direct confession of Nelson's motives comes when the English superintendent says to the blood-spattered RUC inspector, 'But knowing what it would do to the case? . . . Hit him where it would show, knowing . . . Turning on your own –' and Nelson answers, *'He's* my own.' Daldry went to great lengths to stress this moment, by allowing a pause to hang in the air after Nelson's words, by introducing an extreme lighting change at that moment, and by persuading Tony Doyle, the actor playing Nelson, to deliver the line in a single rush of feeling, with the stress on the 'He'. (Doyle, in rehearsals, had preferred a more emotional-sounding but less emphatic reading that broke in the middle: 'He is . . . my own.')

Daldry's production also got us to notice the other intense pairs who inhabit this play. *Rat in the Skull* usually presents an opportunity for virtuoso performances in the two Irish parts, and in this respect Tony Doyle and Rufus Sewell more than held their own. But whereas the two English coppers generally serve as little more than 'decor', in Daldry's 1995 version they contributed to what felt instead like a four-handed composition. Echoing the familial tie between Nelson and Roche (a father–son hook-up which was emphasized, in this production, by the twenty-five-year age gap between Doyle and Sewell) was the far more explicitly paternal relationship between Harris and Naylor. 'Your dear old daddy might be able to give you a pointer or two. If you help him,' Harris says to Naylor near the beginning of the play. 'I object to foreign coppers coming here and screwing up for our lads . . . Trusting little babs, taken advantage of by foreign cops. I object to that. I *object*.' In John Castle's humorous yet forceful rendering of these lines, simultaneously ironic and fierce, one could read a real anger at the visiting Irish inspector as well as a real affection for the young English constable, 'the little slip of a thing who hasn't popped his cherry yet'. And in the Naylor portrayed by Pearce Quigley – a thirty-year-old actor who effortlessly conveyed the innocence and softness of a ten-year-old – one could see exactly how those paternal, protective feelings had been aroused.

All this buried, contorted father–son sentiment gives an extra punch to the moments in the play when Nelson talks about his own father. As we gather from the RUC inspector's brief, bitter musings, Nelson Senior was a staunch Ulster Unionist whose 'rabid' politics caused his son to doubt his own role in maintaining the Union. 'My da,' says Nelson, 'ended up marching along with the mad eyes and the pinched-together bums to the music that says, "We're pissing in the gale of history . . ."' It was the death of his 'old man' along with the subsequent funeral – 'I saw to all the arrangements myself. Went off in a very decent manner. And I know what I'm talking about when I'm talking funerals' – that occasioned the 'leave' from which Nelson has been 'pulled back' to interrogate Roche.

Repeatedly in the course of the play, and starting within minutes of his first appearance, Nelson harps on the subject of funerals. His obsession with death causes the first little rift between himself and Naylor, the naïvely admiring young Englishman who has been 'detailed' to him for the duration of the prison interview. 'I've got a mate with your mob,' Naylor tosses off in his chatty, thoughtless, friendly manner, '. . . wanted to see the sharp end, said it would look good on his sheet in a couple of years time.' 'It'll look all right on the headstone as well' is Nelson's harsh response, causing Naylor to pull back a bit and give him what Nelson calls 'the second look'. The ceremonies of death are, among other things, what bind Nelson to Roche – at first comically ('Your lot do a good send-off and all, don't they?' the interrogator says to the silent prisoner as he offers matching descriptions of RUC and IRA funerals) and then more seriously ('We don't even let each other bury our dead in peace, do we?' Nelson remarks after they've finally begun to talk to each other). And Superintendent Harris's chance discovery of the recent death of Nelson's father is not, or not only, mere grist for his interrogative mill. In one way it's the useful excuse he's been searching for to help him patch up and cover over the beating, but in another and very real way it serves as an important source of connection between the two middle-aged men. 'I lost my old fella two years back,' Harris quietly tells Nelson in response to the Irishman's sudden revelation, and though part of us feels this is just the Englishman's clever way of manipulating the conversation, another part responds to John Castle's palpably sincere line-reading by sensing that Harris really *does* understand what it means to lose a father. That a father is not, in himself, an unmitigated good is made clear in all the play's presentations of fathers and fatherliness; but that the loss of a father is a very deep loss is made equally apparent. Hutchinson views with unyielding clarity the ties that bind us, through both love and hatred, to those who are closely related to us – whether they are members of our own family or fellow Irishmen across the religious divide.

Among the painfully close connections that this play concerns itself with is the relationship between an interrogator and the object of his interrogation. If the central ring of *Rat in the Skull* is about Northern Ireland and the surrounding ring about the relations between two men, then the third circle of this target-like play is about what Hutchinson has called 'the interview as an art form'. Ron Hutchinson had actually worked as an interrogator himself before he wrote the play: as an interviewer for the British Department of Health and Social Security in 1972, he was responsible for sorting out fraud from honesty, lie from truth, real need from simulated need. As a result of his job, he began to notice the dynamic that took over between two people when one was charged with getting information out of the other. 'Both of you get in a strange relationship – you start playing the art form of the interrogation,' he told Daldry's actors during the second day of rehearsal in September 1995. Shifting to a specific discussion of RUC and IRA procedures, he continued, 'They've all been very well trained, so they've got each other boxed in. It's about winning the next hand in the interview – there's no reference to the outside world. And it is about what card can I throw on the table to trump this guy. After being grunted at by the gorilla, Roche has nowhere left to go except to throw a confounding card on the table, which is in a way very Irish: "Let's see what your face looks like when I tell you I'll do it." And then *you're* down one,' Hutchinson said, turning to the actor playing Nelson. 'Those weird, almost surreal dynamics do come into play. Then you have to desperately shuffle your cards and find one to throw at him.'

The longest and most noticeable interview in the play is the one between Roche and Nelson, but the rhythms and strategies of that segment are echoed in all the shorter interviews: between Nelson and Harris, between Naylor and Harris, between Roche and his unseen IRA controllers. One of the key things Hutchinson has discovered about the interrogation is the important role of silence in the conversation. For sustained periods of time – in one case, nearly twenty minutes – *Rat in the Skull* takes the form of a one-sided rant, with one character speaking *at* rather than *with* another. This means that each character, in turn, has to be audience to a monologue. In some scenes, half the actors in the play are functioning as audience members: Roche and Naylor listening, in very different ways, to Nelson's flights of interrogative fancy; Nelson and Roche standing silent and still during Naylor's out-of-time speech; Harris and Naylor sitting quietly on the sidelines while Nelson and Roche play out a crucial scene in their interview. By keeping the temporarily silent actors onstage as much as possible, Daldry highlighted their role as bystanders, witnesses, members of the captive audience. And this in turn reminded us how much the structure of *any* play mimics a one-sided interrogation, with ourselves, the audience, occupying the position of self-enforced silence. Part of Daldry's strategy was to heighten the tension to the point where our discomfort somewhat resembled Roche's. At times we too wanted to cry out, spring out of our chairs, start singing an irrelevant tune, just to drown out the sound of Nelson's unremitting verbal onslaught. And, as with Roche, it was mainly our awareness of the rules that kept us quiet. Roche had his IRA strictures to follow ('I gave them nothing . . . It's in the book. Stick it while you can') and we had the code of theatrical propriety. It didn't need Bill Dudley's clever set – in which the original theatrical circles of plush-covered seats and curved plaster mouldings merged almost imperceptibly into the newly constructed tiers of rectilinear metal grating – to point out that the theatre and the prison have an oddly similar structure. That parallel was built into the play.

Daldry encouraged the actors to address a number of their lines to the audience – whenever possible, to specific members of the audience – in order to emphasize that we too were part of this play. In *An Inspector Calls*, a similar strategy had served an inclusive function: by drawing us into the actors' world, Daldry gave us a sense of complicity and even a feeling of community. But in *Rat in the Skull* the same tactic had a somewhat different effect. Just as speech became an instrument with which the four actors attacked and alienated each other ('The violence of the tongue, yes,' as Roche put it), so it also seemed a weapon used on us. All friendliness of manner, in this production, was suspect; all seeming kindness was really a form of manipulation. There was love in this play, of a sort – the kind of love that could result in self-sacrifice, and sympathetically felt pain, and the desire to overcome barriers between people. But there was no 'acknowledgment of love', in the sense that Stanley Cavell uses the term in his essay on *King Lear*. There was no moment, either in the script itself or in the emotionally faithful production, in which kindness was perceived and returned. This was powerfully driven home to me during a performance that took place shortly after opening night, when an actor made a small slip: 'You're a nice man, Mr Harris,' he said, rather than the actual line in the script, which was 'You're a decent man, Mr Harris.' I realized then that this was a note I hadn't heard before, a tone that was missing from *Rat in the Skull.* Decency – a sense of justice, fair play, doing the correct thing – was something the play could encompass. Niceness, in the form of administered and received kindness, was not. It didn't matter, for my purposes, that Mr Harris wasn't really a 'nice' man ('Even the niceness is unpleasant,' John Castle said about the character he was playing). What mattered was that I had discovered, through this slip, the emotional limitations of the play.

A limitation is not necessarily a flaw. Ron Hutchinson had set out to write a script about interrogations, not conversations – about one-way communications designed to have a practical effect, not moments of communion. As a writer he is in fact very interested in the powers and limitations of speech, and at its outermost ring *Rat in the Skull* seems to me to be a play about language and the impoverishment of language. Moreover, the geometry of the play is such that this outer ring leads directly back to the innermost circles, for the shared language, the destroyed language, is part of what binds the two Irishmen to their land and to each other. The language in question is a Belfast-accented, tall-tale-telling, tongue-lashing version of English, and that too is part of what defines their cultural and personal predicament. For to be Northern Irish is to be, as Nelson says, 'half of everything and nothing much of anything'.

Both Irishmen pride themselves on their use of the English language. 'Mick the Lip', Roche calls himself when explaining how he talked back to the English coppers, but it is Nelson who really turns out to have the gift of the gab, sustaining his twenty-minute unanswered interrogation of Roche through an amazing variety of verbal pyrotechnics. Once the two start talking to each other, they almost immediately resort to linguistic mimicry: 'I'm too fly for that,' Roche taunts, echoing Nelson's earlier 'You're too fly to fall for a copper's trick like that'; 'Nothing. I'm saying nothing,' teases Nelson, reproducing Roche's exact words from one of his moments of resistance. *Rat in the Skull* is filled with dirty jokes and outrageous stories and vicious insults of all kinds – 'heavy verbals', in Roche's phrase – and part of what it requires of its audience is a verbal acuity equal to Roche's or Nelson's. Each of them can tell when the other is lying, or bluffing, or exaggerating; they can hear in the language the difference between a threat and a statement, a joke and a serious remark. If we can't do that as well, we miss half of what the play is about.

Beyond the two Irishmen's delight in words, however, is a suspicion that words have lost their power and perhaps even their
sense. 'Swapping arguments with you is not my line,' Roche tells
Nelson, and goes on to suggest that nothing would be accomplished if he and his fellow soldiers 'left it to the chin-waggers'.
And though Nelson is a chin-wagger by profession – his job, his
speciality, is to use speech in order to extort speech – he too
doubts the capacity of language to express real meaning. 'Don't
tell me you're just a simple soldier, Roche,' he says angrily. 'You
blow the arms and legs off the language, too. You torture the
meanings of things.' Nor can this sorry state of affairs be blamed
entirely on Roche's gang. Whenever Nelson makes a specifically
linguistic or semantic point, he quotes his wife, a graduate of the
Department of English Literature at Belfast University. A trio of
Irish insults are 'each a particular conjugation in the grammar of
hate, as my missis would say'; a typical Irish rant can be characterized as 'the obbligato for wind and spittle, as my missis would
have called it. And often did.' But Nelson's 'missis' turns out to
be 'an English girl' who has left him, as Harris points out, in
order to take up with 'O'Brien, the other sort of Irishman', a
Catholic 'from Roche's side of town'. So her classifications of
Irish speech turn out to be a kind of weapon, too – a dangerously
double-edged weapon, when they are quoted by her cuckolded
ex-husband.

Through the absent character of the former Mrs Nelson, the
playwright aims a jab at all people who take a literary interest in
Irish verbosity, including, or perhaps especially, himself. *Rat in
the Skull* is extremely suspicious of its own enterprise – that is,
the conversion of a spoken, Irish-accented English into literary,
written form. The clearest sign of this suspicion lies in the character of Naylor, who transcribes Roche's impassioned speeches
and in doing so renders them senseless. 'Hefty piece of prose,'
Harris comments about Naylor's shorthand transcription, and
behind that remark we can hear Ron Hutchinson's self-mocking
characterization of his own play.

If the language they share has been tortured, classified, and transcribed to death, the two kinds of Irishman can only be brought together by something behind or beneath language. Words are what keep the existing system going; an informant's confession will, as Nelson says, result in 'the same old jag . . . He'll go along in his parade like me in mine.' This is true of Roche's words and also of Nelson's own: he has begun to hear what he himself sounds like 'as I'm bellowing at Roche', and that's part of what has made him want to break the endless cycle. Since he can't break it through language, he uses his fists. Among its other functions (and they are multiple and complex), the beating is Nelson's way of getting to Roche in a manner that is true and real, his way of reaching beyond the lies and tricks and verbal manipulations. Nelson wants Roche to be aware of him viscerally, physically. 'I'm your fellow countryman. Look at me. *Smell* me,' he shouts, shoving his armpit into Roche's face.

'Paddies . . . I can smell them. Animals, they are.' Harris's final line is an Englishman's disdainful view. But what *Rat in the Skull* does is to turn that disdain on its head, finding pride and strength and a kind of humanity in what someone else considers 'animal'. 'I'm used to the horrors . . . I'm used to what are more the acts of beasts than men, though that's unkind to beasts,' Nelson says, speaking about both his job and his life. He's aware of how the English view their Irish charges: 'The animal bites, does it?' he remarks of the well-guarded Roche. The English may feel their sense of civilization and superiority is defined in opposition to Irish beastliness, but Nelson finally chooses to side with the beasts, those fellow creatures who act rather than speak.

Even the phrase 'rat in the skull', which is Nelson's own figure of speech, gives a new and positive meaning to the proverbial rodent. When we first hear the word 'rat' in the context of this play, we may think of an informant ratting on his friends. We might also notice the distinction Nelson makes between the 'two sorts of Northern Irishman, the farmer's sons and the city rats'. (Nelson himself is a farmer's son, while Roche is definitely a city rat, as Rufus Sewell makes clear in his sniffing, lurking, darting embodiment.) But the 'rat in the skull' refers to something else –

to the doubt that can enter your mind about the whole point of the Northern Irish conflict, whether you're Protestant or Catholic, RUC or IRA. 'You can't afford to doubt, no more than I can,' Nelson tells Roche at the very centre of the play. 'You can't risk letting the rat get in the skull, telling you you're wrong, the fight's not worth the fight and even if it is, why should it be my fight, there are others, I've done my bit, I say no and walk away. But you can't, no more than I can.' In the end, though, it is precisely his own rat that Nelson becomes aware of, and the thing he can't stand to do is simply go on as before, with 'the rat in my head shut up and me knowing there's a chance of something'. To take advantage of that knowledge, that chance, Nelson needs to listen to his own sense of doubt.

Doubt is a funny word. As Christopher Ricks has pointed out, it's a word whose music contradicts its meaning. Nothing could sound more certain than that hard, dentalized, commanding monosyllable, which rhymes with other emphatic words like 'out', 'rout', and 'lout'. And even the status of doubt, as a state of mind, is extremely variable, depending on whether you are practising science (where it is the essential tool) or religion (where it is the cardinal sin). It is typical of Ron Hutchinson's sense of irony that he makes doubt the saving grace in a situation that stems from an essentially religious conflict. 'Fitting usage, you might think . . . the term theological, the religious note again,' Superintendent Harris says about the interrogator's word 'convert', and the same might apply to 'doubt'. The rat in his own skull is what inspires Nelson to want to save Roche – but the salvation can only be complete if he can inspire Roche to doubt as well.

'He's lost his faith,' Stephen Daldry said of Nelson when he first discussed the play's ending with his group of actors. 'But it's about whether ultimately losing your faith is an advantage or a disadvantage.'

'It seems to me,' said Tony Doyle, trying to get at his character from the inside, 'that Nelson has lost his beliefs but he's gained a faith.'

'And what is his faith?' asked Daldry, quizzically.

'Well,' said Doyle, 'that "He is my own."'

'Right,' said Daldry. 'Yes.'

Stephen Warbeck, who had been sitting in on the discussion, at this point made a comment about the lighting Daldry was planning to use in the last scene. (As Warbeck had pointed out to me during an earlier production, 'I have terribly strong ideas – they're not necessarily good – about all aspects of a play. I can't keep quiet about everything but my department.') The composer's remarks bore directly on the whole function of doubt as a positive value in the play. 'If you turn the light out on Roche first,' he said, 'I wonder if the doubt in his mind goes also. If you turn out the light on Roche, he becomes resolved and complete.' What Warbeck was suggesting was that if Daldry wanted to end with Roche in doubt too, 'then turning the light out on him might not be right. The light equals the doubt.'

Stephen Warbeck made this observation during the first week of rehearsals in early September, and the final lighting design was not arrived at until the fifth night of previews. The published script, which was based on Hutchinson's initial June draft, retained the original stage instruction at the end, specifying that Nelson is to be 'alone on the stage with Roche as the lights slowly fade . . . and the waiting Nelson is the last thing we see.' But when *Rat in the Skull* opened on 11 October 1995, the light that flickered on the two Irishmen in the final scene froze and then faded at exactly the same time. They were each allotted their full moment of doubt, and the feeling at the end was one of prolonged suspension in a state of irresolution.

Suspension was, in fact, the keynote of this entire production. Kate Rowland, who saw and loved both Daldry versions of *Rat in the Skull*, commented that the earlier one was 'much bloodier' whereas the 1995 production was 'suspended'. Daldry himself said to me about the Liverpool production, 'There were a lot of things wrong with it . . . I had them shot at the end – both of them.' That closed, pessimistic, violently resolved ending may have been appropriate to the mood of the country and the script in 1987. But by 1995 the political situation had changed and so, therefore, had the play. If Daldry's remounted *Rat in the Skull* existed in a suspended state – between humour and horror, sympathy and hatred, English incomprehension and Irish anger, faith and doubt – that was perhaps because both the nation and the director had become somewhat less emphatic since the mid-1980s. The Irish leaders on both sides of the conflict were beginning to understand that many things were worse than a fragile, uncertain, and gradually prolonged ceasefire; Sinn Fein and the Ulster Unionists couldn't see forward to a resolution, but nor could they willingly go back to the violence that had prevailed before. And Stephen Daldry, too, had reached a point in his life and in his career, '*nel mezzo del cammin di nostra vita*', where he could begin to acknowledge the claims of uncertainty.

7 Anatomy of a Rehearsal

However unresolved it may have been, *Rat in the Skull* emphatically proved the two things which Stephen Daldry needed to demonstrate to those who were weighing his talents – that he could work successfully with a living playwright, and that he could coax intense, nuanced, psychologically complex performances out of actors. He had done both these things together during his years in regional theatre, and in London he had done each of them separately, at the Gate (where the acting in his productions was often singled out for praise) and at the Royal Court (where he had worked exclusively with living playwrights: Howard Korder, Arnold Wesker, Meredith Oakes). But his fame as a director came primarily from *An Inspector Calls* and *Machinal*, both highly theatrical productions which threatened to elevate design and choreography over dialogue and character. That the threat was never carried out, at least in the case of *Inspector*, had somehow escaped most of his critics; its mere presence was enough to make them view Daldry as a kind of highbrow Andrew Lloyd Webber, a superficial master of spectacle and extravaganza. *Rat in the Skull* was his sharp retort to those criticisms.

And, as a retort, it was highly effective. There were a few of the usual carpings in the newspaper reviews, along the lines of the *Daily Telegraph*'s 'Stephen Daldry, flamboyant artistic director of the Royal Court, sometimes gives the impression that he can't walk into a theatre without ripping it apart and starting all over again.' But for the most part the notices were extremely enthusiastic, and even the critics who weren't impressed by Daldry's and Dudley's massive redesign were struck by the script and the acting. It was as if these reviewers saw the play and its performance as something entirely separate from Daldry, whom they had already relegated to the 'visual effects' sphere. They referred to *Rat in the Skull* as if it were an established classic that this director had somehow been lucky enough to stumble on, whereas in reality it had only played in London once, for four weeks in 1984, before Daldry revived it. He wanted the play included in the Royal Court Classics season because he loved it, and his love (along with his public relations canniness) was vindicated when he saw it proclaimed 'a modern classic', 'a thrilling piece of theatre', and 'a blazing, wrathful, compassionate play', 'of its time but not restricted to its time', that 'reverberates long after the last word is spoken'.

Daldry did, of course, pay attention to the technical and visual aspects of the production: it would have been hard for the set to mesh so fully with the script's multiple levels and themes if he had not collaborated so closely with Bill Dudley on the design. But he spent far more time and energy, in the weeks and months preceding *Rat in the Skull*'s opening night, working with the actors and the playwright. It was here that the heart of his production lay, in the rehearsal room – as it generally does with most directors and most plays. This book hasn't enough space to present every Daldry production in detail, from auditions and early rewrites through daily rehearsals to the final tinkerings at previews (nor would you wish it to, since the process can be repetitive in many ways). But I think it's both useful and interesting to focus on rehearsals for one production, and Ron Hutchinson's intensely linguistic four-character play seems well suited to this purpose.

I should stress at the outset that *Rat in the Skull*'s rehearsal period is exemplary, not representative. Part of what a good director does each time he works is to learn a whole new language, physically and theatrically as well as verbally and tonally, in order to speak about a particular play to particular actors. Each play makes different demands on a director, and each cast makes different demands on a play. There are certain strategies and obsessions that are common to all of Stephen Daldry's work, and I will try to remark on them as I take you through *Rat in the Skull*. But there are many things that vary with each production

– that *should* vary with each production, if the director is astute and responsive enough to use the specific materials at hand – and these will be particular to the moment.

Common sense would suggest as much. In my case, common sense was confirmed and augmented by practical demonstration when, in the summer of 1995, I saw Stephen Daldry rehearse the remount of *An Inspector Calls* and then the revival of *Rat in the Skull,* one right after the other. With *Inspector,* he was working on a play he had come to know inside out, he had an Inspector Goole and a Mr Birling who had played the parts before, and he had a cast who shared and understood his perspective on the play. Even the auditions for the 1995 *Inspector Calls* seemed a bit like rehearsals, so thoroughly did he know what he wanted from each character. 'Sorry! I'm fucking directing,' he commented during Helen Schlesinger's try-out for the role of Sheila, as he caught himself leaning forward and interjecting advice during her audition speech.

This intrusive, interruptive, interactive mode of directing was to mark Daldry's approach throughout the *Inspector* rehearsal period. He would frequently jump up to stand in the midst of his actors, calling out questions, instructions, and snippets of advice as they spoke their lines. They in turn would carry on with their roles, incorporating his suggestions instantaneously, modifying their tones, gestures, and movements in mid-sentence. The director's own familiarity with the play transmitted itself to the actors as a kind of momentum, so that they all, actors and director alike, resembled confident, well-trained musicians tightening up their performance of a much-loved symphony. Stephen Daldry himself was the conductor – leaning over this way to elicit more vibrato from the strings, gesturing that way to signal the precise rhythm for the percussion section, or waving both arms to bring up the volume for the finale. This is not to say that the *Inspector* rehearsals contained no surprises; on the contrary, each day brought new insights to a line or new twists to a character's psychology, often provided by the actors. But the basic questions about this production had all been answered before the rehearsals began.

Quite the opposite was true of *Rat in the Skull*. Though Daldry had directed the play eight years earlier, he started work on the revival with a clean slate, including four actors whom he had never worked with before, a new set of political circumstances in Ireland, and, perhaps most importantly, a script which was still in the process of being rewritten. These three sets of circumstances were linked – that is, Ron Hutchinson rewrote the play not only to take account of the historical context in which the performance was taking place, but also to accommodate the specific strengths of the four actors. With the revival in mind, he had already completed a new draft of the play by June 1995; extensive script revisions began in the first week of rehearsals and continued up to the last few nights of previews. The actors found this degree of rewriting unusual, but seemed able to take it in their stride. 'I know it happens,' conceded Rufus Sewell, though he had appeared in premières of Tom Stoppard's *Arcadia* and Brian Friel's *Translations* without experiencing anything like this before. 'With this, it's because we're going back to it ten years later. He had the opportunity to be away from it and see it freshly,' Sewell said of the playwright, and then praised Hutchinson's willingness to make revisions: 'He's not treating it like a sacred object. He wants it to be alive.'

In part because of these changes and in part because of the complicated nature of the script itself, Daldry's work on *Rat in the Skull* was slower, more thoughtful, and in some ways more hesitant than it had been on the remounted *Inspector*. Whereas *Inspector* rehearsals had him constantly on his feet, here he was much more likely to be sitting down, either at a table looking once again at the script, or else watching the actors from in front of the designated stage area. When he got an idea or wanted to give a 'note' about a particular line-reading, he would wait for the end of the unit being rehearsed, stop the action entirely, and then discuss his suggestion with the group as a whole or, more often, the particular actor involved. (Daldry's tendency to confer privately with each actor was something I had noticed in

Inspector rehearsals, but it reached epic proportions when he was working on *Rat in the Skull*, as if this play about secrets and conflicts and contradictory beliefs stimulated in him a desire to create secrets and conflicts and contradictory beliefs. Rufus Sewell, when asked how he felt about this 'confidential' approach to directing, answered, 'I like it. You don't need to know any more than you know. I think it's good for characters to have secrets from each other. I like the idea that one actor's being given one story, one another, because it's an interesting kind of clash that way.') And when one of the actors would stop to ask Daldry for advice about a particular line or scene, the director would be uncharacteristically slow to respond – and, after a long pause, might well say, 'I don't know what the note is.' Even the notes he came up with on his own tended to be proffered somewhat hesitantly, as guesses rather than certainties.

This is not to say that Daldry didn't have definite ideas. But they were the sort of definite idea that was susceptible to modification by everyone around him. The actors felt free to disagree with him and even to tease him, so that despite the difficulty of the play and the sombreness of its subject matter, the atmosphere in the rehearsal room was often lighthearted and relaxed. Pearce Quigley, who had been in several plays directed by Max Stafford-Clark (though not the original *Rat in the Skull*), praised both directors while contrasting their extremely different rehearsal styles. 'It's great,' he said of Stafford-Clark's rigorous methodology. 'But there's no fooling around in his rehearsals. The real jokers have a hard time with it.' With Daldry, on the other hand, Quigley felt free to let loose his zany sense of humour – to such an extent that Daldry dubbed Quigley's version of the play 'Prat in the Skull'. Nor was this permissive manner limited to the social atmosphere; it extended even to dramatic interpretations. 'He's very, very open,' said John Castle, and went on to compare Daldry favourably to the two kinds of directors he disliked – those who had no ideas and those who had fixed ideas. The worst directors, Castle argued, were the 'intellectuals who have these ideas that aren't practical; they're fine on the page but they don't work onstage'. He felt Daldry was precisely the opposite – a director with a pragmatic, flexible, theatrical imagination – and Rufus Sewell agreed: 'He has a strong picture, but he's sensitive enough to adapt it. You can work with directors who you feel have worked it all out in their heads, and they just want to move you about. He's not like that. But there *is* a vision.' On the other hand, Daldry's aura of confident authority didn't unduly intimidate his actors. 'Sometimes I like to guess what he's getting at,' Sewell observed, 'and sometimes he doesn't *know* what he's getting at. Sometimes he's just saying something he's not sure about, to see how it works out. It's quite safe to go with his ideas, because if he's wrong he'll concede it.' Hearing this description of Daldry's directorial technique, I was reminded of what D. W. Winnicott once said about himself as a psychoanalyst: 'A girl of 10 said to me: "It doesn't matter if some of the things you say are wrong because I know which are wrong and which are right."' A good analyst will rely on his patients to choose the most useful interpretations from the range of those offered, and it would appear that a good director relies on his actors in much the same way.

If the director can seem like an analyst at times, he can also mimic the role of an editor, especially when the play is a new work that is still taking shape. More than anything I had seen Stephen Daldry do before, the first week of rehearsals for *Rat in the Skull* resembled an 'editing process'. Day after day, the same eight people (including the four actors, the playwright, the director, the assistant director, and the deputy stage manager) would sit around one long table, going over the words of the script. As the actors read aloud their lines, Daldry and Hutchinson, seated side by side, would compare their marginal notes, tease out hidden meanings and historical references, and weigh the merits of particular words and phrases. Occasionally there were minor disagreements.

'And I thought, below, you wanted "A specialist. A bit of a star in his own way",' Hutchinson commented, offering to restore a piece of dialogue to one speech.

'I wasn't going to have "in his own way",' Daldry answered.

'I was,' Hutchinson gently insisted.

Once in a while the playwright, who relied heavily on the *sound* of the dialogue in his ear, would emphatically resist the director's advice. 'Nelson has brought us to this point, and you're asking us to go two pages back. It's the cello, and you're asking us to bring in the glockenspiel,' he told Daldry. Most of the time, however, they would jointly arrive at a new solution. In Nelson's long rant about his twenty-seven brothers named Sam, Daldry suggested cutting the singular use of the phrase 'Brother Sam' ('I wasn't sure whether there should be more or less than one, but there shouldn't be just one,' he explained) and substituting 'Her Majesty' for 'the Crown'. Hutchinson agreed to the 'Brother' cut immediately; he thought for a moment about 'Her Majesty' and came back with the phrase 'Her Magistry', which is how it ended up in performance.

Throughout the first two weeks of rehearsal, before Hutchinson flew back to California to attend to the rest of his life, the playwright and the director continued this back-and-forth discussion about preservation, elaboration, and excision. It wasn't always the playwright who argued for preservation, either. Sometimes Hutchinson would suggest what he thought was an improvement and Daldry would be extremely nervous about accepting it, as he was when the writer proposed to revise the last two pages of the play. 'I think it's fucking brilliant,' Stephen Daldry said of the ending. 'I love those two pages. So I have a slight anxiety about your changing it . . . But I'd love to see it,' he remembered to add diplomatically. And sometimes the actors themselves would defend lines that the playwright was threatening to cut. 'You're not thinking of cutting it, are you? The rabbit joke?' John Castle said of a line that wasn't even his. 'Because for me it's one of those images that go on and on – the abortion, the miscarriage, the connection with breeding. And it's so horrendous it's funny.' Castle lost this particular battle, but he did succeed in altering one of his own lines to produce what ultimately became the biggest laugh of the play. In both the 1984 script and the original 1995 draft, Ron Hutchinson had given Constable Naylor the speech, 'I say tow that entire fucking wet island and its incomprehensible bleeding tribes into the Atlantic, pull the plug and give us all some fucking peace and quiet,' to which Superintendent Harris replied, 'You've obviously thought this out in the political as well as the civil engineering detail.' After John Castle had read aloud this line, he pointed out to the playwright, in what he characterized as 'purely a whore's question', that 'if it were engineering before the political, it would be funnier'.

'You got me there, sir,' agreed Hutchinson, and instantly made the change.

That Ron Hutchinson was explicitly interested in making this bleak play 'funnier' was one of the strange but characteristic features of Daldry's revival – characteristic of Daldry, that is, and also of Hutchinson himself. 'I added two new jokes and a few new insults,' the playwright told the cultural reporters from London's newspapers and weekly magazines when they asked how he had revised the play. By the time *Rat in the Skull* opened at the Duke of York's, one of these new jokes had been cut entirely and the other had been replaced by a much-abbreviated yarn, yet the feel of the production was – not comic, exactly ('I don't do comedy,' Daldry mentioned to his actors, no doubt recalling his problems on *The Editing Process*), but humorous in a dark, magnetic, shocking way. 'Yours is much funnier,' said Joan Washington, the dialect coach on Daldry's production, who had seen the 1984 première of *Rat in the Skull* at the Royal Court. 'Theirs was very heavy and austere. I'm pleased this one is funny. The humour behind the horror is great.' Stephen Daldry was particularly delighted by the phrase 'the humour behind the horror', which he felt encapsulated what he was trying to convey. It had something in common, I think, with the mood Edmund Wilson was referring to when he wrote, 'Dickens's laughter is an exhilaration which already shows a trace of the hysterical. It leaps free of the prison of life; but gloom and soreness must always drag it back.' Increasingly as opening night approached, Daldry tuned up the performances, particularly Tony Doyle's and Rufus Sewell's, to produce in the audience the kind of painful jolt you experience when you find yourself laughing at something that turns out to be horrifying. In one key scene, for instance, he had Nelson begin to imitate Roche's inarticulate grunts, so that the two actors briefly honked in unison, causing the audience to erupt in wild giggles – a burst of laughter which rang out and then was rapidly quelled by the reprimanding silence that suddenly greeted it from the stage.

The actors varied in the degree to which they could comfortably embrace this dark brand of humour. John Castle took to it like a duck to water. 'Good stuff,' he commented enthusiastically on the third day of rehearsals, when Tony Doyle read off Nelson's scathing series of anti-Catholic insults. ('*Great* stuff', Stephen Daldry amended, to which Ron Hutchinson added, 'And all in the best of taste.')

That John Castle would naturally be drawn to this element in the play had been apparent since his audition, which took place after all three other roles had already been cast. Daldry had thought for a while of making Superintendent Harris a woman, but by August he had given up on that idea and was interviewing a series of middle-aged Englishmen who ranged in self-presentation from the ploddingly plebeian to the blandly competent. And then John Castle appeared in his office. From the beginning, this audition had a different tone from any of the others: it was as if Stephen Daldry came alive in response to this graceful, sharp-edged actor, revealing aspects of himself in the course of taking in Castle's character. John Castle started by mentioning that he had been in another play of Ron Hutchinson's, during which 'I took on the audience one evening – I told them to pipe down'; and this caused Stephen Daldry to respond with a tale from his own childhood. 'I was at school in Somerset,' he told Castle, 'and we took a school trip to the Bristol Old Vic to watch *Hamlet*. And we were yapping away, and one of the actors turned to me in the middle of the play and told me to shut up. It was the most fascinating moment of the play, and terrifying. It was one of my first theatre experiences – I was about twelve.'

As he had done with all the other auditioners, Daldry outlined for Castle his brief theory of the role of Harris: 'What's fascinating about him is that he's really very bright, but he has this take on himself as a dumb English copper who doesn't know fuck all. He talks about himself in the third person. It's a bit like an old theatre director who doesn't really believe in theatre any more, but is still directing plays – which is amusing, and a good defence mechanism, but underneath there's still passion.' Daldry then had Castle read from a scene between Harris and Nelson, apologizing both for doing the Nelson role himself and for having Castle read at all. ('Would you mind?' he asked, as if such things were optional at auditions.) As John Castle read – in a manner that was recognizable even to an untrained observer as galvanizing – Daldry sat forward in his chair, watching the actor with the steady gaze of a serpent about to consume a particularly dangerous prey. 'You're *right* about that,' he exclaimed as soon as the actor had finished reading. Daldry pulled his chair closer to the other man; his face shone with boyish enthusiasm, and as he spoke he punctuated his remarks by excitedly tapping Castle on the knee. 'You're right about that complication. If they both play it like they're aware – that rather than finding it dark, they find it amusing . . .'

'It's wretchedly sad, isn't it?' Castle agreed, as if they had just expressed the same thought.

John Castle had a reputation in the London theatre world as a difficult actor (talking back to the audience was the *least* of his widely reported misbehaviour), and Stephen Daldry was fully aware of this reputation when he chose Castle for the role. But if Daldry was at all anxious about betting on such a wild card, his anxieties were soon alleviated. Within the first week of rehearsal, Castle had shown himself to be the easiest of actors to direct, the quickest to pick up on an implied interpretation, and in some ways the closest in attitude to Daldry's own view of theatre. Castle seemed to stimulate Daldry's innate abilities, and the first visible *directing* on this production, as opposed to mere reading aloud of lines, took place between Stephen Daldry and John Castle on the third day of rehearsals. They were going over Superintendent Harris's line 'Why don't you tell me about your missis?,' which came near the beginning of his interrogation of Nelson.

'I know this is stating the obvious,' Daldry remarked, 'but he's already read his file, hasn't he? He's already manufactured the I'm-going-to-pin-it-on-the-matrimonial-problem. He's pretending to discover it – oh, my, is she English? – but he's building the fantasy and hoping that Nelson will accept it.'

John Castle, in response, drew the director's attention to the stage direction 'Pointed' that preceded the superintendent's line. How did that fit in with his pretending to discover her Englishness? Didn't it seem to acknowledge, instead, that both men knew what was in the file, and furthermore knew that they both knew it?

Daldry agreed, but with a twist. 'Isn't it like the Brechtian unit title that he's giving it? "Why Don't You Tell Me About Your Missus" – that's what we're going to do.'

In this interpretation, as elsewhere, Daldry was leaning towards the view of Harris he had already expressed in the audition, as a figure who was in many respects akin to a director. It was Harris who, in Daldry's production, set the play in motion when he gave his opening speech. As John Castle bellowed his first lines, Pearce Quigley and the two understudies, all dressed identically as police constables, rushed counterclockwise around the clanging metallic ramp, acknowledging the superintendent's barked commands, speeding up as he neared his conclusion, and sliding into position exactly on his final syllable. ('It looks like you're doing your own little circus,' Daldry commented to Castle after he had choreographed this opening. 'I love the pinball effect – it looks like an executive toy.') Like a director, Harris was offstage much of the time and a bystander for most of the rest of the play; he was the only character who, until the very end, never set foot in the patch of dirt that was both Ireland and

the holding cell. His line 'Harris on', in which he self-consciously announced his own dramatic entrance (an entrance that
was accompanied, in performance, by two heavy drumbeats and
a sudden flash of spotlighting), presented him in the guise of
both actor and director – a scripted hint which Daldry proceeded to elaborate. 'I missed "Harris on",' he told Castle during
one rehearsal when the rendition was too subdued. 'You got a bit
serious then. I like it when it's like, oh, hello, lights, action . . .
Which is why it's terribly useful for me when you say "city rats
and farmer's sons", and the lights go up on Roche and Nelson. It
looks as if you're making the lights go up; it looks as if you're in
theatrical control.' In explaining Harris's role to John Castle,
Stephen Daldry even permitted himself a moment of intense
self-revelation. 'It's different versions of being a director,' he said
of the superintendent's various guises. 'A lot of directors, especially when they get older, have this nonsense version of themselves. Because they have a persona of themselves. Like I do. I
act out a version of myself. So it becomes self-conscious. The
feigned innocence, and then the not – and it's the changes, the
spinning on a sixpence.' It would have been impossible to determine from the grammatical structure whether Stephen Daldry, in
that sentence about feigned innocence, was speaking about himself or just about Superintendent Harris.

But Daldry wasn't just projecting his own personality on to
John Castle. It was also the case that they thought about theatre in
similar ways – as a physical, embodied presentation of language,
in which meaning was tied to movement and gesture worked in
counterpoint to words. From the moment he saw Bill Dudley's
model box of the stage, with the rectangular ramps allowing for
constant motion, John Castle knew he was going to enjoy playing
his part. And what Daldry did, in much of his directing, was to
help him use those ramps to the utmost. 'When he says "they
come breezing back",' Daldry said about one of Rufus Sewell's
lines, 'you come breezing around the corner, like this' – and
Daldry showed John Castle how, by making a sharp right turn on
that phrase, he could make Sewell's line narrate his own action.

Once they got into the Duke of York's and were working on the actual set, Daldry's choreographic suggestions increased, and John Castle eagerly adopted every one. '"Great Paddy in the Sky", and you look up,' Daldry showed him, reciting Harris's lines and moving around the ramp as he spoke. '"We ride shotgun on our turf" – use this as the turf.' Daldry pointed to the metallic walkway. Then he showed Castle how to turn the corner on the line 'You step sideways', so that he *was* actually stepping sideways as he said it. John Castle picked it all up as if by instinct.

'Excellent!' exclaimed Daldry. 'It's really clear.'

'I just need to be told how to say every word and where to put my feet,' Castle teased him.

Daldry looked abashed. 'Is that what it feels like?' he asked, laughing sheepishly.

'No,' Castle assured him. 'It's lovely.'

If John Castle exemplified the kind of actor who instantly understood Stephen Daldry's version of theatre, then Tony Doyle was the opposite: a resistant, questioning, deeply internal actor who wanted to bring the character to light in his own way and on his own time. Pearce Quigley may have been the first of the four actors to be cast in his part, and Rufus Sewell may have been the box-office draw, but Tony Doyle was the actor on whose shoulders the entire play had to rest. An Irishman who lived in France, Doyle divided his time mainly between stage plays in Dublin (and occasionally Belfast) and television work in London. He was known as a consummate professional, and Daldry had pursued him for months, finally persuading him to take on this difficult and relatively underpaid role. But then, having won his object, Stephen Daldry was faced with an actor who insisted on pulling the play in unforeseen directions – and who resisted direction (in the other sense) as if it were the devil's teaching. 'The best director I ever had,' Doyle told me at the press launch that preceded the second day of rehearsals, 'was one who remained silent for the entire four weeks of rehearsals. He just watched us work. And from the way he watched us, we could tell how he felt. But he let *us* work everything out.'

This attitude surfaced in the rehearsal room five days later. Daldry had been trying to get Doyle to make a tonal distinction between three different anti-Catholic insults. It was Daldry's attempt to translate into action something that Ron Hutchinson had said on the first day, when the director had asked the playwright about the line 'Mickey, Taig or Fenian bastard', and Hutchinson had suggested that they were arranged in ascending order of nastiness. 'The dirtiest word I can think of is Fenian,' Hutchinson remarked. 'If you're brought up in a Protestant Irish household – when I say that word, I get a phlegm in my throat, because it's a very dirty word.' Daldry wanted to hear something of that progression in Doyle's delivery. But he wasn't getting it.

'Was I not clear about that bit about Mickey, Taig or Fenian bastard,' he finally confronted Doyle, 'or did you not want to do it?'

'No, you weren't watching; I was doing it beautifully,' Doyle mocked him, and then went on to deliver the remark that was to become a touchstone for the rest of the rehearsal period: 'Sit down. It'll be great.' It was the kind of serious joke that contained an admonishment – directors watch, actors act. Later Doyle made the same point more gently but also more explicitly. 'I need to get it clear for myself,' he told Daldry, 'which I promise to do over the next week or two. Until I am familiar, I cannot dazzle you.'

Tony Doyle eventually made good on that promise: he did dazzle Stephen Daldry, and everyone else, with the power and subtlety of his performance as Nelson. But the road to that success was far rockier and more difficult than any of the other journeys made by the actors and the director on this play. At times it almost seemed as if Daldry's and Doyle's versions of *Rat in the Skull* would never come together. And one of the sorest points remained the extent to which Doyle resisted what everyone else, including the playwright, saw as the play's humour. John Castle adored the nasty jokes, Pearce Quigley took every opportunity to play up the slapstick side of his role, and Rufus Sewell commented openly, 'I like the laughs. If the audience feels it can't laugh, you're getting into a dangerous area. If people can't laugh, you get them into a grim silence where they're not listening. It's good to draw people in before you punch them in the face.' But Tony Doyle, though he possessed a devilish wit of his own, persisted in viewing laughter as a violation of the play's serious subject matter. 'One has to be careful about humour,' he warned Daldry during the second week of rehearsals. 'Because otherwise there's a danger that something rooted in terrible reality becomes fictional.' Even on the last Monday before opening night, when Doyle had already stirred several preview audiences to hilarity with his explicitly humorous lines, he was still disturbed about this issue.

'Now, it fucks me up when people start laughing,' he confided to Daldry.

'Why?' asked the director.

'Well, I find it weird that people find cruelty enjoyable. I mean, I know you do. But you're weird.'

'You nut,' Daldry laughed. 'Well, my only note to you is: Let them.'

By this time they had come to trust each other enough to joke about their differences. But in the early stages of rehearsal the vast interpretive gap between them had seemed practically unbridgeable. Their conflicts began as early as the second day, when they openly disagreed about the meaning of Nelson's violent act, his beating of Roche. Doyle was suggesting that Nelson got Roche off so that he could deal with him personally back in Northern Ireland. 'Where I want you is back there,' he told Rufus Sewell, 'so I can tear you limb from limb.'

'No,' Daldry insisted. 'That's a misreading.'

'Well,' said Doyle. 'But it doesn't matter.'

'No, it's crucial. It's the core of the play.' Daldry took a deep breath. 'I'll have to explain what my reading is, then. There's absolutely no intention to do anything but make the turn . . . Getting Naylor out of the room is not in any way a precursor to hitting Roche, but an objection to being policed by him. The irony is that when you get him out of the room, that's when you hit him. It's when you realize that the whole cycle is starting again. It's about getting off the treadmill.'

'But once he's loose and back in Belfast, I have another one of the buggers,' persisted Doyle. 'If we kill enough of them . . . if I can get fifteen of them, why won't I?'

'Because you've given up on the whole cycle of violence,' Stephen Daldry explained. 'You no longer believe in it. And the actual act of violence is also an act of suicide – though I don't know how conscious that is – because he knows he'll probably be killed for it down the line. And it's also an act of love – you're kissing him.'

At this point, Daldry still had in mind an image of the play that was linked to his Liverpool production: the image of two men fighting together in the dirt, growing muddier and muddier as they held each other in an embrace of intimate hatred. Bill Dudley had picked up on this image in his first computer-designed sketch, which had two naked Francis Bacon figures struggling in the pit of peat; and, throughout the design process, Daldry and Dudley had planned on this climactic moment of physical action, which they referred to as 'the rumpus'. But that fight was never to take place. When Stephen Daldry finally understood the personality of the actor he had chosen to play the part of Nelson, he altered the role to suit the man. In the production at the Duke of York's, the crucial beating took place in darkness, in the audience's imagination.

I suspect that Tony Doyle's resistance to Stephen Daldry's interpretation of the beating had many sources. He was an Irishman standing up against an Englishman's opinions about the nationalist struggle, and he was a Catholic who, though he was playing a Protestant in the play, still couldn't bring himself to credit the Protestant view. He was, at the same time, a puritan objecting to what seemed to him the hedonistic irresponsibility of a humorous or fictionalized rendering of reality. He was also an explicitly heterosexual man resisting what may have struck him as an implicitly homosexual interpretation. He was an older man defying the younger man who had been placed in a position of authority over him, and he was an actor standing up for his artistic rights against the opposing guild of directors.

Perhaps none of this would have mattered much, though, if Daldry had not made certain kinds of physical demands on Doyle's acting. A central difference between the two men lay in their attitude towards theatrical movement. For Tony Doyle gesture was a mere accessory to language, a naturalistic appendage to the effective delivery of lines. But for Stephen Daldry it was an essential dramatic tool.

One of the battlegrounds on which they waged this particular war was the scene in which Nelson first got Roche to speak. For the preceding twenty minutes, Nelson had carried on a punctuated monologue, interrupted by occasional speeches from Naylor and a few seconds of self-imposed silence. Now Daldry wanted a change of mood – a shift to something less public and professional, more casual and personal. For the most part he had kept the actors at a distance from each other, projecting across the entire stage area so that they could be heard clearly in this theatre-in-the-round. 'The one thing we should really avoid doing is getting close,' he told two of the actors about their scene together. 'It's probably me as well, my taste. I'm always interested in keeping people as far apart as possible.' But for this crucial scene between Nelson and Roche, Daldry asked Tony Doyle to get as close as possible to Rufus Sewell.

'Can you break personal space?' Daldry urged.

Doyle gave him a quizzical (or was it mock-quizzical?) look. 'Break person space?'

Stephen Daldry rolled his eyes (this gesture, too, a combination of real and feigned exasperation) and stepped into the marked-off rehearsal area to show Doyle what he meant. Sewell was seated on the ground at the edge of the dirt square, hunched over and facing away from the centre. Daldry had Doyle stand directly behind him, almost leaning over him, and practically whisper the line, 'Tell me you never heard it scuttling around between your ears . . .'. At the sound of this new note from Tony

Doyle, the director's face brightened with pleasure. 'Yes, yes, yes! I love it,' he said. 'It's so intimate.' And he went on to intensify the sense of intimacy by having Doyle sit down in the dirt, his back almost touching Sewell's back, before he began to speak.

Tony Doyle hated sitting down on the ground. He was an actor who, when he hadn't yet learned his lines, would remain rooted stolidly in one position, script in hand, as if the firm foundation of his planted legs could alleviate the anxious uncertainty of his performance. Even when he had learned his lines, at which point his verbal delivery took off, Doyle's range of physical gestures was limited to a slow perambulation around the edge of the stage and occasional intense arm-wavings. In asking him to sit on the floor – and a dirt-covered floor, at that – Stephen Daldry was violating what Doyle considered to be his professional dignity. 'With my ass exposed to the audience,' he pointed out to the director, 'I can't help feeling it diminishes my incisive intellectual argument.' But Daldry wanted him, in this scene, to let go of some of that incisiveness, to seem off-duty, somewhat vulnerable, even a bit childlike. 'In my weird world,' Daldry told him at one rehearsal, 'you go down not to speak to him, but before that.' As he spoke, Daldry himself sat down on the rehearsal-room floor, his legs extended out in front of him. 'I know you won't do it,' he continued, 'but in my weird world you sit down and make a mud castle' – and Daldry proceeded to demonstrate this, patting together a pile of invisible peat with both hands.

The sitting-down episode remained a major if eventually humorous bone of contention between them. ('As soon as we get rid of you, after press night, I'm going to stop sitting down,' Doyle jokingly threatened, to which Daldry replied, 'Ah, but what you don't know is that I've had monitors installed in my house, so I can watch you . . .') But there were other bits of physical direction that more aptly demonstrated their differing approaches to theatrical language.

Towards the end of the fourth week of rehearsals, a few days before the company began to occupy the Duke of York's, Daldry started to focus on the way the actors moved. For Daldry, stage gesture had always been a way of highlighting or counterpointing a play's verbal meaning, as when he had Edna usher open the house in *An Inspector Calls*, or Eleanor climb up on the stool in *The Editing Process*. With *Rat in the Skull*, he tried to find places where the language itself could invite the next move. For instance, immediately after Constable Naylor ended a scene by saying about Roche, 'And could he have a sandwich, cheese or ham,' Daldry had Superintendent Harris enter the next scene chewing on a cheese or ham sandwich. This kind of thing didn't make literal, naturalistic sense, but it made perfect sense in a stylized, conjuring, theatrical way, and the other actors (particularly the sandwich-chewing John Castle) loved it. Tony Doyle, however, hewed to the literal as if it were God's only truth. It seemed to puzzle and even offend him when Daldry began to introduce these verbal-physical puns, as he did in profusion during that fourth week of rehearsals.

Daldry began with Nelson's speech about the typical RUC funeral. Addressed to a silent Roche and a witnessing Naylor, it included the lines, 'All the cameras on her as her legs go under her outside the church. Pan, zoom, big close-up on the kiddies leaning against her . . . Any kids? . . . Roche? Do you have parental responsibilities or just explosive ones?' What Daldry wanted Doyle to do during this speech was to imitate the motion of a television camera lens – suddenly zooming in towards Roche on 'pan, zoom', leaning towards him on 'big close-up of the kiddies leaning', and turning away in a pivoting motion to ask Naylor, 'Any kids?' before flipping the same question back to the IRA man on 'Roche?'

'So it feels as if you're coming in, out, then in again, before you spin it away,' Daldry told Doyle. Speaking with the precision of a dance instructor, he asked for a turn that would pivot in a specific direction and then back the other way, so that 'it's an inversion of what you've just done . . . It's something new, something we haven't seen yet.' Then he began to add similar gestures to other speeches of Nelson's. On the line 'Ignorance. You can't beat it for making you feel all warm and cosy and snuggled up inside,' he asked Doyle to move in close to Sewell, as if he were somehow snuggling up to him. 'There's something about being snuggled up *with* it . . . as in, "Ignorance – I love the word",' Daldry suggested. When the moment came for Nelson to recite the Orangeman's classic toast (which concluded with 'whoever denies this toast, may he be slammed, jammed and crammed into the muzzle of the Great Gun of Athlone, and the gun fired into the Pope's belly, and the Pope into the devil's belly', and so on in a similar vein), Daldry tried to get Doyle to make a cannon-ramming gesture.

'It's like you're jamming *him*,' the director said, indicating Roche's impassive figure; and then, as an afterthought: 'Tony, tell me if I'm wrong, but there's nothing you can do with your feet, is there, to go with this?'

Tony Doyle had reached his limit. 'You want me to do an Irish jig?'

Daldry utterly ignored the sarcasm. Immersed in his stage picture, or else feigning immersion, Stephen Daldry went on, 'No, just . . .' and proceeded to demonstrate a little grapevine step, a slow weaving in and out that would take Nelson around Roche as he recited the toast.

Doyle didn't even deign to attempt it. Instead, he chose this moment to challenge Stephen Daldry's whole approach to marrying language with gesture. 'The words aren't saying what they mean, you mean?' he said.

'I don't understand,' Daldry answered.

Witnessing this exchange, I thought of Randall Jarrell's description of children's speech, in which 'a word has the reality of a thing: a thing that can be held wrong side up, played with like a toy, thrown at someone like a toy'. Stephen Daldry, in this sense, was like a child (or, as the poet Jarrell would have been the first to admit, like a poet): words to him were playthings, toy weapons, magic talismans that could be used to conjure up whole imaginary realms. And Tony Doyle, in contrast, was the sternly scientific adult, insisting that words should perform their proper job of transparently conveying reality. For the adult, there was only one reality, with nearer and further approximations to it in the theatre; but for the child, the theatre had its own kind of reality, separate from and simultaneous with the reality that we might experience outside it.

Daldry tried to convey something of this to Tony Doyle when he talked about Nelson's first entrance on the lines, 'Belfast bound or Belfast been you're set apart. Cut out from the other arrivals and departures. Corralled off.' The director acknowledged that Nelson did, in real-life terms, seem to be coming through or from the airport on those lines. 'But the situation we have in this theatre is a similarity,' Daldry pointed out, 'and I wonder if it's possible to play the analogy. So you're walking along this metal gangway in the theatre, with all these people looking up at you. And you've been cut off from the other arrivals. So the first moment is a marrying of the convention. And then you arrive and your speech is, Oh, so this is the set. It's also to Harris, but it's . . .' And Daldry let his voice trail off, as if to indicate the inexpressibility of the two simultaneous, conflicting, but none the less present realities. The blending of two worlds, in this case, was as powerful and as illogical as religious ritual; and the irony here was that Tony Doyle, the Catholic Irishman, was playing the Protestant sceptic to Stephen Daldry's theatrical Roman Catholicism. In this respect they were mimicking the roles set out for Protestants and Catholics in the Irish conflict itself. 'This attitude to language in the Republic of Ireland infuriates the Unionists in Northern Ireland . . . ,' wrote Colm Toibin in his essay 'On (Not) Saying What You Mean'. 'They call it hypocrisy. A community which longs for the Bible to mean exactly what it says feels that it has nothing in common with a group of people – Catholics – who believe that the bread and wine becomes the body and blood of Jesus Christ while at the same time knowing it does not.' Tony Doyle may have been a Catholic by upbringing, cast against type in the role of Nelson; but in terms of his theatrical attitudes he was squarely in the tradition of the Protestants who, from Cromwell onwards, had always mistrusted the transfigurative powers of the theatre.

Anyone who has ever spent time watching a play in rehearsal knows that sooner or later the themes and characters and speeches begin to ease out of their fictional constraints and invade the actors' and director's real lives. People begin to take on aspects of their dramatic personae, or to make alliances based on those personae; particularly apt lines of dialogue become touchstones or frequent jokes; and issues raised within the play become issues in the rehearsal room. As with all plays, this happened with *Rat in the Skull* – not only in regard to the peculiarly Irish conflict over language, but in terms of many other themes as well. So it should have surprised no one that Stephen Daldry's relationship with Tony Doyle began to take on the intimate, edgy, fraught quality of a family conflict. In rehearsing this play, which was, among other things, about fathers and sons, the two men fell easily into their generational roles, with Daldry respecting, resenting, and at times gently bullying the powerful, grudgingly affectionate, disapproving dad embodied by Tony Doyle.

This meant, of course, that he was learning from Doyle even as he was fighting with him, for he was too clever a director to let this demonic angel go without obtaining some kind of blessing. Stephen Daldry knew that Tony Doyle was a professional of the first order, and if he hadn't known it before, he would have perceived it when they began to rehearse the 'Belfast bound' speech. At first, Daldry couldn't figure out where to place Doyle in the stage area; no location seemed appropriate.

'I feel it's coming from a long way off, from down the corridor,' Doyle said. So Daldry let him try it that way, and it worked.

'How did you know?' Daldry asked.

'Instinct,' smiled Tony Doyle.

When the time came to stage the scene where Constable Naylor stepped into the centre of the cell to pick up the chair Roche had overturned – a very important scene, because it represented the first violation of the 'rule' that kept the Irishmen inside the dirt square and the Englishmen outside it – Daldry again relied on Doyle's instincts. He told the three actors to 'try it out, do what you want', and he stood back to watch them. As if on an impulse, Tony Doyle physically took charge of the scene, placing his body protectively between the agitated Roche and the fearful Naylor; then he gestured Naylor into the square as he delivered the line 'Easy with that chair.'

'OK, good,' said Daldry, eagerly accepting someone else's choreography if it solved the problem at hand. 'I love it. It's absolutely fab, because it's so professional.'

If Daldry played the son to Tony Doyle's Nelson, he played the father to Pearce Quigley's foolish, naïve, but unremittingly lovable Naylor. Whenever he wanted to move Quigley around on the set, Daldry would take him by the hand and lead him to the desired spot, just as if this six-foot-tall, beanpole-thin, immensely capable actor were actually a small child. Whenever he gave Quigley his notes, there was something world-weary, condescending, and at the same time amused in his voice. 'It's a master class from PC Naylor about interrogations and why you don't want to be involved in them,' Daldry advised him about his long monologue, urging him to play it up. 'I'll let you know when you've gone too far.' When Quigley *did* go too far, Daldry pulled him up short with the stern tones of a strict parent. '*Don't* get cocky,' he warned him sharply, as if addressing a sassy son.

Pearce Quigley responded to this treatment by exaggerating his resemblance to a child, at least in Daldry's presence. He came across as sweet, vulnerable, eager, whimsical, and ready at any moment to play the class clown. In one rehearsal, for instance, Daldry had him read aloud his transcription of Roche's speech in as flat a voice as possible. 'Flatter,' said the director. 'And with all the words given equal weight. *The* martyred dead. All those words – the, those, for, that – emphasized.'

Quigley did the speech as requested, and then added, in the same robotic voice, 'Exterminate.'

'You hate it,' translated Daldry.

'It seems odd,' Quigley admitted.

'When you get people reading to you in translation, it *is* odd – not natural,' the director explained, as if speaking to someone with a slight mental deficiency.

'What about making it interesting?' Quigley mischievously proposed. 'Can I do that this go?'

'Can I . . .?' was Pearce Quigley's constant refrain. 'Can I have a "But" there?' 'Can I look at Nelson in this scene?' 'Can I just do it?' It was a mode of address that a child might adopt with a kindly but occasionally strict adult; none of the other actors used anything like it in their man-to-man dealings with Daldry. Yet Pearce Quigley was only five years younger than Stephen Daldry – which made him three years older than Rufus Sewell, the other 'juvenile' in the play.

But Rufus Sewell, in the context of the rehearsal room, seemed years if not decades senior to Quigley. This was partly due to his role: unlike the soft, smooth-cheeked, endearingly direct Naylor, Roche was tough, unshaven, street-smart, brutal, sentimental in a romantic sort of way, and self-consciously, self-congratulatingly cocky. Partly, however, it was due to Sewell's own presence as an actor. A strikingly handsome man who, at the age of twenty-seven, was already well known in Britain for his work in films, plays, and BBC serials, Rufus Sewell had the self-assurance of someone much older. He also had an ease of manner which made everyone, from the twenty-three-year-old assistant director to the fifty-something John Castle, feel like an old acquaintance. 'I like him as a man,' Castle commented, remarking on Sewell's surprising lack of film-glamour veneer. And it was as another grown man, a straightforward equal, that Stephen Daldry dealt with him. If Tony Doyle performed the role of Daldry's father in these rehearsals and Pearce Quigley played his son, Rufus Sewell occupied the position of his brother. (In real life, Stephen Daldry has no son, no brother, and – since the age of fifteen – no father, but this only made it easier to imagine him taking on the abstract characteristics of those roles.)

From the beginning, Daldry focused his work with Sewell on the issue of Roche's responsiveness – to the other characters, to imagined interrogatory voices, to members of the audience, or to some combination of those. In each case, he was going after precision and specificity. On the first day of rehearsals, when the director spoke about Roche's opening monologue, he said to Sewell, 'It's that key thing about when you're talking to the audience, who *are* you talking to? I always hate it when it's just "I'm talking to the audience."' And one week before the move into the Duke of York's, Daldry was still talking to him about aiming his remarks: 'The only thing you have to keep in mind,' he told the actor, 'is your speed of working backward and forward.' For it was Rufus Sewell who had to carry most of the burden of the theatre-in-the-round structure. Planted in a swivel chair in the middle of a nearly empty stage, he had to distribute elements of his story in all directions, turning this way to make a joke, that way to deliver an important piece of information, swivelling on a syllable's notice from front to rear and back again. For much of the play he also had to be silent, and Daldry worked with him on making Nelson's twenty-minute monologue into a 'conversation' by having Roche's facial and bodily expressions speak for themselves. Once Roche had started to talk, Daldry wanted him to be continually on the verge of an outburst. 'When he's talking to you,' Daldry said about Nelson, 'speak back. Don't just be passive. You're always looking for the chink in, where you can speak. It's still too batonic,' he went on, suggesting an analogy between a staged conversation and a relay-runner's baton. 'It should be both of you trying to speak at once.'

In much of this collaboration between actor and director, Daldry either built on Rufus Sewell's own inventions or else stimulated Sewell to move the performance in a particular direction. His mode with this actor was mainly to invite rather than to demonstrate. 'Yes! That's fab,' he exclaimed about one of Roche's nervous, twitching mannerisms, to which Rufus Sewell replied, 'Yes, because I've come back as a rat.' Later, when Daldry suggested another physical gesture to Sewell, the actor responded, 'What does it look like? Because that's what I thought I *was* doing.'

'Ah!' answered the director. 'Well, that's probably why I'm suggesting it. I'm serious – I usually suggest things that people do.'

Often Daldry, when working on a unit with Sewell, would rely on one of his favourite ploys, the elaborate metaphor. For instance, to give him an idea about the tone of Roche's initial cross-cutting dialogue with Harris, Daldry suggested that he think of himself as 'talking to the Junior Roches' about his experiences in Paddington Green. 'People are going to write songs about me, about how I got away from the fucking police,' Daldry characterized the attitude. 'I'm in the history books. So I think you can play up the "Before I became the hero of Western civilization I was just an ordinary lad like you" . . . *Good*. It's coming,' he commented, after Sewell had delivered the lines, and then went on to modify his instructions between each repetition of the speech. 'Can you just do it again, and educate me. I'm ten . . . He's having the best of times. This is the happiest he's ever been, telling this story . . . Ah! So in the lecture he's got artefacts, and one of the prime artefacts he's brought back is the copper. You can wind him up. And the great thing about this copper is that you can chop him up in pieces at the end of the lecture and give the pieces to the children.' As Rufus Sewell spoke his lines, Stephen Daldry sat directly in front of him, responding to each sentence with the appropriate facial expression – as if he *were* ten, and excited at learning all about the Paddington Green coppers. Sewell laughed when he finished. 'I'm going to have to have you sitting in the audience pulling me that face,' he told Daldry.

The two of them spent a great deal of time trying to figure out what was going on in Roche's mind when he finally agreed to talk privately with Nelson. Was he ready to turn, or was he simply, as he himself said, going 'along for the ride . . . just to see how they work the informer ramp'? In order to arrive at the appropriate physical action for the part – the action that would make the internal motivations manifest – Sewell first had to understand what was going on inside the character. One of the things he found most confusing was that the transformation from apparent resistance to apparent capitulation was so sudden. To help him work it out, Daldry said, 'I'm trying to think of an analogy (only because I like them). You're working in a theatre – a socialist co-operative – and then the Disney Corporation comes in and offers you a million-dollar deal to make movies. On the one hand there's the adrenaline, and on the other hand the fear. It's that panic.' Daldry got up out of his seat and started imitating the two voices in his head: 'I could afford to buy that Winnebago – but no, can't go down that road.' As he mimicked the two sides, the deal versus the resistance, he paced back and forth, gesticulating all the while with his hands.

'This is quite good for you as well,' Sewell joked.

'All plays are therapy,' answered Daldry, in a tone that was slightly less joking than Sewell's had been. 'All plays are about your own therapy.'

If, in eliciting performances from his actors, Stephen Daldry gave away huge chunks of his own inner life, then that too was part of the art – not only the art of directing, but of interrogating. As a drama, *Rat in the Skull* is very much about the kind of information that has to be given away before one can get anything valuable; and in this respect as in others, the rehearsal process mirrored the play. As Daldry put it on the second day of rehearsals, in talking about Nelson's character, 'Part of his objective in the interview is to get Roche to let his rat out. Nelson knows what his own rat is, but he's got it shut up. But in getting Roche to explore *his* doubt, he's got to explore his own doubt at the same time. To do it well, you have to become emotionally engaged. The inverse of that is that he exposes his own doubt.' At the end of the rehearsal period, two days before opening night, he was still discussing this issue with Tony Doyle. As they sat in the Green Room on the morning before the second-to-last preview, Daldry told Doyle about a woman who had been arrested and imprisoned as an IRA suspect. 'She was saying the strongest relationship she'd created was with the interrogator.

When he died, in a helicopter crash, she wept for him. And he'd actually organize the shopping, buying birthday presents for her relatives –'

'It's rather freaky, isn't it,' said Doyle, 'that you have to make love to someone you're going to kill.'

'Yes. Well, it's that to get something you have to give of your-self,' responded Daldry. He could have been referring to directing as well as interrogation: to do it well, he had to explore and expose his own doubts.

Mostly, with *Rat in the Skull*, Stephen Daldry's doubts had to do with the conflict between theatrical intensity, on the one hand, and narrative clarity, on the other. In choosing this play, Daldry had selected a script which was extremely complex to begin with – not only in terms of plot and character, but with respect to the playwright's own aims. Ron Hutchinson had written a political allegory which was also a personal history, and the two were so intermingled that each set of ambivalences made the other set impossible to resolve. In rewriting the play for its 1995 revival, Hutchinson had taken to heart Daldry's sense that it was 'really a poem', and had pared away all the explanatory, connective tissue. What remained was stark, emphatic, and musically beautiful, but as a sequential plot it was even harder to grasp than the 1984 version had been. To this, the playwright had then added a number of elements in response to what he saw taking place in the rehearsal room. These included some new speeches for Constable Naylor ('Because Pearce is so good, and because you've blown the play open with the staging, so it just seems as if some of the duets should be trios,' Hutchinson told Daldry), some new images from his own mem-ories of Belfast history and geography, and some new jokes. Encouraged by this rich material, Daldry had opened out the play even further by adding a 'mad scene', in which Roche burst out of the dirt square and tore around the metallic walkway, all the while singing an old Irish song at the top of his lungs, while Nelson whipped him up with a forecast of his twenty-five years behind bars, and Naylor (after briefly taking refuge in one of the stage-level boxes) threw down his notebook in disgust and loudly complained about his job. What *had* been a difficult play to understand – with its rapid-fire Irish accents, its obscure political references, and its complicated sets of motivations – became, in this scene, utterly impenetrable. But this moment at which all hell broke loose onstage was also the most theatrically exciting episode in the play.

Half of Daldry wanted to create more moments like that, to convert *Rat in the Skull* into a series of intense, immediate, gripping encounters that would draw the audience in emotionally while remaining impervious to easy interpretation. But the other half felt a strong obligation to narrative clarity. Increasingly as he moved towards opening night, Stephen Daldry wanted to make sure people in the audience understood *what* was happening in the play and *why* it was happening. And in order to accomplish this, he was willing to jettison theatrical devices that had formerly seemed to earn their own keep.

A process that illustrated this tendency, and that also underlined in a particularly visible way Daldry's collaborative approach to theatre, was the development of the interval. *Rat in the Skull* was originally performed without an intermission in 1984, and Daldry's 1987 Liverpool production had no break, either. But on the first day of rehearsal in September 1995, when the company sat around the long table reading Ron Hutchinson's script, the director stopped them at Naylor's line, 'He said. And could he have a sandwich, cheese or ham.' The line follows Roche's most heartfelt, rebel-rousing speech ('He said' being Naylor's reference to his transcription of that speech), and it precedes a new scene between Harris and Naylor which Naylor opens by saying, 'Notebook entry signed with date, place and time, Morris Brian Naylor, Number MP 752,' to which Harris's response is 'Hefty piece of prose, that.' Pausing in the space between Naylor's two comments, Daldry remarked, 'If there's an interval, I suspect this is where it is.' Hutchinson, who had no theoretical objections to having an intermission, agreed that this spot – about one hour into the play and forty-five minutes from the end – would be a good place for a break.

A few days later, when he was rehearsing the actors in this segment of the play, Stephen Daldry asked Rufus Sewell, 'Can you just start, after the interval, with the word "violence"' – and he pointed to the place midway through Roche's long speech – 'as if it's a rewind.' In other words, he wanted the same actor who had given the full speech just before the interval to start the second act by repeating the latter half of that speech, as if to remind us exactly where we were taking up the story. (Daldry had used a similar device for the non-intermission in *An Inspector Calls*, where the curtain fell and then instantly rose again on a mimed, orchestrated repetition of the dialogue that had just taken place.) At the end of that day's rehearsal, Ron Hutchinson came back to the question of the intermission. He suggested that it might be more interesting, when the second act started, to have *Naylor* delivering Roche's speech this time, as if he were reading from his transcript, and to have Roche in turn asking for his own sandwich. 'Move the camera,' as Hutchinson put it.

'Oh, *yeah*,' Stephen Daldry said enthusiastically. 'Why didn't I think of that?' And it was this version of the interval – with the role-reversed rewind, as it were – that appeared in the rewritten script which Hutchinson presented to the actors at the beginning of the second week of rehearsals.

On the Friday of that week, however, further tinkering began to take place. Pearce Quigley was working on Naylor's delivery of Roche's speech, but he was having trouble making it as flat as Daldry wanted it. Hutchinson remarked, 'Maybe it isn't flat. Maybe it's like Chinese to him. It's this weird tablet from Mars and he's trying to understand it. It's not only from Mars, it's written in Cyrillic alphabet.'

Daldry nodded. 'That's the note I should have given you,' he told Quigley. 'It's like you're translating.'

Then the director and the playwright took a moment to confer, and Pearce Quigley sat down to rest his lanky frame in the swivel chair recently vacated by Rufus Sewell. Hutchinson glanced up and said, 'You know, when Pearce sits there, it does something to the theatrical space. Like the play hasn't started yet and there's this one page of the script that's fluttered down from somewhere, and this young man is trying to understand it.'

Then Rufus Sewell suggested, 'Why doesn't Pearce do me, like in a school play?' and Quigley instantly took up the suggestion, adding an overlay of exaggerated mimickry (including an imitation of Sewell's acquired Irish accent) to the last few lines of his delivery. Everyone excitedly got in on the act, with Hutchinson adding a new line for Quigley to say after he'd done the speech ('Bollocks!') and Daldry rearranging all the actors' post-interval entrances. 'If we pursue it, it's like showing what's going on in the interval,' the director explained, meaning that Quigley's playful little rendition would seem to be happening *between* the acts rather than at the start of the second act. Daldry was blithely cutting out lines so as to move immediately from Naylor's 'Bollocks!' to Harris's 'Things I knew and things I didn't know when I got here two hours back,' when he happened to glimpse the expression on the face of the deputy stage manager.

Emma Basilico, the DSM, had never worked with Stephen Daldry before this job. A freelance stage manager with an excellent reputation at the Young Vic and elsewhere, she had been called in at the last minute to replace someone else who had fallen through. Once the performances at the Duke of York's started, her job would be to cue all the technical people and, if necessary, the actors; she would be responsible for keeping the production on track in the face of all the usual disasters, and in that sense she would be the director's eyes and ears during the run. For now, in rehearsals, her main task (other than getting the right actors to the right rehearsals on time) was to follow the script closely and prompt people when they needed a specific line.

'What's the matter, Em?' Daldry said when he saw her doubtful expression. 'You don't like it.'

'Well, it's just . . .' hesitated Basilico. She knew Daldry only by reputation, so she couldn't be sure how he would deal with a contrary opinion.

'Tell me,' he urged.

'Well, it's just that without those three lines you're cutting – "Notebook entry . . .", "Hefty piece of prose", and "First prize shorthand typing . . ." – I think the audience is going to be lost. They've just had a few drinks in the bar and they've come back from the interval, and you're asking them to make leaps that I think are beyond them. They need those lines to locate themselves and give them the context of what's happening . . .' She let her voice trail off.

Daldry looked down at the script. Then he looked up at her with his beady blue stare. 'You're right,' he said, and reinserted the lines he had been about to discard.

In the end none of this mattered, because one week before previews, having rehearsed the interval all along, Daldry decided to do the play without an intermission. He had to persuade everybody – in particular the playwright, who had become very attached to the interval – that the play worked better as an uninterrupted piece of music. After watching several run-throughs, Daldry had determined that the ticklish pleasures of the second-act opening were outweighed by the need for narrative momentum. He was probably right, and in the end he persuaded the others that he was. So the interval became a phantom interval, a non-existent event. Still, the experience of working on it in that collaborative way left a residue in the mind of everyone in the company. What struck the actors about Daldry, as illustrated by this particular episode, was his combination of authority and flexibility, openness and strength. As Rufus Sewell put it, 'You're quite confident in his authority, because he doesn't try to put it across.'

Benefiting from other people's perceptions was nothing new to Stephen Daldry. He was used to relying heavily on his technical collaborators – Ian MacNeil (or, in this case, Bill Dudley), Rick Fisher, Stephen Warbeck and, in the recent shows, Paul Arditti. 'What's great about the productions,' Rick Fisher told me about their work together, 'is afterwards we can't remember what is anybody's idea . . . We're all very respectful of everyone. Maybe the person that we're least respectful of is

Stephen, because the director has to get into everything.'

I saw how this worked in practical terms once the *Rat in the Skull* company had moved into the Duke of York's. Prior to that, Daldry's collaborators had only seen a single runthrough of the play, which they attended exactly one week before the technical rehearsal. Fisher, Warbeck, and Arditti then had seven days to come up with their respective plans for lighting, music, and sound – plans which would be extensively revised and elaborated once the actors actually got on to the set and the preview audiences started responding to the play. 'It's not a technically difficult show,' Daldry told the actors on the day before their move into the theatre, 'so what we'll do is sketch it in and develop it over a few days. As usual.' That development, which was almost invisible to most of the actors, consisted of getting the technical details honed to a precise edge. In this Daldry was greatly aided by the nearly telepathic level of his communication with Fisher and Warbeck. 'Rick, can you change the colour on Roche so he feels in past tense to me?' Daldry would say, and Fisher would do it without another word, shining a bluer, dimmer light on Rufus Sewell while leaving the other actors in normal lighting. 'We need to work out exactly how many of those sounds we need before "Belfast bound",' Daldry told Warbeck, referring to the series of loud drumbeats that introduced Nelson's first appearance; and when Warbeck answered, 'I would say two less,' Daldry agreed, 'That's what I was going to say: two less.' The composer and the lighting designer were also in tune with each other, as Stephen Warbeck illustrated when he asked Daldry, 'When we go to Harris, should it be snap to Harris? And should we' – by which he meant the sound people – 'signal it as well?'

'Correct on both counts,' affirmed Daldry. 'So your first note should go to Rick, your second to Paul. And just tell me what you're doing so I can tell John.' It was Daldry's job, as director, to maintain the links with the actors, warning them when to pay attention to the technical changes. Or, in some cases, when *not* to pay attention: when the director pointed out to Pearce Quigley that one of his lines had been 'consistently late', Quigley answered, 'I think that's because I've been aware of the lighting change.'

'Thank you,' said Daldry, using his typical rising intonation (in which the phrase sounded like 'thang-*cue*' and meant 'I should have thought of that myself'). 'That explains it. Don't wait.'

Negotiating among the actors and the technical people, polishing the staging details in the rehearsals between previews, Stephen Daldry really came into his own. His visual imagination appeared to reach a new pitch of intensity when he got into the theatre and at last saw the actors moving around on the stage. Daldry's theatrical 'vision' was as much an internal process as an act of physical seeing, but it seemed to need the sense of place to set it off. During one rehearsal in the Duke of York's, for instance, he was trying to work out Harris's exit and Nelson's entrance when he suddenly announced, 'Stop. I'm getting confused. I must have a think.' Left alone on the stage, he sat down in Roche's empty swivel chair and stared in a rather glazed way at the rear walkway. While he considered the problem, his eyes flickered back and forth along the deserted metal gangway, as if he were counting the laps run by an imaginary figure. Then he stood up, having resolved the choreography to his satisfaction. 'Good,' he said to himself.

The one piece of the play that continued to worry Stephen Daldry up to the very last moment was the ending. Often referred to as 'the coda' by the playwright and the director, these last few pages of the script had a different feel from the rest of the play. There was something unreal or at least dreamlike about them, something quiet, detached, and peaceful, almost elegiac. This last scene is set in an imagined or imaginary future, months or even years after Nelson has beaten up Roche and thereby freed him. The two of them are back in Ireland, alone onstage in that patch of dirt; but though they speak in alternating lines, those lines at first do not appear to be addressed to each other. 'There was nothing said but "Let's be getting on." Sure, what

could be said, him to me, me to him. The crime is breathing,'
Nelson begins, to which Roche responds, 'A straight brutality it
was, on the jumping bleeding heart of Jesus. What else could it
be? My crime is breathing, for the likes of him.' Nelson's next
comment starts in mid-argument – 'Because that would say I led
him on, he took the hook and that could get him killed' – while
Roche, in *his* next line, definitely seems to be speaking to an
invisible third party: 'Your man's not just a thug in size fifteens,
you're saying? . . . He meant to get me off?' And the fifth and last
speech in this mysterious exchange, the final piece of non-
explanatory explanation, is similarly aimed outwards. 'He can't
afford,' says Nelson, continuing to refer to Roche in the third
person. 'Come on now, do you want to get the wee skitter
killed?'

The tone of the scene then shifts, as the two men begin to
speak directly to each other ('We've a date, you and me . . .' 'Oh,
ay. I'll be seeing your skinny malink malojam legs and thin
banana feet again . . .'). They briefly taunt and mimic each other,
and then there's another sudden tonal shift, introduced by
Nelson's line, 'There was a chance, once. Once, there was a
chance' – a move towards quiet thoughtfulness that is echoed in
Roche's 'Now, my friend, it's just who keeps hating longest.'
After a brief pause, the mood breaks again, with Roche setting
Nelson up for assassination ('That's him. The blue Sierra with
the roof rack and yellow plates . . .'), a line that in turn is followed by Nelson's Pat-and-Mike joke, the final speech of the
play. So these few scanty pages could really be viewed as four
different subscenes: the first five lines of cross-cutting dialogue;
the direct attack; the brief moment of pensive reconsideration;
and the death warrant. What was absolutely clear in the script –
and what remained consistent from first reading to last preview –
was the rhythm of these internal breaks, their musical and tonal
relation to one another.

But that was all that was clear. What did those last two or three
pages *mean*, especially those mysterious five lines at the beginning? (Hutchinson, when asked such questions, would simply

shrug.) And how were they to be rendered on the stage – to be 'physicalized', as Daldry put it on the third day of rehearsal? 'Now, OK, I'm thinking. In terms of what you want,' he had said that day to Tony Doyle, referring to Nelson's motivation, 'just for the moment of supposition, the aim of what you're getting to is that when you meet again, when you find this inevitable moment that he's going to kill you – he doesn't. What's got to happen to him is that *he's* got to come to a realization that you're *his* own. And that's the half a chance. Let's do it, just as an exercise. What would happen if you literally did physicalize it now?' And at this he had the actors move away from the table and into the performing area, for the first true bit of rehearsal.

He placed Tony Doyle and Rufus Sewell on either side of a seated, silent John Castle, who for the purposes of the exercise was given a role that didn't exist in the script – the role of listener to Nelson's and Roche's speeches.

'I can't tell if he's God or the chief of staff,' Doyle cracked.

'Chief of staff – of the IRA,' Daldry answered seriously.

'And who am I?' asked Doyle.

'I don't know. That's what I'm trying to find out,' said Daldry. He had Doyle deliver his first line of the scene, 'There was nothing said but "Let's be getting on . . .",' to Castle.

'OK,' commented Daldry, 'so that's the first example of why it doesn't work. So say the line to him.' He pointed to Sewell. After they'd accomplished several back-and-forth exchanges, he told Doyle, '*Him*. Talk to *him*,' and indicated John Castle again.

'You told me not to talk to him,' pointed out Tony Doyle. 'You're confused in your thinking.'

'You can talk to him after the first one,' Daldry amended. After the actors had worked through the whole scene once, he said, 'Thank you. It's sort of fighting for his soul, is what it feels like.' Weeks later, he would refine this notion by telling Doyle to think about the scene as if Roche and Nelson were each 'arguing with a Good Fairy. He's saying to the Good Fairy, "No, I didn't think that," and you're saying to the Good Fairy, "No, of course he couldn't afford to think that – do you want to get him killed?"' But for now, on the third day, Daldry simply told Rufus Sewell, 'Roche can't really afford to think that way. It would be the end of his faith.'

'But it would be his salvation,' interjected Ron Hutchinson.

'And Nelson knows that,' Daldry added. 'It would be his salvation, and Nelson's willing to sacrifice himself for that redemption. And that's why the music at the end is –'

'Beautiful,' said Stephen Warbeck, who had dropped in on the rehearsal that day.

'Beautiful, rather than *Terminator 2*,' agreed Daldry.

At this point a new voice entered the discussion. 'It's like mathematics,' said Raeda Ghazaleh, the twenty-three-year-old Palestinian woman who was working as Daldry's assistant director. 'He can't save himself, so he has to save him. Because they are the same one.'

'Yes, that's absolutely right,' said Daldry.

Stephen Daldry had hired Raeda Ghazaleh (if 'hired' is the right word for an unpaid theatrical internship) after getting to know her through the Royal Court's International Summer School, a British-Council-funded event which brought young theatre professionals from all over the world to work in Sloane Square. Young as she was, Ghazaleh had already put in many years as an actress, director, and playwright with her own theatre company in Jerusalem; she had seen and absorbed the work of Peter Brook, Robert Wilson, and other luminaries of the theatre world; she had a strong sense of herself and even stronger opinions about theatre; and, of course, she came from a part of the world that was plagued by a religious war similar to, if not identical with, the conflict between Catholics and Protestants in Northern Ireland. But what made Daldry pay special attention to her comments was the usefulness and accuracy of her perceptions about the play.

On the Monday before opening night, after four previews had already taken place, Raeda Ghazaleh took Stephen Daldry aside and told him her opinions about the ending. 'This is wrong,' she told him about the current version, her less-than-perfect command of English and her innate straightforwardness combining to produce a level of bluntness that was virtually unheard of in the London theatre world. What she didn't like, in particular, was the physical movement he had given to Roche on those final lines. Daldry had Sewell delivering the assassination instructions and then looking wildly from the audience to Nelson, as if waiting for someone from the boxes or the dress circle to shoot the RUC man dead. Ghazaleh felt that Roche should exhibit more pain at having Nelson executed – that he should go along with the plan because he believed in the cause, but regretfully, unwillingly. After giving the description, she argued, he should turn his back on Nelson so as not to see him killed; and then, when he heard Nelson telling his Pat-and-Mike joke, Roche should turn his head to look back at him on the joke's final line: 'I hope nothing's happened to him.'

Daldry listened to Ghazaleh's suggestion and agreed to try it. He put it into effect in the Monday night preview, and he left it in place as part of the finished production. Her proposal did indeed address some of the central emotional issues in the play, and to that extent she made a major contribution to the ending. But Raeda Ghazaleh's choreography did not really resolve the problems of narrative clarity in the play's final pages, because these pages, as rewritten by Ron Hutchinson, were *intended* to be obscure. In the 1984 script, Superintendent Harris's final speech to Naylor, after the line 'Animals, they are,' had gone on to include the words, 'Statement, on a straight brutality. There was nothing said, take it from me' – meaning: Nelson didn't get Roche off on purpose; there was no deal, no move towards confession, and therefore no attempt to silence a confession; it was just a garden-variety case of a Protestant cop beating up on a Catholic prisoner, 'a straight brutality'. With this line in place, it had been possible in the coda to hear both Nelson's first line ('There was nothing said . . .') and Roche's first line ('A straight brutality it was . . .') as theatrical echoes of Harris's last speech. They didn't have to have a clear meaning, because the echo *was* the meaning. But for the 1995 script Hutchinson had cut out Harris's line and left Nelson's and Roche's unchanged, so that the coda seemed to come out of nowhere. Had either of them really wanted the ending to seem limpid and resolved, the playwright or the director could have proposed restoring Harris's lost line, as they had restored so many other lines from the earlier script. But neither of them did. To both of them, the mysterious poetry of the stark, abbreviated version, dependent as it was on good fairies and invisible chiefs of staff, was preferable to the original ending.

None the less, over the last few days of rehearsals Daldry continued to rework and clarify the ending, prevailing on Hutchinson to insert lines like Roche's 'There was nothing said' and Nelson's 'Nothing offered, nothing taken.' With Hutchinson's collaboration, Daldry also went back to earlier scenes and introduced with greater explicitness the idea that Roche had been successfully 'turned', had perhaps even begun to talk, and had only been saved from his act of betrayal by Nelson's act of violence. Roche's formerly ambiguous remark when he was finally left alone with Nelson – 'Well, now there's just the two of us, let's be getting on' – was amended to include the blatantly informative 'Names. Dates, is it? Faces?' And Superintendent Harris, in his final interview with Nelson, was given the explanatory line, 'We wanted Roche. We had him. And you deliberately arranged for him to walk. To go free.' (When I asked Ron Hutchinson if he would include these last-minute changes in a finished version of the script – given that they had been imposed on him, with all due respect, by Daldry's search for clarity – he answered, 'Yes, because they represent a record of what happened in this space at this time. And they fit with the stage picture Stephen has created.')

But despite Daldry's efforts, the play remained opaque to large portions of its audience, including some of the critics, who concluded that Nelson's violence stemmed from either his marital difficulties or his generic hatred of Catholic terrorists. I asked one member of the audience – the London fireman who, in accord with municipal law, was assigned to guard the theatre each night – why *he* thought Nelson had beaten up Roche. 'At first I thought it was because of his problems with his wife,' he said. 'But when I saw it again tonight, I decided it was because he wanted to get him off. It was that line about "You *deliberately* arranged for him to go free."' So Daldry's revisions did have an effect in at least one case. The problem was, though, that they only worked on an audience member who had a chance to see the play more than once.

'I want it so that people like my mum can understand it,' Daldry said as he tinkered with the play during the last few previews. But this remark was only half true. If one side of Stephen Daldry was the charming ringmaster who sought to make theatre accessible to the crowds, an equally strong side was the rebellious tough guy trying to make life difficult for his audiences. 'He's my own,' Nelson said about the man he had just punched in the face, and Daldry may have felt some of the same ambivalences about the people who came to his productions. He implied as much in a joking remark he made during a post-performance talk on the evening after *Rat in the Skull*'s opening night. One of his listeners had asked him why he chose to put members of the audience practically onstage, in those seats located between the outer metal walkway and the inner square of dirt.

'Oh, because it freaks them out,' Daldry answered. He also had a theatrical reason, he admitted, that tied back to his image of the play as a struggle in the mud. 'You go to a boxing match and you see all those fucking guys rooting for that violence. I wanted those seats only to be available to men wearing DJs,' he went on, alluding to the standard boxing-match attire, 'but I was told I couldn't do that because we'd be breaking all sorts of rules and laws. You're meant to be so big about audience and access. I think if people want to come to your theatre' – and at this he began to grin demonically – 'they should apply for admission and you should get to choose. Exclude them!'

8 The Theatre and the World

Exclude them is what he proceeded to do with his next production. 'Production' is not exactly the right word: Stephen Daldry's next piece of theatre was actually a work in progress called *Body Talk*, performed at the Royal Court's Theatre Upstairs on three successive nights in July 1996. Since the Theatre Upstairs held only 70 audience members, and since a number of seats at the three sold-out performances were taken by repeat attenders from among the Royal Court staff and friends, fewer than 200 people ever saw *Body Talk*, which turned out to be Daldry's only new theatrical project in 1996.

He had intended to do more directing. The filming of *The Wasp Factory*, which was to be his cinematic début, had originally been scheduled for the summer of 1996, but the project was delayed by disputes over the option rights. Daldry had also planned to direct a Beckett play in either the spring or the autumn, but that too evaporated. He kept in his hand by occasionally supervising the road show of *An Inspector Calls* – a quick trip to California in May, for instance, allowed him to rehearse Kenneth Cranham and Stacy Keach for the Los Angeles segment of the American tour – but in the nine months between *Rat in the Skull* and *Body Talk*, Daldry had been much more a theatre administrator than a theatre director.

Nor had he planned to do *Body Talk* when he did. For a long time he had vaguely intended to do some kind of piece about men's (and perhaps women's) bodies – a stage work created entirely out of interviews, using the verbatim theatre techniques developed in England by Peter Cheeseman and in America by Anna Deveare Smith. 'He planned to do it *sometime*,' Marieke Spencer told me on the morning before the first performance of *Body Talk*, 'but then it was included in the Barclays New Stages

Festival programme, and suddenly he had to do it now.' Neither Spencer nor anyone else at the Royal Court had been privy to the three weeks of rehearsals, which had taken place in an empty warehouse in Clapham. All they knew was that it was a verbatim piece about men's bodies, and that everyone, including the director himself as well as the male stage manager, had been obliged to rehearse naked. 'Half the building is going tonight, to see what he's been up to,' said Spencer with a smile.

Half the building did, indeed, seem to be there when *Body Talk* had its first performance on 4 July. Among the dozen or more staff members squeezed on to the benches at the Theatre Upstairs were James Macdonald, recently promoted from associate director to deputy director of the Royal Court; Graham Whybrow, the theatre's literary manager; David Lan, the writer in residence; Vikki Heywood, the general manager; and Stella Hall, director of the Barclays New Stages Festival. Paul Arditti, the Court's sound designer, sat in the control booth co-ordinating the sound effects he had quickly put together for this production; Colin Grenfell, the deputy technical manager of the Theatre Upstairs, handled the lights; Ian MacNeil, who had provided what the one-page programme described as 'design help', sat on the far right-hand side of the tiny auditorium, next to where Stephen Daldry eventually perched himself; and a number of the men who had been interviewed for the play's material occupied seats in the first and second rows. A few members of the so-called general public, including playwrights Caryl Churchill and Wallace Shawn, had also managed to obtain tickets, but there was probably no one there that night who had not had *something* to do with the Royal Court's or this performance's previous history.

And there were no members of the press, at least in their official capacity. 'I doubt there will be any written material on *Body Talk*,' said Anne Mayer, the Court's press officer, in a fax dated 12 June. 'Stephen regards it as a work in progress and has discouraged press attendance. There won't be any reviews.' Depending on one's perspective, this made *Body Talk* either the ultimate theatre experience or a complete non-event.

The piece began with a brief speech by Stephen Daldry, who announced, 'This evening's show is very much a rehearsal.' He went on to explain how the material had been collected: the actors had interviewed forty to fifty men, including each other, about their attitudes towards their own bodies; some of these men had been gay, some straight, but all were alike in having agreed to take their clothes off during the interviews. 'Everything that's in the show is verbatim – it was said by one of the people interviewed,' Daldry assured us. 'And the good news is, we're not showing you everything we've got, so the show will only last about forty minutes.'

Then, as the lights dimmed, the sheet-like curtain was pulled open by a white-haired, white-bearded man who until this moment was sitting unobtrusively in a chair located just to the side and in front of the curtain. Neatly dressed and wearing gold-rimmed spectacles, the elderly man stands and pulls the material in evenly measured armfuls towards himself – a gesture that is somehow less evocative of a curtain opening than of billowing laundry being gathered in. Having accomplished his task, he silently returns to his chair, where he sits with an expressionless but none the less attentive look on his face: the mildly incurious look, perhaps, of an audience member waiting for a play to start.

Behind the curtain, lined up in a row, are five virtually identical cast-iron bath tubs, of the sort that one might find in any unremodelled Edwardian-era bathroom. Resting on their stunted legs on the slatted wooden flooring, they narrow in shape from head to foot, so that the five men reclining in the tubs are framed by the white rims, like babies in cradles or bodies in coffins. At the narrower end of each tub, closer to the audience, a board resting across the cast-iron rim holds items such as cigarettes, a lighter, a mirror, a bar of soap; on a single board, the one on the central tub, there is also a lighted candle. Four of the men who lie back in their tubs have their eyes closed and are cloaked in relative darkness, so that, despite the cigarettes dangling from their mouths and other signs of immediate, contemporary life, they seem strangely unfinished, like bodies about to be awakened with new souls – or, more pointedly, like dramatic characters on the verge of coming into being through the theatrical alchemy of actors and words. Only the bather in the centre has his eyes open, and the spotlight that shines on him alone, intensifying the light cast by his single candle, emphasizes his difference from the other four shades.

Suddenly there is the sound of music: taped music, with a female vocalist singing about angels and lambs and cherubim and seraphim. (Among the *cognoscenti* this would be instantly recognizable as Julie Andrews's Christmas album, a recording so patently camp as to have, in certain circles, its own form of authenticity.) At the word 'angels', the open-eyed bather in the centre begins to mouth the words along with the singer. On a crescendo in the music, he sits up slowly in his tub; his lip-synching has by now become exaggeratedly and falsely theatrical (though it is accompanied by real effects, in that it apparently brings up the light on the other four bodies). He spreads his hands before him, as if to offer the performance to an imaginary audience, pausing only briefly during this gesture to examine his nails for cleanliness. But before the song is even over, the central figure seems to tire of this self-amusement: he lies back down in his tub, takes a swig from a nearby bottle, and spits through his teeth into the water.

And then, before our eyes, he transforms himself. When the music ends he sits up again, not as a campy performer this time but as an ordinary man in a bathtub. He cocks his head and stares hard at something – not precisely at us, because his focus is somewhere off to our left, but at something that engages him as much as a mirroring audience. He is looking, we gather, at his own face in a mirror. One eyebrow rises quizzically, the jaw sets in a characteristic pose, the head swivels in a fleeting, utterly paranoid backwards glance, and even before we hear the first line ('You lookin' at me? You lookin' at *me*?'), we know we are seeing Robert De Niro in *Taxi Driver*.

But wait a minute. How did a line from a Martin Scorsese movie make it into this supposedly verbatim performance piece? Did one of the men who was interviewed actually recite that De Niro speech?

'They *all* did,' said Daldry. 'When we asked them, what do you do in the bath. At least, the straight men all did. Not the gay men.'

For Stephen Daldry, a central motive behind this theatrical endeavour was to use Peter Cheeseman's verbatim technique. To the small crowd who assembled for a discussion after the first performance of *Body Talk*, Daldry explained that in the 1970s Cheeseman had used this strategy – interviewing steelworkers who were about to be thrown out of work, and then performing their words – to keep the Sheldon Bar steel mill open. 'I've always admired the absolutism of his work, and the fact that it was the only time the written word changed political history,' Daldry said, practising a little absolutism of his own.

Producing a verbatim piece takes an enormous amount of work. As Daldry pointed out, there were six hours of rehearsal time for every minute of theatre in *Body Talk*. He himself did seven of the interviews before casting the five actors, and he then sent them out to do the rest, using a standard questionnaire amplified by their own individual follow-up questions. The actors, who were required to transcribe their interviews within an hour of having taped them, would present their characters the next day at rehearsal, complete with accents, gestures, and whatever else they might choose to include. Daldry would then select from the performances. 'I would edit that, roughly as I heard it – "Keep this, don't keep that" – and then that would be typed up, by character and also by category,' he noted.

The result of all this labour, though, was a piece of theatre whose dialogue never lived up to the opening promise of De Niro's borrowed speech. *Body Talk*, especially in its bloated middle section, was filled with lines like 'I love my dick' and 'Anywhere, absolutely anywhere, I will show my dick off. I love people looking at my dick' and 'I love knobs and I love boys – I really love them all.' ('Just technically, my girlfriend thought it really slowed down on cocks,' one actor mentioned the day after the first performance. 'Yes,' agreed another, 'mine too. She switched off on dicks, really.') Even with the unspoken invocation of gay rights and the tip of the hat to free speech, it's difficult to see why this material should require – or deserve – the same kinds of theatrical strategies that Peter Cheeseman developed to combat unemployment and Anna Deveare Smith used in response to the Crown Heights and Los Angeles racial conflicts. In comparison to its predecessors in the genre, Stephen Daldry's verbatim piece was not only notably apolitical; it was also singularly devoid of meaning, in a literary or linguistic sense.

Of course, *Body Talk* was still a work in progress, and therefore to a certain extent exempt from the obligation to satisfy in the manner of a completed play. It was not, however, a 'rehearsal', as Daldry had suggested in his opening speech. A rehearsal implies something private, fluid, interruptible, done for practice only, whereas *Body Talk* was very much a presentation to an audience, frozen at a single point in its development for scrutiny by outsiders. There was nothing transitional or improvised about its three performances: they resembled each other as closely as any three evenings in the run of a West End play. When Stephen Daldry rehearsed the actors on the afternoon between the first and second evenings of performance, he 'worked bits' in very much the way he would between normal previews. In fact, he made fewer changes in the dialogue than he normally would, because of his concern for the verbatim text, and he made no changes whatsoever to the structure of the piece.

Structure was the most salient and pleasing quality of *Body Talk*. In that respect, it probably makes more sense to compare it to a piece of music than a language-based play. And, as the editor who had produced the whole by listening to and rearranging the various parts, Daldry himself played the part of the composer this time. (His usual composer, Stephen Warbeck, wasn't even aware of *Body Talk*'s existence until he happened to drop by the Royal Court on the afternoon before its first presentation, and he never did see any of the performances.)

Stephen Daldry's own musical ear was evident in the way the

lines had been selected and arranged in the text – echoing each other at scene endings, leading from one topic to another through sound rather than meaning, providing theme and counterpoint (sometimes even choral counterpoint, with all five actors chiming in on a given word), or hanging unanswered in the air, like an elegiac coda. And musical structure was even more evident in the overall shape of the piece, which essentially broke down into five parts.

First there was the dialogue-less prelude, ending with the De Niro speech, which starts as a solo ('You lookin' at me?') and ends with the introduction of other characters ('I'm the only one here,' says the actor, still using De Niro's words, and then he looks around at the other four figures, one of whom now opens his eyes). Next comes an allegro sequence in which the dialogue jumps rapidly and amusingly from elbows to wrists to arms and their sensory/sexual uses, thence to cosmetics and vitamins, onward to body fat (with all the actors scrambling out of their tubs in unison, as if the fearful fat is something that surrounds them in the water), then to food, torso shape, personal trainers, and finally prostitution. This first and most enjoyable 'movement' ends with a phone call, which also serves as a theatrical joke. We hear the ringing of a cell phone and at first presume that it belongs to some forgetful audience member, someone who has ignored the sign posted outside the theatre (which reads, in full, PATRONS ARE REMINDED TO SWITCH OFF MOBILE PHONES BEFORE THE PERFORMANCE. THANK YOU). But then the elderly man, the curtain attendant, discovers the ringing phone under his chair and, after a brief exchange, hands it to one of the actors, who proceeds to describe into the receiver his selling points as a rent boy, while the old gent pulls the curtain closed.

The curtain opens again almost immediately, and we are at the beginning of the long adagio movement. In the short time afforded by the scene change, the actors have shed the wet jeans they wore in the first sequence, and they now stand facing away from us, completely naked. There is a relatively brief bit about bums and bottoms ('I prefer to think of mine as a bottom, not a bum,' says one actor), and then, as they turn around to face us, we are launched on a seemingly endless discussion of cocks and willies and dicks and knobs. The closing line of this section is 'It's like my access point to a dream world.'

Another curtain then leads into the last movement of dialogue, whose pace might be characterized as moderato. Here there is more physical motion than in earlier sequences and, perhaps as a result, there is also a rising sense of audience involvement. When one actor soaps another thoroughly and then chucks a bucketful of water at him to rinse him off, we in the first few rows get sprinkled if not soaked. When a different actor stalks riskily across the slippery rims of all five bath tubs, his balancing act induces in us a nervousness that is akin to, but not the same as, the feeling produced by his exposed nakedness. And when still another actor climbs a pole at the back of the stage, lifting himself above the level of all the previous action, we have an indefinable sense that the piece is moving towards its close.

Meanwhile, the section's intertwining monologues veer between two primary subjects: the joys of youth and infancy (there is a good belly-button speech), and the horrors of old age. Then the dialogue comes to rest on the subject of death, with the actor who has climbed the pole taking on, for the moment, the voice of a character with AIDS. In his final lines, he speaks to the other four men, or perhaps to the auditorium at large, or to no one in particular – the intended audience is not really clear, since one effect of the verbatim splicing technique is to detach remarks from their original context. 'Wouldn't mind coming back as an owl, though,' he says from his perch. 'Then I could watch you all on Hampstead Heath.'

These are the last words spoken in *Body Talk*. By this time, all five actors have put on their clothes or at least draped themselves in towels, so they are no longer naked in front of us, and that gives rise to a certain amount of subliminal relief. But Daldry hasn't finished with us yet. There is a final movement of the piece that is totally silent, and in this movement the elderly curtain-puller comes on to the stage area and begins undressing – slowly, carefully, with a kind of painfully inward focus – under the still, steady gaze of the other five actors. He seems oblivious to their presence, and to ours, but (or perhaps therefore) we are galvanized with discomfort, especially on behalf of the now-clothed actors, who have just recited a litany of insults about old, ugly, decaying bodies, with their 'saggy tits' and 'shiny calves' and 'bent things, slow things, grey things, difficulty, loneliness'. As we watch, the white-haired, bespectacled old man removes the last item of clothing – his underwear – and folds it neatly, placing it on the top of a careful pile. Moving slowly, he climbs into the central bathtub and sits down in the water. Only now does he look to his right, directly into the faces of the staring actors, who exchange a long glance with him. Then he lies back in the tub and his gaze focuses on the back wall of the theatre, somewhere just above our heads. And that is the end.

The moment is charged with powerful feeling and, intermittently, with a kind of transformative grace. As Stephen Daldry said about this scene, 'He comes on, and when you realize he's going to get undressed you think, "Oh, no," and you sit there waiting to get through it. And then, somehow, it changes.' That is true, and yet . . . and yet, one wants something more out of a piece of theatre. One doesn't ask of a Bach sonata, 'What does it mean?' and one doesn't require of a John Cage silence that it have some relation to the language surrounding it. Music is singularly well equipped to preserve and celebrate the moment in pure expressive form, to make the feelings it arouses the only feelings that matter, at least for a time. But theatre has other demands. Because it uses the language of our daily speech, and because it uses the human bodies of actors to represent characters we think we can know, theatre insists on making connections between its own noises and other noises, other speeches, other meanings. It wants to become a part of our ongoing conversation, to give us something we can take away with us and ponder or worry over or enjoy. What it wants to say can't be reduced to mere statements of principle or fact – if that were the case, the theatrical experience itself wouldn't be necessary. But theatre, though it is very much of the moment, also has longings to go beyond the moment; and plays, which are notoriously confined to their wooden O, want to reach beyond that stage space to encompass a bigger sphere, the world.

All of Stephen Daldry's work has played with this particular quality of theatre – its desire, its tendency to reach out into the world of its audience – and *Body Talk* was no exception. By definition, the verbatim form itself calls attention to the relationship between the world onstage and the wider world, in that it draws its theatrical dialogue from language that was not initially spoken in a theatrical context. We are told that these are the true thoughts and expressions of people as real as ourselves, and at the same time (especially in Daldry's use of the genre) we are encouraged to think of the speakers as fictional constructs, stage creatures snipped and sewn from the whole cloth of reality. 'They're actually creating fictional characters in a sense,' Daldry said of the actors, 'because all that you're using of character is a speech pattern . . . The character becomes more vivid when re-presented by the actor than the real person would be. And then, you get the interference of me,' he went on, alluding to his directorial shaping role. 'It's my choice that he gives his little belly button speech and then puts his finger in the other guy's belly button.'

Through a combination of editing and choreography, Daldry was repeatedly able to give the verbatim lines a meaning other than what they had in their original setting. For instance, there is the scene in which all five actors anxiously scramble to their feet, trying to escape something frightening that apparently surrounds them in the water. ('Their fat,' explained Daldry afterwards. 'This awful thing, their body.') The first line spoken after they all stand up, when they are posing before the audience as if before a mirror, is 'It's all right.' When the actor says this line, the other four visibly relax; they are soothed by the calming assurance. But there is another meaning to the phrase, and the implied mirror-gazing brings it out. As originally spoken, the line was clearly an answer to a question like 'What do you think of your body?' It was meant as an evaluation ('it's all right') rather than a soothing remark. By staging the comment the way he did, Daldry left just enough evidence of its origins to give us both meanings at once: we could understand the remark's contextual role in the scene and at the same time grasp its evaluative import. So this moment in the performance of *Body Talk* simultaneously referred to two different historical events, the past-tense event of the original interview and the present-tense moment in the theatre.

A similar tension was created by having the actors move fluidly from one character to another, adopting first one accent or one speech pattern or one set of opinions and then exchanging it for a different one. For most of the play (until they were allowed to put on their own clothes at the end), the five speaking actors were dressed identically, first in jeans, then in nothing. In both the programme and onstage, they were presented as an indistinguishable group, not as particular men playing particular roles. (Their names, for the record, were Peter Darling, Ian Gelder, Alan Gilchrist, Richard Kill, and Glyn Pritchard – and, in the role of the elderly man, Jimmy Gardner.) But even the five younger actors were of varying ages and body types, and often those types were in conflict with the lines they were speaking, so that a thin body would be referred to as fat, a bulky torso compared to 'a pencil', a straight or a thick or a short penis described as bent or thin or long. One effect of such discrepancies was to make the requisite point about the inaccuracy of self-image (everyone thinks he's too fat, everyone thinks his penis is too small); a more interesting result was to emphasize the difference between actor and character. Sentences that had perhaps been truthful when first spoken became lies in the mouths of actors. The self referred to in a first-person statement had been usurped by another and different self. It was, in a way, a commentary on the instability inherent in all theatre productions, where relatively static characters are constantly being transformed by the particular actors who take them on. It was also, obliquely, a commentary on the weird ethic governing the stage professions. A playwright or a director or a designer can hide behind his talent and his intelligence, but an actor, though he may benefit from talent and intelligence, is finally dependent on and subsidiary to his own body. And the unfairness goes deeper than that. The actor's primary job is to display himself to an audience which has no corresponding obligation to display itself in return.

This inequality, built into the very structure of *Body Talk*, was highlighted by a curtain speech that each night interrupted the audience's applause. At the end of the play, after the old man had lain back in his bath, one of the other actors would pull the curtain closed. Stephen Daldry would then get up from his seat in the audience and open the curtain, at which point the theatregoers, sensing the convention of a curtain call, would begin to applaud. The actors would smile in acknowledgment, as if the play were indeed over, and then one of them would raise his hand for silence. 'I have been thinking sometimes,' this actor would say in an endearingly unidentifiable European accent, 'how all this conversation would affect you and me if we were going to fancy each other. The fact that I was naked and you were dressed . . .' He is looking directly at the audience, speaking *to* the audience. 'If I were dressed maybe I would have lied more about myself. And something I have been thinking all the time is: how's *your* body?'

This speech (which, as with all the dialogue in *Body Talk*, was actually said by an interview respondent, though obviously in a very different context) cleverly engages the audience in at least two different ways. First, its cue is our applause. Before the speech can have its impact, we must play our role properly, doing our bit to signal the transition from stage world to real world by clapping our hands. (The fact that the audience performed its part correctly on all three evenings shows just how well trained, as theatrical participants, we are.) But second, the speech makes overt what all of us in the audience, men and women, have been thinking throughout the play. How would *we* stand up to this kind of close scrutiny of our bodies? What feelings – of identification, of protection, of exploitation – are created by the fact that the actors are naked and we are clothed? And how is theatrical nakedness different from real-world nakedness? What, in this context, is the role of shame, or embarrassment, or tact?

The master theoretician on the subject of theatrical tact is Erving Goffman, whose book *The Presentation of Self in Everyday Life* acutely elaborates the connections between dramatic convention and daily social existence. 'We find that there is an elaborate etiquette by which individuals guide themselves in their capacity as members of the audience,' says Goffman, referring to real-life interactions but encompassing theatre as well. 'Audiences are motivated to act tactfully because of an immediate identification with the performers, or because of a desire to avoid a scene, or to ingratiate themselves with the performers for purposes of exploitation.' One of the social situations cited by Goffman seems particularly pertinent to the closing moments of *Body Talk*:

> Whenever the audience exercises tact, the possibility will arise that the performers will learn that they are being tactfully protected. When this occurs, the further possibility arises that the audience will learn that the performers know they are being tactfully protected . . . [A] moment in the performance may come when the separateness of the teams will break down and be momentarily replaced by a communion of glances through which each team openly admits to the other its state of information. At such moments the whole dramaturgical structure of social interaction is suddenly and poignantly laid bare, and the line separating the teams momentarily disappears.

This passage seems to allude not just to the moment after the applause, when the actor spoke directly to the audience, but also to that somewhat earlier moment when the now-naked old man and the now-clothed actors engaged in 'a communion of glances'. That old man was, patently, a stand-in for the audience: he sat on our side of the curtain, observed the action along with us, and remained silent throughout the performance, as we did. When he stepped onstage and began to undress, it felt like a violation of the theatrical contract we thought we had entered into. And it also served as an uncannily exact illustration of another of Goffman's remarks, his reference to those moments when 'audiences are inadvertently given glimpses behind the scenes of a performance'. At such points, says Goffman, the audience may discover 'a fundamental democracy that is usually well hidden . . . Behind many masks and many characters, each performer tends to wear a single look, a naked unsocialized look, a look of concentration, a look of one who is privately engaged in a difficult, treacherous task.'

As we watched *Body Talk*, we may have thought we were seeing nakedness in the younger men, but that was just a performed nakedness, an undressing behind a drawn curtain. Only when that rabbinical old man began to take off his clothes in front of us, wearing that inward-turning expression, that 'look of concentration', did we feel for the first time the shame of seeing real, unstaged nakedness. And even then, of course, our feeling was the result of an illusion, a theatrical effect created by Stephen Daldry and his actors.

'If I were dressed maybe I would have lied more about myself,' said the actor in his curtain speech, implying some kind of equation between nakedness and truth. But this line is itself a lie. The naked actor was following a script; had he been clothed, he would equally have been following a script, and hence lying neither more nor less. Moreover, the lines he spoke while naked had their own special brand of falsehood, for he was applying other men's descriptions to his own body in a way that was patently inappropriate to it. We were intended to enjoy the confessional quality of his words and at the same time understand them as lies.

Something of this is inherent in all theatre. Writing about the Dover Cliffs scene in *King Lear*, in which Edgar persuades Gloucester to believe the unbelievable, Stephen Greenblatt has pointed out:

But the audience at a play never absolutely accepts such fictions: we enjoy being brazenly lied to, we welcome for the sake of pleasure what we know to be untrue, but we withhold from the theatre the simple assent we grant to everyday reality ... the theatre elicits from us complicity rather than belief.

To which Anthony Dawson has retorted that, at least in Shakespearean theatre, 'complicity and belief are inextricably intertwined and involve each other'.

Dawson's response is too quick and easy to cope with all the complexities raised in Greenblatt's assertion, but in questioning the firm distinction between belief and complicity, it does touch a nerve. Is it really possible for us to 'withhold' fretful anxiety at Desdemona's impending fate, instinctive disgust as Gloucester's eyes are poked out, or grateful relief when Hermione's statue comes to life, and still feel we are getting the theatrical experience offered by *Othello*, *King Lear*, or *The Winter's Tale*? It is true that theatre grants us a degree of voluntary removal from its dangers and fears that life (at least, sane life) forbids us: we can place ourselves either riskily inside the performance or safely outside it, committing our emotions temporarily to its service or viewing the whole thing as just a conglomeration of words. But if, as Stanley Cavell says, you go to the theatre to see Mrs Siddons survive rather than to see Desdemona die, you must be a very strange theatre-goer indeed. The theatre needs some kind of collaboration from its audience if it is to work on us at all, and there's no point in paying good money for the ticket if you're not planning to grant your assent to its premises. That this is not the same as the 'assent we grant to everyday reality' is undeniable: we wouldn't think of it as theatrically induced belief if it were identical to *non*-theatrically induced belief. But both theatre and real life ask us to make leaps of faith. Something more complicated than acknowledgment of empirically visible facts is required every time we profess a belief in the existence of, say, God, or true love, or a corporate entity: 'This company's not for real,' as the character in *The Editing Process* correctly observes.

One difference between theatrical belief and its ordinary-life equivalent may be that the former doesn't disintegrate when we are forced to recognize its deceitful or at any rate artificial underpinnings. The events onstage can be fiction, but the emotions and realizations they produce are real enough, as Sheila Birling passionately points out in *An Inspector Calls*. So theatre allows us a very special freedom: the freedom from disillusion. Understanding the artifice behind the effect doesn't, for once, puncture the pleasure of the effect. We can possess both the truth and the lie at the same time, admiring the form even as we are absorbed in the content. And we can continue to invest in the ongoing emotions of a play even if we have already seen it once, or twice, or ten times. Perhaps because it takes place in real time, or perhaps because it presents us with the real bodies of human actors, a play is even better able than a novel to draw us in repeatedly. The wonder of Hermione's revival is not ruined for us if we know it's coming; on the contrary, we wish for it every time, and then we get our wish. (On some level we may also wish for Desdemona's death and Gloucester's blinding, but because those wishes are too destructive to acknowledge, we experience them as anxiety.) In any case, theatre lets us have it both ways: we know the magic is a trick, and yet we still find it magical. To have our credulity cushioned in this way is a great gift, rarely available in the life outside art. No wonder, then, that the theatre-goer pays for the opportunity to be lied to, begs to be lured into complicitous belief, longs to be seduced by the theatrical fiction.

Seduction – another area where belief and complicity are often but not always intertwined – is one of theatre's central metaphors, and *Body Talk*, with its naked actors talking mainly about sensual pleasures, makes it explicit. The link between credulity and desire, between longing to believe and pure longing, infects our feelings about the actors in any theatre performance; and in this kind of verbatim theatre, it also affects the actors' relation to their characters. 'What I loved about this process is the actors would go out and meet and respond to different people,' Daldry commented after the first performance of *Body Talk*. 'And they would form an emotional attachment, because the interview process is so intimate. And they would love the character . . . and we would all fall in love with the character.'

'Falling in love' and 'lying' might be seen as the two poles around which *Body Talk* shapes itself, and the ways in which they are connected say as much about theatre in general as about this particular play in progress. *Body Talk* is, or seems to be, about self-exposure, about the intimacy and openness and deep connection that are only possible when someone chooses to bare himself to another. But the self-exposure, in this case, is refracted through and therefore undercut by the highly artificial conventions of the theatre. The fixed performance time, the curtain, the audience's applause, the exact repetition of the same dialogue night after night – these characteristics announce the presence of illusion, which is central to the definition of theatre. (You can look at a piece of film and not know whether you are seeing documentary or fiction, but you cannot have that confusion about a performance onstage; theatre, in this respect, is always fiction.) So to undertake a theatre piece about honest, unmediated self-exposure entails, by necessity, a complicated and collaborative form of lying.

Part of the deceit stems from the fact that we can never precisely pin down whose self is being exposed. The actor is presenting someone else's nakedness even as he displays his own, and that presentation has in turn been shaped by the manipulative figure behind the scenes, the director. Stephen Daldry would have been the first to admit that *Body Talk* was a strongly autobiographical piece, even though none of the words in it were actually his own. 'What's weird is doing something that's entirely me and not a play,' he told me on the day after the first performance. And by this he meant not only that he had constructed the piece through a very active 'editing process'; not only that it dealt with issues linked to his own mainly-gay-but-sometimes-straight sexuality; but also that he had been obliged repeatedly to put his own inner life on the line in the course of developing *Body Talk*. 'We talked a lot about Gestalt psychology and archetypes and sublimated personalities,' Daldry said about the rehearsal process. 'The actors are having to expose not just the person they discuss, but their own little dodgy selves. That's when it gets dangerous, of course.'

As a director, Daldry doesn't have to expose his own little dodgy self in quite the same way, but he relies heavily on its existence. Fictitious confession and seductive tale-telling are central to his personality, both inside and outside the rehearsal room. He is notorious for his small, harmless, but none the less persistent lies, like the way he consistently gives his age as one year less than it is. Among his tall tales, one of his favourites (to judge by the frequency of its telling) is the story of how, as a boy, he derailed a train by putting an obstruction on the tracks. When pressed, he sometimes adds that at least one passenger was killed. There is no hard evidence for this event, and one suspects that this is a case of Daldry's theatrical and fictional memories interpenetrating real life, for a train derailment was central to the plot of his first London production, Ödön von Horváth's *Judgement Day*, while Iain Banks's *The Wasp Factory*, from which he intended to make his first movie, featured a murderous child as its protagonist. At any rate, no one connected with Daldry's past can remember an actual train derailment during his Somerset childhood, not even his mother, Cherry Daldry.

Instead, she recalls Stephen's lifelong capacity to charm. 'When he was three-and-a-half years old, I remember,' she said, 'he was at the house of a friend of mine, a woman who had five children all under the age of seven. She was standing at the kitchen sink and he said to her – he used to lisp then – he said, "Oh, Mrs Birley, you look *wonderful*!" And she said it made her day.'

When his mother first told me this anecdote, on the eve of *Rat in the Skull*'s West End run, I connected it with Stephen Daldry's mistrust of sentiment. As a story about the too-easy efficacy of charm, it helped explain his preference for the harsher theatrical emotions as opposed to the more tearful and cathartic ones. But later, when I considered it in light of *Body Talk*, it seemed instead to be a story about the link between falsehood and seduction. People wanted to be lied to, people longed to be charmed into believing the unbelievable, and Stephen Daldry, with his still-boyish manner of open ingenuousness, knew how to give them this pleasure.

Of course, *Body Talk* was not really Daldry's autobiography; like all the plays he has chosen to direct, it merely had certain autobiographical elements. Whether Daldry is attracted to specific theatrical material because it echoes facts in his own life, or whether he remakes the facts to fit his dramatic creations, becomes a moot point. 'You're in the theatre because it enables you to reconstruct your life over and over again,' remarked the director Chris Barton, who himself confesses to a certain degree of exaggeration and tale-telling. 'Yourself, or your life, or your world. The proscenium arch is the most obvious model of that process. It's in a picture frame – there's this little environment you can control.'

The connection between that physical environment and Daldry's artistic work as a director became especially pointed during July 1996, for *Body Talk*'s rehearsal and performance happened to coincide with a particularly intense period in the plans to remodel the Royal Court. Ever since the National Lottery's sixteen-million-pound grant had come through in September 1995, Stephen Daldry had been working steadily and primarily on the remodelling process. The architectural firm of Haworth Tompkins and the theatrical design firm of Theatre Projects Consultants, who jointly issued the grant-winning feasibility study on 31 March 1995, had continued to collaborate with the Royal Court on the refinement and development of the design. Open meetings involving playwrights, directors, and designers had been held in October and November; opinions had been solicited from every branch of the Royal Court staff; and numerous wild possibilities had been explored and (mainly) discarded. By the summer of 1996, architect and client had reached a consensus on a final design that closely resembled the initial feasibility study, and the theatre company was preparing to move to its temporary location – two theatres in the West End, the Duke of York's and the Ambassadors – so that reconstruction could begin in the autumn. *Body Talk* was, in fact, the last production scheduled for the Theatre Upstairs before the move, the last piece that would take place in that space before it was completely rebuilt. But during the month of June the expected planning permission was twice put on hold, which meant that Stephen Daldry, in addition to directing *Body Talk* for eight hours each day, was also attending early-morning brainstorming sessions and lengthy evening meetings. 'That this got done at all,' said David Lan after *Body Talk*'s last performance, 'with what's been going on with the building the last three weeks, is amazing.'

A particular irony lay in the fact that though the building's remodelling plan was what was distracting Daldry from his work as a director, it was also crucially tied to the kinds of theatre ideas played out in *Body Talk*. 'We are building in more options which can be taken up as alternatives to the normal inverted comma production,' said Steve Tompkins, the lead architect on the project; and when I questioned him about the wonderful phrase 'inverted comma production', which seemed to refer simultaneously to the visual structure of a proscenium arch and the theatrical structure of a play's text, he elaborated in words that explicitly if unconsciously linked his architectural project to Daldry's most recent theatrical project. 'The norm has been discussed by everyone as a kind of verbatim away from which things can move,' explained Tompkins. 'There is quite a strong sense in which the auditorium in its everyday clothes is suitable for most occasions. We're taking away carpets and leaving floors that are bare board; the seats will be leather rather than cloth; the rails will be black bars rather than shiny brass. So there is a comfortable astringency about the whole interior design – we described it as an unmade-up face.' Or, one might add, an unclothed body: an artificially composed nakedness lending itself to the varieties of theatrical illusion.

The physical environment in which a play takes place has always been, in Stephen Daldry's terms, part of the play itself. In taking apart and rebuilding the auditorium space for *Rat in the Skull* and *The Kitchen*, or in exploring the nature of the stage machinery and its enclosing frame in *Machinal* and *An Inspector Calls*, Daldry was incorporating architectural and technical design into the dramatic experience. Helping to redesign the Royal Court was simply an extension of that approach. And if he went beyond the auditorium itself to give advice on the entrance foyer, the box office, the restaurant and the bar, then that too was consistent with his vision of going to the theatre. As Ian MacNeil put it during a panel discussion on stage design in 1995, 'If you take a child to the theatre and ask them to draw what they've seen, they'll draw the cables holding up the set and what happened to them in the foyer. *All* that is part of going to the theatre for them, and not just what happens in this little box. We've learned to block all that other stuff out.' But Daldry, with his childlike tendency to see everything, was now putting it all back in. The new design for the Royal Court, according to Steve Tompkins, would point to 'the dialectic between the public front of house, the formal rituals of going to the theatre, and the more private aspects of theatre production, a sense of private shared endeavour away from the more frivolous public ceremonies'; but if Stephen Daldry recognized this division, he also sought to break it down, and if he shared Tompkins's serious sense of purpose, he could also throw in a good word for frivolity. 'More than any other London theatre,' Daldry wrote in his section of the feasibility study, 'the Court needs to be a home for clowns as well as ensembliers, a place for fun and games as well as shocks and sermons.'

The feasibility study which was completed in March 1995 included, in embryo form, virtually all the elements that were to appear in the final design approved by the planning commission on 16 July 1996. 'Most of the ideas that were contained in the feasibility study we've had the chance to test out, and most of

the ideas have held up,' Tompkins commented about the intervening process. 'The scheme has simply evolved as we have
talked more to the staff of the theatre and investigated the technical detail of the proposals.' That 'scheme' included more and
better-organized office space for the Royal Court staff, a
redesigned foyer and box office, a previously non-existent
Green Room and expanded dressing-room space, a rebuilt stage
and substage area, some wing space where there had been none
before, a new grid and flying equipment, vastly improved
lighting, electrical, and sound systems, a higher ceiling for the
Theatre Upstairs, additional and relocated toilets, wheelchair
accessibility throughout the building, and a large underground
bar/restaurant extending outwards from the tiny existing Stalls
Bar, with access to and from the middle of Sloane Square.

In coming up with the plan, the architects were strictly confined by the physical limitations of the site, for the old Royal
Court had been built into a space bordered on one side by the
Circle and District Underground Lines and on another by the
Victorian-period Ranelagh Sewer. As remodellers of a living
theatrical monument, they were also inhibited, or at any rate
strongly guided, by the Royal Court's history and reputation. In
fact, the playwrights associated with the Court, when they were
called together to give their opinions about the remodel, voted as
a group against making any alterations whatsoever. 'The authors
demanded the money be handed back because they didn't want
any changes at all,' said Bill Dudley, who had been involved in
the redesign as an independent consultant. 'All joking aside, I
thought that was very selfish of them. It's not understanding
what theatre is, what theatre artists can do with space.'

One of the writers' primary fears was that something would
be done to alter the seemingly magical proportions of the Royal
Court's mainstage theatre. In that respect they had little to
worry about, for the people chosen to work on the remodel were
eminently concerned with preserving that magic. Iain
Mackintosh, the project's official theatre consultant, had already
gone on the record in his book *Architecture, Actor and Audience*,

where he attributed to the perfect proportions of the Royal Court its role in producing 'much of the best new writing in Britain since the middle 1950s'. And Steve Tompkins, though he had never before designed or remodelled a theatre, was fully aware of the virtues of the Sloane Square building. 'The Royal Court is my local,' he told me. 'I live round the corner, and as luck would have it I've seen more productions at the Royal Court than anywhere else.' It was therefore with some authority – as an audience member as well as an architect – that he was able to say, 'The form of the auditorium is beautiful, peerless in some senses: the intimacy, the relationship between actor and audience, the ease with which energy is transferred from the stage to the audience and back again, the acoustics.' Tompkins admitted that in the course of examining all their presuppositions, the design team 'went through a very long process which included swilling around in our mouths the idea of a radical demolition of the auditorium – spent hours and hours on the stage with the great and the good. But the auditorium as it stands has been incredibly potent, so that remains.'

Bill Dudley described the redesign as 'like having the same model of car, but a bigger engine. The proportions will be the same as the old Royal Court. The way we're doing it, you'll be able to have the auditorium look pretty much the way the old Royal Court did, if you want to.' But the remodelling would also allow designers and directors to 'go more readily into the round', or 'go three floors down, or you can rake it. And we've acquired some wing space on one side. It's the sort of thing critics wouldn't necessarily notice, but it's a godsend.' And, added Dudley, what might be considered by the writers to be an excessive expenditure on design was actually something that could *lower* the design costs over the long run: 'It's building design flexibility into it with this capital outlay, so that future productions can be mounted more cheaply.'

As artistic director of the theatre, Stephen Daldry was a constant presence in every aspect of the remodelling process; he was, as one fellow participant said, 'very much hands on'. In this respect, his role in the redesign was like his collaborative direction of a play, only more so. 'It's mainly that he has more people to consult,' said Bill Dudley, defining the difference between the two directorial positions. 'When he's in charge of a play, he can make most of the decisions himself. But when you've got these things – the economics of people, how they move, marketing research, all the rules and regulations of new buildings these days – it's much more complicated than just doing a play. And it's permanent.'

According to Dudley, one effect of the gigantic windfall of money – 'this bizarre thing, the Lottery' – was that it 'made us all lose the confidence of decision-making, to some extent. You don't want the curse of future generations.' But Stephen Daldry, though he consulted widely and deliberated judiciously, didn't seem to display any diminution of self-confidence; by all reports, he leapt into the architectural endeavour as fearlessly as he had into any theatrical one. 'Stephen, being a theatre person, isn't aware of the more banal constraints under which most architects work,' remarked Steve Tompkins, 'so he can say the unsayable, he can ask the unreasonable, without appearing arch, simply out of enthusiasm and curiosity. And that's very liberating, because it forces you to examine certain design orthodoxies. And often there's a very good reason why you can't do something, but it sometimes makes a difference.'

Tony Hudson, the project manager who had been hired by the Royal Court in the autumn of 1995 to oversee the remodelling through to its completion in 1998, gave me a few examples of some of Daldry's wilder contributions to the discussion. 'One of his ideas was to reoccupy the theatre halfway through the construction process,' Hudson grinned. 'Other ideas he's had – Stephen wanted a bloody great window between the underground café and the tube tunnel, so you could sit there having a drink and a meal watching the trains thunder by. And if he couldn't have his window on the tube, could we open up a window on the Victorian sewer at the back of the stage?' But Hudson wasn't complaining, or if he was, he was complaining in a tone of pure admiration. 'His main role is he's a visionary,' he said of Daldry, 'and that means he's both invigorating, exciting, and also frustrating. When you work on a building, you're moving from the infinitely possible to a single conclusion, and the whole of that process is a narrowing down to a single point. Stephen, of course, turns that on its head, and wants to know at every point if there's something we're missing – what if we did it *that* way?'

Both Tony Hudson and Steve Tompkins described Daldry as a collaborative worker, though they seemed to mean somewhat different things by the term. 'He's very collaborative, but make no doubt about who actually makes the final decision,' said Hudson. 'He consults very widely, and if he finds himself iso-lated, he reconsiders. Sometimes he reconsiders and drags the rest of us to where he is . . . He ultimately says what it is he wants. Of course, he's answerable to the board, but they have great respect for what he does; he's been able to take them with him.'

But the portrait drawn by Tompkins was of a less assertive, more co-operative figure. 'In my dealings with him – and this is probably an area where it has worked because there's a lot of mutual respect – he is very happy to allow certain things to be our call,' noted the architect. 'It's not a question of just letting us get on with it, but so far he does trust our judgment, and so far we've all been happy with the things we've come up with, including Stephen. He's a very astute critic, so presenting things to him is actually a rigorous workout, which is just what the scheme needs.'

The people who watched Stephen Daldry and Steve Tompkins work together on the remodelling seemed to feel that the per-sonal chemistry between them helped a great deal. The two of them were roughly the same age – Daldry had graduated from Sheffield in 1982, Tompkins from Bath in 1983 – and, in this world where 'the great and the good' were almost entirely prod-ucts of Oxbridge, they may have felt some kinship as relative outsiders. Like Daldry, Tompkins had travelled after graduation, working in Italy and India before taking up a job in England in

1985; and, like the director, he was already the head of his own shop by 1991. But more than any of these biographical features, the two men seemed to share attitudes and approaches. 'They're sympathetic to each other's ideas, the way they think,' one participant in the remodelling process commented.

'I would be wary of describing the whole process as some meeting of two great minds – it doesn't work that way at all,' Steve Tompkins demurred. 'I am simply the spokesperson for some twenty very talented designers working on the project. I wouldn't want to put myself forward as the great man, the individual genius. There has to be an energy, there has to be direction, and I think Stephen and I share a sense of pushing against obstacles as hard as we can. When you push that hard, you don't always overcome the obstacle – it might mean a retraction, it might mean a redesign – but it usually leads to somewhere interesting.'

Still, there was more to their collaboration than their combined energy. Tompkins and Daldry also shared what one might call, at the risk of sounding pretentious, an aesthetic. As a landscape painter as well as an architect, Tompkins could appreciate Daldry's strongly visual approach to theatre directing. He *had* appreciated it, long before he took on the Royal Court job, for he had seen both *Machinal* and *An Inspector Calls* at the National and had even been to some of Daldry's productions at the Gate. It was clear, when he described his specific response to one Daldry production, that Steve Tompkins saw analogies between what he was trying to do with buildings and what Stephen Daldry was trying to do with plays.

'I enjoyed *Rat in the Skull* very much, his most recent production at the Duke of York's,' Tompkins said. 'Having seen the original Court production, it was fascinating to see a different approach. I had seen the first play as intensely claustrophobic and almost voyeuristic, but the new production and Bill Dudley's design involved the audience completely in the action; to me it was pure theatricality without threatening or devaluing the text. There was a rawness, a directness in the production, like being at a bear pit, which I found very refreshing in such a bijou auditorium – which, coincidentally, was designed by the same original architect as the Court. It made me think of parallels between the interventions we're making, looking at a set of quite radical new moves which try to complement rather than repeat the past life of the theatre. I think we share a feeling that going to the theatre might sometimes be a dangerous and thrilling experience, not just intellectually satisfactory.'

If Tompkins and Daldry were both interested in making 'radical new moves', they were also, and equally, infused with a feeling of respect for the pre-existing text. In Steve Tompkins's case, of course, that text was a building, and the question was how to give it a whole new life without destroying it in the process. 'The fabric of the building is totally inappropriate to what the Court wants to do, and yet it's haunted,' Tony Hudson told me. 'And part of the puzzle is to find out what that is, what is the spirit? Steve is good on the line that needs to be trodden before you take away so much that you've lost everything.'

In describing how he located that line, Steve Tompkins resorted to a literary metaphor. 'What's important about the Royal Court,' he said, 'is not so much bricks and mortar as a sort of narrative continuity. We are trying to plug into that narrative sense: what's the theatre's story, what is the line of history, what is the story on to which one can write the next chapter? As long as one has a clear idea about it, then it's relatively simple to extrapolate into detail. We have been able to clear away quite large areas of built material without feeling uncomfortable, and we have been able to add large areas, particularly at the back, but we've been quite careful to preserve areas that seemed important, architectural bits of magic. But the proof of the pudding will be the eating of it. One can discuss a building being sensitive and appropriate, but it's quite another thing to realize it, particularly within the constraints of the modern building programme.'

A theatre production, too, can be judged only in its final form, and not on the basis of the ideas that went into it. But here, in the lapse of time between conception and execution, is where the analogy between the two endeavours begins to break down. Even the simplest building project takes months – more often, years – to reach completion, whereas a theatre production is expected to go from first readthrough to opening night in four or five weeks. Prominent theatre figures in both Britain and America have been objecting to these commercially imposed constraints since the time of J. B. Priestley and Harold Clurman. A very few, like Peter Brook and Declan Donnellan, have succeeded in forming their own companies so that they can rehearse a single work for months and years on end. But with the exception of the Royal National Theatre and the Royal Shakespeare Company, which generally give their directors six to sixteen weeks of rehearsal time, the norm in British theatres is still a four-week rehearsal period.

In his own elusive way, Stephen Daldry had already begun rebelling against this limitation – mainly by returning to plays he had previously staged and giving them new productions, so that he had double the rehearsal time and, more importantly, many intervening years to rethink the problems. Now, however, he had found two new projects which openly enabled him to stretch the normal preparation time. On the one hand there was the Royal Court remodel, the stage design to end all stage designs, where for once he had the time to explore and discard every alternate possibility before coming up with the right solution. And on the other hand there was *Body Talk*, which at the end of three weeks of rehearsal was still in its infancy as a theatre production.

Both of these burgeoning sprouts required Stephen Daldry's careful attention and, like rival siblings, they sometimes made their loudest demands at exactly the same moment. A single image from one rehearsal of *Body Talk* might serve as an apt emblem for Daldry's divided sense of paternal solicitude. It was the Friday afternoon between the first and second performances, and the director was rehearsing his six actors in the Theatre Upstairs. As they rehearsed, a huge and unexpected rainstorm suddenly intruded on the warm July day. There were no windows in the Theatre Upstairs, but you could hear the water pounding on the roof and then, increasingly, you could see it begin to trickle through the decrepit old ceiling on to the empty cloth-covered benches of the auditorium. When one of the leaks had reached a steady drip, Stephen Daldry – without taking his eyes off the actors' ongoing performance of a scene – picked up a bucket from beside the stage, walked over to the heaviest leak, and set the bucket under it. But at the first loud plop, which threatened to drown out the speaking actor's line, Daldry hurriedly cupped his hands under the drip instead, so that the water would fall softly into his palms before draining quietly into the bucket. For the duration of the cloudburst, he stood there, slightly stooped, his hands cupped over the bucket and his eyes trained on the actors, tenderly protecting both of his works in progress.

9 Collaboration and the Individual Talent

Like the architect who characterizes himself as 'simply the spokesperson for some twenty very talented designers', the director is in many ways merely part of a team. Yet he is also the person who 'ultimately says what he wants'. Between these two extremes lies the truth of any collaborative art form. What makes theatre directing strange, and interesting, is that it can be so markedly individual even as it relies so heavily on a group effort. 'Stephen Daldry' may seem at times to be a corporate name applied to a team of four, or eight, or sixteen (once you start counting actors, prompters, and stagehands along with designers, composers, and sound technicians), but a Daldry production is always distinctive and recognizable no matter who his collaborators may be. Something of the man's own vision in each case structures the theatrical experience, even though he needs to get other people to elicit it.

One cannot predict exactly *how* he will work with and through them; there is no general form this collaboration takes. It varies not only with the specific role of Daldry's collaborator (composer, set designer, lighting designer, assistant director, playwright, or whatever) but also with the specific personality, so that his manner towards one actor, for instance, will be totally different from his behaviour to another person in the same role. Some of his collaborations are ongoing while others are much more temporary, but with all his collaborators he works to find the common ground that will allow him to use their skills and desires to express his own theatrical intentions and obsessions. But 'works' implies an exercise of the will, whereas in Daldry the collusion appears effortless.

Let's begin with the example of stage music. Stephen Daldry has done his best to live up to Pater's dictum that all art should aspire to the condition of music, in the sense that all of his productions, in some form or other, have operatic aspirations. In part, this has been due to his own preference for spectacle and choreographed movement, his own leanings towards a kind of *Gesamtkunstwerk* that would, through words, music, set design, and theatrical atmosphere, embody a whole world. In part, it has also been due to his long-term collaboration with Stephen Warbeck, the composer who has worked with Daldry on all his major productions since 1989 (and on a few before that). And, in part, it has probably been due to both men's Brechtian allegiance to 'epic theatre', their desire to fashion a theatrical art which would employ sometimes strident, always noticeable, often unconventional music as one of its chief 'alienation effects'.

Besides directing plays so that they *seem* like operas, Daldry has in fact done one real opera – the first project he ever did with what was to become his core group of collaborators. In 1990, Stephen Daldry worked with Stephen Warbeck, Ian MacNeil, and Rick Fisher on a production of *Manon Lescaut* in Dublin. 'He's only done that one,' Rick Fisher told me, 'and he didn't have a particularly happy experience, largely because of the results. But it was never as bad as he thought it was. Two acts were very good, one was OK, and one – Act Two – was not right. But by the time we knew what was wrong, it was too late to fix it. We needed to have used our time better, and we needed less wooden singers, sexier singers.' As he spoke, the lighting designer showed me slides of the 'somewhat sexually graphic' production, which had been set in Vichy France, with Manon fleeing from the Nazis. 'In Act Two the set revolved, and it was kind of like in a Deco office,' Fisher explained. 'Act Three was my favourite, I think. It's normally done on a wharf. We did it as if it was in a secure mental hospital. The set again revolved, and there were hospital beds. In Act Four the set was destroyed, and there were the typical Stephen Daldry refugees walking at the back – this mass of humanity.' Though Daldry now deprecates this production, one can none the less see in it the seeds of much of his later work – the revolving set he used in *Damned for Despair*, *Search and Destroy*, and *The Editing Process*; the focus on sexual commerce implicit in *Figaro Gets Divorced*, *Machinal*, and *Body Talk*; and, most noticeably, the Second World War setting, the destroyed set, and the 'typical Stephen Daldry refugees' that were to distinguish his production of *An Inspector Calls*.

Daldry's production of J. B. Priestley's play was heavily dependent on Stephen Warbeck's live music – so much so that, as in an opera, the musical element became central to the play's effects and meanings. And when, in a cost-cutting measure, the live music was replaced by a tape for the touring and West End productions, Daldry's version of *An Inspector Calls* seemed diminished, if not utterly effaced. If *Inspector* could remain its essential self even without the rain (as it was when I first saw it at the Olivier), it could only be a shadow of itself without the live music. In the original productions at both the National Theatre and on Broadway, Warbeck's music for cello, piano, trumpet, and percussion was played by highly visible musicians who were either perched under the set (in New York) or suspended in stageside boxes (in London). As such, the live music contrasted noticeably with the taped *Vertigo* music that seemed, in the opening sequence, to emanate from the old radio set. Theatre, in this implied comparison, entailed human presence, spontaneity, the possibility of openness and change, whereas film specialized in the fixed, the ghostly, the pre-recorded, the eternal. The comparison did not necessarily elevate one element over the other: both were central to Daldry's conception of *An Inspector Calls* – which, after all, drew many of its inspirations from 1940s *film noir*, from Hitchcock, and from the movie-screen shape of the stage for which the production was originally designed. 'When we first did *Inspector Calls*,' Stephen Daldry mentioned in 1995, 'it was at the Lyttelton Theatre, which is really a very badly designed cinema space. The interesting thing about doing *Inspector* within a cinema is that it was written for theatres like this,' and he gestured around him at the Victorian-Edwardian grandeur of the Duke of York's, where he was currently staging *Rat in the Skull*. 'So you always had a three-tiered dialogue going on: a cinematic convention, an Edwardian theatre convention, and the rather surrealist conventions of the play itself.'

That dialogue, that sense of tension between conventions, was palpably evident in the earlier productions of *Inspector*. But when live music gave way to taped accompaniment, the balance was thrown off. 'I hate the *Inspector Calls* in London for its being recorded music,' Stephen Warbeck said about the West End production. And this was not just a composer's pride speaking. Warbeck is used to composing music that functions beautifully as taped accompaniment: he has, for instance, done the scores to all of the *Prime Suspect* television shows. But he knew that to accomplish its assigned role in *An Inspector Calls*, his stage music had to be performed live.

In his essay 'The Modern Theatre Is the Epic Theatre', Bertolt Brecht wrote:

> When the epic theatre's methods begin to penetrate the opera the first result is a radical *separation of the elements*. The great struggle for supremacy between words, music, and production – which always brings up the question 'which is the pretext for what?': is the music the pretext for the events on the stage, or are these the pretext for the music? etc. – can simply be by-passed by radically separating the elements. So long as the expression 'Gesamtkunstwerk' (or 'integrated work of art') means that the integration is a muddle, so long as the arts are supposed to be 'fused' together, the various elements will all be equally degraded, and each will act as a mere 'feed' to the rest. The process of fusion extends to the spectator, who gets thrown into the melting pot too and becomes a passive (suffering) part of the total work of art. Witchcraft of this sort must of course be fought against. Whatever is intended to produce hypnosis, is likely to induce sordid intoxication, or creates fog, has to be given up. *Words, music and setting must become more independent of one another*.

That is Brecht's own emphasis; and a few lines later he added, 'Music plays the chief part in our thesis.'

Stephen Warbeck is the most overtly Brechtian of Daldry's collaborators. He has done the music for the staged versions of a number of Brecht's plays, and speaks excitedly about the beauty and wit of Brecht's dialogue in its original German. He is also the most European of the four, in the sense of being the least English (though two of the four collaborators, Rick Fisher and Ian MacNeil, are in fact American). This allegiance to Europe has to do with temperament rather than birth or upbringing. Warbeck – who studied French as well as drama at Bristol University – is always looking across the Channel for wider, wilder influences, and when he complains about a play, as he did about *The Editing Process*, it is likely to be on the grounds that it is too English. One can also trace the international influence on the music performed by Stephen Warbeck's own little freelance band, the hKippers (spelled that way 'to distinguish it from the fish', says Warbeck). In some of the band's pieces, his partner Sarah Homer plays virtuoso clarinet in a style that mixes klezmer with American jazz; in others, Warbeck himself, jauntily wielding his accordion, performs *faux*-music-hall tunes sung in an outrageously hoarse, emphatically loud German or French that bears no resemblance to his quiet English speech. It is as if, during these performances, the intense, unbridled sources of Warbeck's music come nakedly into view, even as he himself retreats behind the mask of a 'character'.

Of the four collaborators, Warbeck is the oldest (by only a year in Rick Fisher's case, but by seven years in relation to Daldry and MacNeil). He has also worked with Daldry the longest, having met the director on a regional *Canterbury Tales* production in 1986. But mere chronology can't entirely explain the force of his personality on the rest of the group. They all mock each other's suggestions, but most of Warbeck's ideas are at least considered seriously. 'I'm not a serious person,' he protested at one point, 'I just have serious eyebrows.' But whatever the cause, other people – both within Daldry's group and beyond it – look to Stephen Warbeck as some sort of wise man. 'He's a genius,' enthused Ian Rickson, who had just collaborated with Warbeck on the enormously successful première of *Mojo*, after doing three or four previous productions with him. 'He's like someone from another century. He's medieval. He's like some sort of little prophet, with all sorts of wisdom.' And Kate Rowland, when I asked her why Daldry had used Warbeck on every one of his projects, answered, 'If you knew Stephen Warbeck, *you'd* want him to be on every project. I've worked with him myself. Stephen Warbeck is such a generous person. He's open. He has a huge talent, and he's very experimental. He's not a competing ego. That doesn't mean he's any less than – but it's probably what makes it possible for them to work together. He has such integrity about his work, and Stephen Daldry trusts him because of that.'

Warbeck's fondest memories are reserved for the work he did with Stephen Daldry at the Gate and, above all, for *Machinal*, where, as he said, 'we had a lot of time in rehearsal, improvising with musicians'. About a third of *Machinal*, he estimated, was underscored with live music, often played very loudly. In contrast, the scores for both *The Editing Process* and *Rat in the Skull* were little more than brief, taped segments of sound. 'I'm not excited about doing a few little bits of music as the revolve goes around,' he said during the previews of *The Editing Process*. 'I tried to get them to have a live musician, but they said there wasn't enough money, and as it's turned out there isn't much music in the play at all. It could really be done entirely without music . . . I'd like to do something with ten musicians in the pit, where the spoken word is not supreme.'

His method of collaborating with Daldry has varied from play to play. Warbeck describes Stephen Daldry as 'reasonably musically literate. I think he *feels* what it should be.' But the feeling doesn't always translate into specific musical notes. 'On *Inspector Calls*,' Warbeck commented, 'he would say, "I think it needs do-do-do-do-do," and I wrote something like that, that sounded very close to his do-do-do-do-do. And it didn't work.

It was a lesson for us both on how *not* to do it.' On subsequent plays, Daldry's suggestions about the music tended to be much more abstract – and, where concrete, often challenged by Warbeck and the other collaborators.

It was Warbeck, for instance, who summarized where and how the music would go in *Rat in the Skull*, after he, Daldry, Rick Fisher, and Paul Arditti had sat through one of the earliest complete runthroughs of the play. 'I thought – there are just a few bits of music – a low bass note at the beginning, as the din subsides; it would be gone by Roche's first speech,' Warbeck said to the other three. The four of them were seated at the director's table, conferring in quiet, almost secretive tones while the actors waited patiently at the other end of the room for Daldry to give them their post-runthrough notes. 'And I thought – there's no good reason for it, but trying some overlapping . . . And there are one or two other small places that could have music.' The composer then indicated them in his copy of the script.

But Daldry wasn't yet satisfied. 'Well, there's more music than what you just said.'

'How will I know where it is?'

'Wherever you want it,' the director answered. Daldry did have one specific suggestion, though: he wanted the final music, where the script now said *tin whistle*, to 'break into voice'.

'Why?' asked Warbeck.

'Well, it just feels that if you've had the tin whistle, it should break into one other thing. I feel it should be a child's voice. It needs to be a pure thing.' Daldry went on for a bit about how the boy singer should have to strain to reach the notes, so that we would really feel a sense of tension. He even hummed a little tune, to show how the voice would barely reach the high points.

'And then do you want him to do a little dance?' Rick Fisher impishly interrupted.

At this Daldry jumped on Fisher and pretended to beat him up. 'Yes, you might be right,' he admitted. 'It might be too much.' He turned back to Warbeck. 'What's your tin whistle like?'

'Hauntingly beautiful,' smiled Stephen Warbeck, bringing out the little phrase that had been their half-serious joke since the first week of rehearsals. And in the final performances it was in fact the tin whistle – emerging unexpectedly from a string-and-accordion background, and sounding a new note because of that – which constituted the music's 'one other thing'.

But Warbeck's effect on any given production is likely to reach far beyond the musical sphere. At that same runthrough of *Rat in the Skull*, he watched for the first time while Tony Doyle and Rufus Sewell, as Nelson and Roche, physically played out the tension between them – or rather, in Warbeck's view, *failed* to express that tension in adequate visual terms. Musing on this problem, Stephen Warbeck described to Stephen Daldry a fight he had witnessed in a pub a few evenings earlier, a quarrel between two men that had suddenly turned ugly and violent. 'They had their arms around each other, they had their mouths close to each other, they were saying the most unbearable things to each other,' Warbeck observed. 'But if you just saw a photograph, you'd think they were lovers.' Daldry listened to this account of the fight as if he were barely registering it. But from that day forward he began to direct Tony Doyle so that he moved nearer and nearer to Rufus Sewell, so that sometimes he was actually standing between the seated man's legs, and so that at one point, memorably, their two faces were frozen in facing profiles, their mouths close to each other, almost as if they were about to kiss. Warbeck's pub story had become a part of Daldry's theatrical picture. If music was secondary in this production, the composer was none the less central, for he had a hand in constructing the essential Daldry element, the *look* of the play.

'What Stephen was famous for, at the Gate,' commented his friend and fellow director Julian Webber, 'was spending more money on the set – that is more money per square foot of stage area – than any other theatre in London.' Since the Gate's stage measured less than 200 square feet, this wasn't quite as amazing as it sounded. None the less, the remark points to something significant about Stephen Daldry's career. Ever since 1989, when he had his London début with von Horváth's *Judgement Day* at the Old Red Lion in Islington, Daldry's productions have been singled out for their astonishing sets.

Daldry is often described by other theatre people as a director with 'vision', and by this they seem to mean not so much (or not only) a vivid imagination or an underlying aesthetic ambition, but rather a specifically visual take on the world. Sometimes this praise has been given backhandedly, even fearfully, as if the emphasis on design is bound to overwhelm the play itself. 'There's a kind of phony equation between text and design,' Ian MacNeil once commented, 'that somehow text is this vulnerable little bird that's going to be crushed by too much design.' It's an attitude with which MacNeil and the other Daldry collaborators obviously disagree. But Daldry himself has frequently had to contend with it, and occasionally he has made directorial choices which sacrifice his own most spectacular effects in order to preserve what he considers the identity of the play.

Take, for instance, the oft-recalled story of the boy who flew. Late in the rehearsals for the Broadway première of *An Inspector Calls*, Stephen Daldry came up with a new variant on the *faux*-interval, that moment when the curtain dropped on the argument between Sheila and Gerald and then almost instantly rose, to the accompaniment of the *Vertigo* music, on a mimed, replayed version of that argument. Normally the director brought the curtain up by having it tugged into motion by the little boy (that unspeaking but crucial figure whom some identified with Daldry himself – the child of the future looking back on these events of 1945 and 1912). But now, on Broadway, he decided to have the little boy fly up *with* the curtain.

It was an amazingly dramatic moment, both magical and terrifying. As the Bernard Herrmann music swelled in the background, the child, seemingly hanging on to the rising curtain with one hand, was lifted above the audience's rapt, upturned faces until he disappeared behind the high proscenium arch. (Actually, the boy was supported by a very elaborate and expensive harness;

Daldry went through two of them in the course of previews, at a cost of about $5000 each.) After experimenting with this scene during the dress rehearsal and three previews, the director gathered the cast together in Rosemary Harris's dressing room and announced, 'Tonight will be the last time the little boy flies.'

'Oh, *why*?' pleaded one of the actors. 'It's such a great effect.'

'It *is* a great effect,' agreed Daldry, 'but it doesn't have anything to do with the play.' And he was right. It was a case in which one aspect of his 'vision' – the side connected with intuition, subtlety, and negative capability – came up against and defeated his more commonly acknowledged talent for visual effects.

It is tempting to trace this director's love of spectacle back to his period with the Italian circus: he does, after all, have a particular fondness for theatre in the round, for spectacular lighting effects, and for gymnastic, obstacle-course sets. But Stephen Daldry's ten-month sojourn with the Circo di Nando Orfei doesn't seem sufficient to explain the powerful visual sense that is at the core of his strong reputation as a director. 'What I've liked about all his work is the painting glorious pictures,' said Stella Hall. Stephen Evans recalled having dinner with Daldry shortly after he saw *Machinal* and urging him, 'Well, surely, you have this strong visual sense, you'll want to make films.' And Kate Rowland summarized Daldry's special talents as a director by remarking, 'He has vision. He exudes energy. It's about putting energy onstage, so that you feel you're entering into something new, you're going to have an experience.'

As Rowland's words suggest, the visual in Daldry's work quickly merges into the experiential. The audiences at his plays are not simply looking at a picture; they are being surrounded by a whole new world. Rowland went on to make this explicit when she talked about a production of *The Ragged Trousered Philanthropist* he did in Liverpool – a remounting of his first great Sheffield success. '*Ragged Trousered Philanthropist* caused such an uproar in the theatre,' she said, 'because he was trying to do the usual create-the-whole-world, with very complicated tech, real painting and decorating, and even some dangerous things.' The technical over-ambition caused certain difficulties, with the result that the play opened late – a problem which has by now become so routine with Daldry's productions that his regular collaborators have practically memorized his first-night apology speech. It varies in its specific elements, but the gist of it was already there in his speech for *Machinal*, recited to me some years later by Rick Fisher. 'This play hasn't been seen for sixty years,' Fisher recalled Daldry saying to the assembled audience, 'and even *we* haven't seen it yet. I hope you like it, and if you do, tell your friends. If you don't like it, tell all your friends you went to see *Inspector Calls*.'

The reason Stephen Daldry has had to perfect a first-night apology is that he generally makes substantial changes in the choreography, the technical effects, and even the content of a play once he gets it into the theatre. In Daldry's case, the most intense phase of directing begins just prior to the first preview, during tech and dress rehearsal. (Sometimes, if he's making enough last-minute changes, the first preview *is* the dress rehearsal.) The intensity of this period is exacerbated by the technical complexity of Daldry's sets – the fact that there is always an eight-ton ceiling that needs to be lowered and raised, or a house that needs to fall apart and reassemble itself, or a revolve that needs to move exactly on cue, or an entirely new seating section that needs to be massively reconstructed and then approved by the safety inspectors. Both of these factors, the last-minute changes and the complicated sets, are in turn tied back to Daldry's overwhelmingly visual sense of theatre, for it is only when he actually sees the set in action, with the actors moving over it, that he can be sure what he wants it to do. It is a visual sense, however, that does not dominate at the expense of words or music, but that, as Stella Hall has pointed out, works with them to 'create a very satisfying theatrical whole . . . a seamless marriage of word, sound, image'. In describing the eventual success of the technically troubled *Ragged Trousered Philanthropist*, Kate Rowland used a word of Daldry's own to convey this overall theatrical effect. '*Zhush*, they call it – an idea that him and Julian love. These wonderful moments of theatricality that he would put into something and no one would ever expect.'

Zhush apparently has strong affinities with what some might call cheap showmanship. 'When we first met there was a kind of vulgarity to his approach to theatre,' Ian MacNeil told me, half-admiringly and half-ironically. 'I was more of a purist, which I've got over. My taste has expanded. And he respects my aesthetic: sometimes I'll say we should do something just because it's beautiful, and he'll go along with that. Before I met him my work was pretty static. I wasn't into sets that did things.'

Stephen Daldry's effect on Ian MacNeil's designs is easy to see; what's less instantly visible, perhaps, is the impact of the quiet, thoughtful, and dedicated MacNeil on the boisterous, excitable, excessive Daldry. 'The idea was his, but the look was mine,' MacNeil said about the exploding house in *An Inspector Calls*, and when I saw the attentively arranged period 'chromos' on the interior wall of the Birlings' house, I had some sense of the powerful but secretive visual perfectionism he had contributed to the design. It is impossible, in any case, for an outsider to distinguish who contributed what to such a close working relationship. In an interview Daldry and MacNeil jointly gave to the *Independent on Sunday* in April 1996, Stephen Daldry said about their partnership, 'We always say in public that our ideas merge, that we can't remember who thought of what, but in fact it's remarkably clear who came up with what. We don't become one when we work together. When you're trying to imagine the world of a play, it's like handing over the baton to someone else. One runs with it for a while and then they pass it on and the other runs with it then passes it back. Unless you put in a huge amount of time together, it just doesn't work, which is why it's an obsessive working relationship.' To a certain extent, this obsessive connection continues to operate even when they are *not* working together. For instance, when Daldry came into a *Rat in the Skull* rehearsal and announced that he wanted Nelson left alone onstage at the end 'because it's

a – what do you call it? *Tristan und Isolde* – a transfiguration,'
this was not because Stephen Daldry is in the habit of citing, or
imitating, Wagnerian opera; it's just that Ian MacNeil was at that
point engaged in working on the design of *Tristan und Isolde*.

As a pair, Daldry and MacNeil form a classically divided personality, with Daldry taking on all the extrovert qualities and
MacNeil playing the introvert. In part this is due to their professional roles: a director's job involves speaking with everyone and
mediating between various departments, whereas a designer is
likely to spend a lot of time alone in his studio. MacNeil made a
version of this point when he participated in a panel discussion
about stage design in June 1995; he had just been asked by a
rather belligerent member of the audience to explain the
designer's relationship to the public. 'Does a painter talk about
his public?' MacNeil retorted. 'People respond to a piece of
work because the person who created it said what they wanted
to say. It's the conundrum of theatre: I do the work at home as if
I am a painter, and yet it has to come across to the public.' But
this attitude is itself indicative of the kind of set designer Ian
MacNeil is. It reflects temperament as well as ideology, character
as well as profession. Rick Fisher pointed out that 'Ian is more of
a fine-artist designer,' whereas Bill Dudley, whose work he also
respects, is 'more of a craftsman-designer who knows how
things work'. Along with MacNeil's fine-artist quality goes an
element of reticence, a hesitation to engage in the argumentative
give and take of the normal rehearsal process. Johanna Town,
who had worked separately with both MacNeil and Daldry
before she worked with them together on *The Editing Process*,
made a specific observation about the relationship between the
shy man and the outgoing one. 'What Ian achieves in the end
with his look is always very good,' she said, 'but he can be bul-
lied when Stephen's not there to protect his ideas.'

Designer/director pairs who live and work together are
nothing new or unusual in the English theatre world. Among
Daldry's and MacNeil's predecessors in this mode are George
Devine and Jocelyn Herbert, the parent figures of the Royal

Court; and among their contemporaries are Declan Donnellan and Nicholas Ormerod, whose seamless collaborations (on works as diverse as Tony Kushner's *Angels in America*, Brecht's and Weill's *Mahagonny*, and the Cameron Mackintosh extravaganza *Martin Guerre*) show the benefit of their long and fruitful association in the Cheek by Jowl theatre company. What makes Daldry's partnership with MacNeil unusual is that it is not an exclusive one. Since they began living together in 1989, MacNeil has worked on a number of projects without Daldry, designing for many different directors and in various art forms, including dance and opera as well as theatre. And Daldry, during the same period, has done major shows designed by Tim Hatley, Mark Thompson, and Bill Dudley. Sometimes the choice of another designer has to do with MacNeil's unavailability; sometimes it has to do with Daldry's desire not to rock the domestic boat. 'When we work together on a show,' he told Nicola Bacon, the *Independent*'s interviewer, 'it's not just "Let's do a show," it's "Let's tear the relationship apart and rebuild it while we do a show." If it works, it's fantastic. If it goes wrong, it's awful.'

When I asked him why he wasn't working with Ian MacNeil on *Rat in the Skull*, Daldry's answer was simply 'I can't' – meaning, I assumed, that he couldn't bear to go through that mutually destructive procedure again so soon after *The Editing Process*. But he may have had other motives as well. When Stephen Daldry selected Bill Dudley to design the first show in the new Royal Court Classics series at the Duke of York's, he knew that the old Victorian theatre space would have to be dramatically redefined to contain Hutchinson's 1984 play. Daldry had met Dudley through their work together on the Royal Court remodel, and he also knew that the designer was involved as a consultant in the ongoing reconstruction of Shakespeare's Globe. Bill Dudley was, in fact, the stage designer most likely to be associated with overall theatre design. As Iain Mackintosh noted in his book *Architecture, Actor and Audience*, 'One designer, William Dudley . . . successfully and accidentally turned theatre designer with his realisation in 1990 . . . of director Bill Bryden's dream: "We build a ship – a liner – in fact and at the end of the evening it is launched."' Praising Dudley's achievement in *The Ship*, Mackintosh went on to point out that the 'towering four-floor steel structure' launched at the end of each night's performance 'was not so much a liner as a courtyard theatre' – in other words, a direct descendant of the kind of traditional British theatre space designed to bring audiences in close contact with the players. This ancestry was certainly intentional on Dudley's part, for he cited Elizabethan courtyard theatres and Victorian music halls in his programme notes for *The Ship*. When Stephen Daldry was choosing a designer for *Rat in the Skull*, he no doubt took account of Bill Dudley's reputation as a full-scale theatre designer along with his other useful qualities (including an extremely high level of craftsmanship and a good-tempered openness to collaboration). In the event, Daldry's faith in Dudley was both earned and returned. Speaking to me about skilful directors in general and Daldry in particular, Bill Dudley characterized the director/designer relationship by saying, 'They feed you.'

Feeding the designer, either with concrete ideas or an overall sense of the play, is precisely what many directors apparently fail to do. 'It's amazing, the number of directors who sit down with you at a design meeting and you get the feeling they don't really know why they wanted to do the play,' Ian MacNeil commented. In any production, the extent of the designer's involvement is essentially up to the director. 'Designers are invited to the talk table,' said MacNeil, referring to the initial planning stages of a production, 'but maybe not. It's up to the whim of the director how much they're included. The better ones welcome it.' But even when a director doesn't actively welcome a designer's contribution, the set designer can still have an enormous effect on the play. 'It's a terrifying thing,' remarked MacNeil, 'that you're asked to turn in a model box before rehearsals' – before, that is, you even know how the actors will be moving around the stage. But this terrifying responsibility has its positive side as well: 'You influence the director.'

The set designer's work is intimately bound up with that of

the lighting designer, so that even though the director selects each designer separately, he needs to ensure that they can work well together. Though they may do an entire play without once exchanging explicit instructions, the two designers must understand and respect each other's intentions for the set to succeed. Like Ian MacNeil, Rick Fisher has been involved with many but not all of Stephen Daldry's productions; he has worked with MacNeil on *Manon*, *Inspector*, and *Machinal*, and without him on *Rat in the Skull*. Fisher is also a longtime friend – he and his partner, a doctor named Cornelius Kelly, even considered buying a house with Daldry and MacNeil at one point – so when the three of them work together on a project, it's a much more intimate process than the usual one. 'Usually when Stephen and Ian are doing something, I'll see some ideas,' Fisher told me. 'That's unfortunately uncommon with director/designer pairs. And it's true that most of the time I don't want to be shown things at that stage; I'm just too busy.' Though he works closely with the director and the designer, Fisher's job is not simply a matter of translating their preconceptions into lighting terms. 'Stephen and Ian don't actually give me a huge amount of this-is-what-it's-going-to-look-like-at-this-moment,' Fisher commented. 'I feel like I have a pretty free hand. But then, that may be the genius of a great director, that he makes people feel like they're doing exactly what they want to.'

Johanna Town, who did the lighting for *Search and Destroy*, *The Kitchen*, and *The Editing Process*, seconded the *laissez-faire* characterization of Daldry's approach. 'He doesn't give you any ideas at all, and expects you to put your mark on it,' she told me. 'He doesn't necessarily put *his* mark on it. He gives you a clue and then lets you do it.' But this didn't mean the lighting designer could produce a self-contained work of art. She had to be constantly alert to the director's needs and intentions in the production, constantly willing to change things. 'The thing about Stephen is, he'll change things up until press night,' Town observed. 'So you have to be flexible. What you see in rehearsals isn't necessarily the final thing.' In fact, the real collaboration between Daldry and Town has taken place mainly after they've moved into the theatre itself. 'He doesn't give you any guidance at all until you get to the space. And then, if you come up with something, he'll reblock it to take advantage of the lighting. Most of the things, we've always just tidied them up.' But occasionally, she recalled, Daldry's last-minute changes led to a major re-design. 'In *Search and Destroy*, he said, "Right. Costumes are coloured in Act One, lights black and white. Coloured lights are right in Act Two, because the costumes are black and white." So then we went back over it all to make it fit that pattern.'

For Rick Fisher, this freedom to alter things at a late stage is one of the particular advantages of working with Stephen Daldry. 'What's great about the productions is we start out with strong ideas of what the show is going to be, and then you end up responding and making it up in the theatre. A lot of the best bits of *Inspector Calls* came to us in the theatre. There's a high level of trust,' Fisher noted, 'and we feel we can be spontaneous.' But if they all contribute so much to the production, what justifies the director's role as the lead figure? Rick Fisher thought about this question before answering. 'Certainly the style of the production comes out of his head,' he concluded. 'In a void, I don't think I've got particularly brilliant ideas. I'm better at reacting. He puts things together in a way I couldn't.'

'The thing about directing is, it's like sex,' said Julian Webber. 'You know other people do it, but you don't know *how* they do it.' Richard Eyre, in his introduction to the Royal National Theatre's Platform Paper on Directors, picked up on the same analogy. 'Most of us have an indecent curiosity about what other people do in private,' he began. 'My own particular corner of prurience concerns the work habits of directors.' That directors do not, on the whole, ever see each other direct was confirmed by the habits of Stephen Daldry and his two associate directors at the Royal Court, James Macdonald and Ian Rickson. Though the three of them shared an office so tiny they were practically sitting on each other's laps, and though they selected scripts and allocated directing assignments with what they described as 'organic' ease, not one of the three had ever watched the other two direct.

The exception to this pattern is the role of the assistant director. Assistant directors can be anything from student-level gophers to highly competent professionals. On smaller productions, they may not even be necessary; on larger ones, their primary job (aside from watching the director) may be to work with the understudies, the extras, or the children. What is unusual about Daldry's assistant directors is that they tend to be people who are already fully fledged directors in their own right. From twenty-three-year-old Raeda Ghazaleh to thirty-six-year-old Chris Barton, Daldry's assistant directors have been too good to keep: it is rare for him to work with the same AD for more than one or two productions, because the people he chooses for the job are too talented to remain satisfied with such a subordinate position. Drawn to Stephen Daldry by their admiration for his work, these younger (and sometimes not-younger) directors learn what they can from him and then move on.

One such person is Julie-Anne Robinson, who worked as Daldry's assistant director on *The Editing Process*. 'He's a great director,' she told me, 'because his mind is so unusual. He doesn't think in a straight line: he thinks that way or that way or that way.' Her arms moved to match her words, spreading wide on one phrase, pointing up and down on the next. 'And he never takes the easy option. Instead, he finds the best way, whatever that is. And he inspires great loyalty. He allows actors to do things in rehearsal that they've never done before, by making them think in new ways. He goes further and further and further, and then he uses the most bizarre things. That's why he's the most exciting director I've ever worked with.'

If Daldry has taught other directors, he has also learned from them – and not just those with whom he has worked as assistant director. Several people pointed out to me that Kate Rowland had done a production of *Machinal* years before Stephen Daldry staged the play at the National, and that Daldry must certainly have been aware of hers. 'Oh, yes, he'd seen my video, he'd got all my notes, all my research,' Rowland told me. Yet she had received no mention in the programme, no credit of any kind. 'Ian was very upset with him about that,' Rowland observed, but she herself seemed more resigned. 'I really do believe it's about taking ownership of the idea. They really think they've had the idea. Stephen's incredibly strong, and he will trample. He will just go from A to B. But people want to be got from A to B; the Gate was a powerhouse when he was there . . . He's an incredible combination of innocence, childlike relish, and arrogance. The arrogance is confidence, but it's also this insecurity – we all have it – that you're going to fail this time.' The problem for Daldry, Rowland pointed out, is that 'he believes in his own myth', a myth that derives, in part, from his notoriously seductive charm. 'He makes people love him,' she added, 'or think they love him.'

In part because of Daldry's tremendous charisma, it's not always easy to track which way the influence is flowing. Daldry's method can be so attractive, his enthusiasm so infectious, that some of his fellow directors see him as a mirror of their own theatrical ideas. 'When I saw Stephen directing the recast of *Inspector Calls* in London,' said Julian Webber, who was about to take on the job of associate-directing the touring production, 'it was like watching myself direct.' But this identification can be an illusion, a corollary of Daldry's empty-vessel persona. ('Everyone reads his own politics into Stephen,' as Rick Fisher noted in another context.) According to the actor Nicholas Woodeson, who worked with both Julian Webber and Stephen Daldry on *An Inspector Calls*, the two men are actually very different as directors, and the only reason their work matched up so well on this production was that Webber was doing his best to carry out Daldry's intentions. 'They know each other well, and Julian has a strong sense of what Stephen wants,' Woodeson told me after one *Inspector* rehearsal, during which Webber had handled the morning session and Daldry the afternoon. 'Their directing styles are different, because Julian isn't directing so much as interpreting. Julian concentrates on the guts of a scene, the way the characters clash against each other. Stephen's direction is of a piece. He doesn't make a distinction between the way it looks, how the characters sound, what the line means. When he gives a specific direction, he has in his mind already the whole world of the play. The what and the how are the same thing with Stephen: what's going on and how it is being done . . . I think it's true of him in general. The worlds in his productions always seem to me to be imaginative responses to the texts.'

Those texts are, in most cases, the creations of individual playwrights; and the relation between the director and the playwright, whether living or dead, is one of the most complex aspects of theatrical collaboration. A few directors feel free to ignore anything the writer may have intended. A few others believe that their only obligation is to transmit the writer's exact words, whole and unmediated, to the audience. But the vast majority of directors find themselves somewhere on the spectrum in between. 'So much of directing is responding to the imagination of the writer and translating it for the actors,' wrote William Gaskill, who ran the Royal Court Theatre in the period between George Devine and Max Stafford-Clark. 'Jonathan Miller thinks it is impossible to know a writer's intentions and that it is not the director's business to try. I think this is plainly untrue . . . I do know that the director is on a quest of creating something that has already existed in the writer's mind.'

Elsewhere in *A Sense of Direction*, Gaskill formulated the problem slightly differently. 'The attempt to create images and concepts separately from the play makes for cumbersome and inelegant work,' he argued. 'I believe that every play has an identity that it is the director's job to reveal.' I believe this too; but when one separates 'the play' from 'the writer', as Gaskill's syntax has done here, one begins to perceive the true dimensions of the problem. The 'identity' Gaskill refers to may be something that the writer herself can't or won't identify – or can't, for a variety of reasons, translate into stage terms. Even William Gaskill, who sees the director as essentially the writer's stand-in, admits that most playwrights 'lack the craftsmanship, the overall sense of theatre, the ability to combine the different strands which make up a performance'. So some kind of collaboration, some shifting of the responsibility from playwright to director, becomes necessary, especially when the playwright is no longer around to specify his intentions.

And even living playwrights acknowledge that they can't retain control over their writing once it leaves the page. Speaking at a public lecture in San Francisco during April 1995, the playwright Tony Kushner commented on the essentially collaborative nature of his work. 'Playwriting is a good form for someone who is lazy and scatterbrained,' said Kushner, with typical self-deprecation, 'because you can just put together this mess of words and ideas and hand it over to this whole other group of people, who then get all sorts of things out of it that you didn't necessarily put into it.' But later, with equally typical sharpness, he added a caveat: 'After you see what some people have done with your work, you want to put stage directions after every *word*.'

Some directors violate authorial integrity by accident; others set out to do so. 'There are directors who are making their own devised pieces, as if with found text, like Robert LePage,' Meredith Oakes told me in 1994. 'I wouldn't much fancy providing text for that purpose. I'm too pigheaded.' Yet her 'pigheadedness', as she called it, did not prevent her from accepting many of Stephen Daldry's suggestions when they worked together on *The Editing Process*.

'There were all sorts of changes he suggested,' Oakes said about the director, 'and others that I introduced as a result of the atmosphere he created.' Among the changes she cited were the alteration in the handyman's role and the condensation of all the second act's action into a single day. 'He's extremely practical – a good dramaturge, though I never really thought of him in that light. He sees writing always in terms of the energy he can find from it. He's always looking for that one thing.' As a novice playwright, Oakes was particularly grateful for Daldry's visual skills. 'I don't visualize much,' she pointed out. 'I stay inside the text. That's what I can do. I've got a lot of feelings, but terrible eyes, so I need someone to show me what the feelings look like.' She was also emphatic about the ways in which her own conscious intentions didn't necessarily define or limit the play's meanings. 'A lot of the correspondences are involuntary,' she commented about the script's echoes and resonances. 'You make the connections unconsciously . . . I was very keen to write a play that gave opportunities to a director, that has metaphorical possibilities, that isn't just rooted in the here and now.'

None the less, some observers felt that Daldry was hampered by his respect for Oakes's text – that, in his accommodation to the playwright's wishes and intentions, he failed to make the play his own. But this problem stemmed as much from the nature of the script itself as from the presence of a living playwright. With *Rat in the Skull*, he clearly felt free to push and nag and cajole the playwright, and even to tinker with the play's structure and language during the writer's three-week absence from the set. His attitude towards this text was no less respectful than it had been with *The Editing Process.* It was just that with Hutchinson's script, Daldry had a much stronger perception of the 'identity' of the play (to borrow Gaskill's term) and hence a much firmer sense of how to reveal that identity to the audience.

To a certain extent, such identifications and perceptions are based on shared beliefs; they depend on there being common ground between the director and the playwright. But the overlap needn't be total. While directing *An Inspector Calls*, for instance, Daldry found himself in explicit agreement with Priestley's socialist message, but somewhat less enamoured of other aspects of Priestley's thought. When one of the actresses auditioning for the role of Sheila Birling asked him, 'Why does he make Sheila, do you think, the one who's able to learn?' Daldry's answer was both revealing and self-revealing. 'He's a romantic,' he said of Priestley. 'He always saw women as seers. Of course it's bosh, but there we are.' Daldry went on to explain the connection between Sheila's visionary characteristics and Priestley's other ideas. 'It's about these spurious time theories that Priestley believed in – Dunne's theory of parallel time, and Ouspensky's

Buddhism. So that you could see the future. In real terms, a policeman is ringing up at the end, and they've seen that in advance. And if you can see it, you have the possibility of breaking out of the cycle and going up the spiral to Nirvana. But the tragedy of the play is that only one person sees, and takes that on board. It's all pooh, really.'

As usual with Daldry's statements, only part of what he was saying to the actress represented his true opinions. Or perhaps the problem was that his own opinions varied so widely that, from moment to moment, he could never adequately represent them all. At least for the duration of his work on the play, Daldry seemed to have taken on board many of Priestley's ideas. And not just for the duration. One of the things he failed to mention to the actress was that he himself had been a practising Buddhist for several years in his early twenties, and still felt some allegiance to Buddhist ideas. Nor was the romanticism about the young female character solely Priestley's. Or rather, in Priestley's case as in Daldry's, it was a romanticism mixed with much more complex ideas about women. Daldry's triumph with *Inspector* stemmed in part from the way he had unearthed this complexity – had turned flat, allegorical characters into individual people with psychological histories. And nowhere had he done this more clearly than with the female characters.

As he explained to each of the auditioning actresses, Sheila's role divided into 'three different units in the play. The first unit is about making her as horrible as possible, delaying the realization. Then she drives the play for a long time, an impotent driver. And then in the last unit she changes.' For their audition, he asked each of the actresses to read a speech from the first unit – Sheila's story about getting the shopgirl sacked from Millward's, which is also her confession about her own part in Eva Smith's decline. 'The basic premise,' Daldry told one of the actresses, 'is that she thinks she's right. I want you to do two things. I want you to make me collude with you: *this fucking girl*. And I also want you to get angry. She's an hysteric, so the anger itself reminds her of what she felt, and alters her. She actually becomes ugly.' And when he saw Helen Schlesinger – the actress who eventually got the role – read this speech, Daldry had a further realization. 'I've just discovered something I never realized before,' he told her. 'I think Daddy rather likes it when she loses her temper. Mother might not like it, but Daddy likes the tantrums.'

If Sheila Birling was one pivot for Stephen Daldry's interpretation of the play, Mrs Birling was the other. Daldry's production of *An Inspector Calls* depended on having a physically effective, psychologically terrifying actress in the role of Mrs Birling: 'a fully rigged vessel sweeping around the harbour', as he put it in one metaphor. Later, he was to rely on a much more loaded comparison when explaining the relationship between Eric Birling and his mother. 'It's as if your mother was feeding the ovens at Auschwitz but you only discovered that piece by piece,' Daldry said to one auditioning Eric. '"You mean you were in Germany? You were there at the camp? You did *what*?" And then you realize your mother is a monster.'

Along with sailing ships and Nazi camp guards, Stephen Daldry drew on analogies much closer to home. 'It's literally my mum,' he told Susan Engel, the actress playing Mrs Birling, when he was trying to get her to deal forcefully with the Inspector. 'It's my mum storming down to the leafy suburbs and saying, "If you fucking come near my son again . . .". She is defending her family, which is why she gets so angry. In my experience, with my mother, the worst thing was always when she was protecting the nest. And she protected it brilliantly.'

Daldry went on to show the actress how she should physically embody this aggressiveness by 'breaking the Philip Prowse rule'. He explained the famous stage designer's dictum, which was 'never to hitch up the dress, but to let it trail, because otherwise it ruins the line of the dress. But I want you to break that rule. It's kind of like you're hitching up your dress all the way.' Daldry then got out of his seat and demonstrated, walking in a swaggering, Annie Oakley manner as he held imaginary bunches of skirt out to his sides with his hands. 'You've ditched Philip Prowse,' he said as he walked, 'and become Steven Berkoff.'

He also showed Susan Engel how to fold the Inspector's coat with the proper degree of distaste when she was getting ready to dismiss him. Engel, watching the director's lengthy, detailed rendering of the gesture, commented, 'He *loves* this. You love this, don't you?'

'I do,' Stephen Daldry laughed. 'It's all those years of watching the way bourgeois ladies behave at jumble sales. It's fear of your own poverty, and the more middle class you are, the more fear there is.' Then, in a rapidly improvised demonstration, he showed how a middle-class lady at a jumble sale would take an item of clothing offered by a poorer woman, turn to her tablemate, and disdainfully set its value at a mere twenty pence. 'Twenty p,' mimicked Daldry in appropriately haughty tones. 'And then Mrs Jones from the leafy suburbs comes in, and it's two pounds.'

'I always felt when he did his little bits of Eleanor, he looked so attractive,' said Caroline Harker, the actress who played Eleanor in *The Editing Process*. 'He got his ideas across through demonstrations, not through line readings.'

One could see this instantaneous transformation take place again and again as Daldry worked with his actors in various plays. Never having been an actor himself, he would have readily acknowledged that he had no capacity to sustain a role over the course of a whole performance. But he loved to immerse himself briefly in each character. This came through especially clearly during one of the rehearsals for *An Inspector Calls*. The scene was the one in which Sheila Birling delivered her long speech about getting Eva Smith sacked from Millward's – the same speech Daldry used for the Sheila auditions. Now, to show the actress what he wanted, he was imitating Sheila himself, using a mixture of her exact lines and the ideas behind those lines to convey the character's attitude towards the uppity shopgirl. 'No, actually,' he interjected in a soft, high voice, 'you wouldn't *believe* what this fucking bitch did. Anyway –' He tossed his head coquettishly. As he assumed Sheila's mannerisms and thoughts, he took on an exaggeratedly female posture that was markedly different from his own usual manner. The hand gestures, the way his head rested on his neck, the movement of his chin were all those of a silly girl rather than an athletic, graceful man.

Next, seating the actress in one chair and himself in another chair opposite her, about two feet away, Daldry asked her to deliver the whole speech directly to him. As she talked, he leaned forward and gave her what would have been, under other circumstances, a hilariously intense response. His play of facial expression was so exaggerated as to seem demonic; smiling, nodding, eyebrows raised, eyes crinkling, he constantly interjected remarks like 'That bitch!' or 'What did you do?' The actress kept her eyes glued to his face throughout, like a mouse hypnotized by a snake.

Then he had her do the speech again, but now his face remained completely expressionless. 'This time I'm not responding,' he explained. 'It causes anxiety. You're not getting a friend here' – he pointed first to the Inspector, then to himself – 'and you're not getting a friend here. You're friendless.'

Suddenly the actress understood. 'So the shame is partly the shame of it *now, here*.'

'In front of a thousand people,' Daldry assented. 'And it's horrific.'

'My impression, from seeing *Inspector Calls*, is that it's terribly important for the actors to hang on to the reality and truth of their parts and, if anything, try to achieve a documentary style of acting, which is very difficult in terms of what Stephen demands,' Prunella Scales told me between rehearsals of *The Editing Process*. 'I think the juxtaposition of documentary-style acting and the bizarre, surreal qualities in his direction is what makes the play work.'

But did he, in *The Editing Process*, push her to be more bizarre and surreal?

'Yes, yes,' she confessed. 'I've resisted, and I hope his fears have been allayed.'

Such resistance was typical of Daldry's more naturalistically inclined actors: he would work to push them over the top, and they would work equally hard to keep the melodrama level down. When he was rehearsing the touring production of *An Inspector Calls*, for instance, he pushed especially hard on the actress playing Mrs Birling. Particularly in her major scene with the Inspector, where the two characters were arguing over Mrs Birling's behaviour towards and responsibility for the pregnant, impoverished Eva Smith, he repeatedly urged the actress to display more anger, more unremitting opposition.

'I didn't like her manner,' said the actress, delivering her line about the charity-seeking girl.

Daldry corrected the emphasis. '"I didn't like *her* manner." And I don't like yours either,' he added by way of explanation, showing how the line was really meant to be a rebuke to the Inspector.

Mrs Birling tried it again, but again Daldry interrupted her. 'No, stronger. This exchange has nothing to do with the girl. It's all to do with you and him.' He asked her to deliver the lines at top intensity, but without shouting; throughout, he insisted, she should remain stonily resistant to the Inspector's argument. 'Granite,' he told her.

'I don't know,' said the actress. 'I've got to shape it.'

'Don't worry about shaping it,' Daldry urged. '*We'll* shape it. Just worry about control.'

Julian Webber interjected a suggestion. 'It's like throwing furniture, but in a controlled way.'

'But that's, then, blitzkrieg, blitzkrieg, blitzkrieg,' objected the actress. 'And that's not what it is.'

'But it *is* that, more than you think,' explained Daldry. 'Much more than you can feel comfortable with. I can't modulate you till you get there. Then I can take you down.'

'People forget that drama works according to rules, and the rules of theatre are not the rules of television,' commented Nicholas Woodeson, who played the ruthless executive in *The Editing Process* and the sternly humanitarian Inspector in *An Inspector*

Calls. 'There must always be a sort of pulse that's specific to theatre. If you look at *Oedipus* literally, it doesn't make sense; if you look at it logically, in terms of its theatrical progression, it makes sense perfectly.

'I like working with directors who really know their own minds, who have a strong visual and dramatic sense, and who are in charge, but who also ask me to respond imaginatively and with freedom, so I'm not either taking orders or just doing what they want. I think it's my job to bring in possibilities and choices, and his to say, "I like that, and I think that's better than that one."

'There are two or three people I've felt imaginatively free with, I've enjoyed working with, and he's one of them. It's often easy to miss that Stephen's theatrical taste is very mature. People get the idea that it is very visual, primitive and naïve, but it's not. The worlds of his plays may not be naturalistic worlds, but they're very human. They cut to the heart of a particular human preoccupation.'

In *An Inspector Calls*, such individual preoccupations were perhaps most evident in a scene from which Woodeson himself was absent – the scene in which Inspector Goole has just left the stage, the house has exploded, and a light rain has begun to fall on the four members of the Birling family. In Stephen Daldry's staging, Mr and Mrs Birling are huddled together on one side of the stage, while their two children, Sheila and Eric, are grouped together on the other side. Rehearsing the four actors in this scene, Daldry stressed the psychological dimension of their performances.

'When in doubt, stay in your own world,' he advised. 'When you read it, it sounds like they're having a conversation together, but they're not. They vaguely hear echoes of each other, but it's two separate conversations.'

Turning first to Mr Birling, the director proceeded to give this apparently flat character an unexpected degree of interiority. He pictured how Birling might have felt when he first learned of his possible knighthood. 'You see the whole thing clearly,' he told the actor, 'the public announcements, the newspaper articles, the family celebration, telling it to your son, so that for the first time your son appreciates just how outstanding his father really is. You can see it all, you've had it all planned out for years. And now this is all that's left of it, and when you tell your son, he just laughs. So then your subsequent line – "Nothing matters to you" – is really about the relationship between you and him, about your sense of hurt. All that's got to be in it.'

Then he turned to Sheila, giving her a series of tender gestures to accompany her conversation with Eric. 'Take the blanket and put it over him,' Daldry instructed the actress. 'Now take the hankie out of his pocket. Now clear his face. This can actually be quite beautiful. It's like the scene in *The Borrowers*, where the kids get together and work it out.'

He widened his remarks, now, to include the other three actors as well. 'It's really tricky, this scene, because there's no direct narrative drive. Because when the Inspector goes, chances are the audience thinks it's the end of the play.' In one of those instantaneous demonstrations, he mimed an audience member standing up, looking for his coat, checking his watch. 'And then there's this delicate scene, for six or eight minutes. It needs to be so perfect, to exist without narrative, before Gerald comes.'

The audience is Daldry's final collaborator. This is true to a certain extent of all theatre directors, but it is emphatically and explicitly true of Stephen Daldry. Whether we are playing the ghosts of the future in *An Inspector Calls*, or the witnesses to an execution in *Machinal*, or restaurant patrons in *The Kitchen*, or a combination of mirrors and voyeurs in *Body Talk*, we are essential to the performance. As Steve Tompkins noted about *Rat in the Skull*, Daldry's production of the play was different from the original Royal Court performance precisely because of the way it 'involved the audience in the action'.

It's common to hear people speak of Daldry as an extremely visual director, and at times I've adopted that language myself. But his productions are really more experiential than visual, or rather, their strong visual quality is simply one of the elements that goes into making the Daldry experience. That sense of immersion and involvement – of having been present at an event, and crucial to the completeness of that event – is only possible in the live theatre. If Daldry translates his enormous visual talent to film-making (as he evidently plans to do), he will find himself unable to create quite the same effects. The power of his work depends on our being right there.

The down side of this is that, as one-time performance attenders, we may not be the ideal artistic collaborators. How is the director to distinguish between an intelligently bored audience and a lazy, inattentive one? Does he play to the lowest common denominator, cater to the select few, or try for the middle ground? As the secular inheritor of religious ritual, the theatre still has some allegiance to the notion of a communal response, and if the director were a priest or a minister he would certainly be trying to save *all* our souls. But what kind of 'community' does the modern-day theatre audience represent, composed as it is of largely unconnected individuals? How can the director decide whether our failure to respond to a line (or a scene, or a play) is his fault rather than ours – and what difference, in any case, should that attribution of blame make to his actions? Should he change delicate or complicated moments just because we don't, on first glimpse, understand them, or should he hope that we'll gradually be educated by the play itself? Finally, what kind of self-respecting art form can be dependent on such unreliable collaborators?

It is an old question, whether a theatre that relies on the theatrical audience can in fact be considered an art. Henry James went into it thoroughly in his novel *The Tragic Muse* (a novel written in 1890, well before his own drastic theatrical failures, when he still harboured personal hopes for the medium). Through the character Gabriel Nash, who attends yet despises theatre, James voiced his own worst fears. 'The dramatist shows us so little, is so hampered by his audience,' Nash complains, going on to attack

the essentially brute nature of the modern audience . . . the *omnium gatherum* of the population of a big commercial city, at the hour of the day when their taste is at its lowest, flocking out of hideous hotels and restaurants, gorged with food, stultified with buying and selling and with all the other sordid speculations of the day, squeezed together in a sweltering mass, disappointed in their seats, timing the author, timing the actor, wishing to get their money back on the spot, before eleven o'clock . . .

'It's a commercial and social convenience which may be infinitely worked,' Gabriel Nash says of the theatre. 'But important artistically, intellectually? How can it be – so poor, so limited a form?'

To which Henry James offers, in his characteristic fashion, two answers:

'Dear me, it strikes me as so rich, so various! Do you think it's poor and limited, Nick?' Sherringham added, appealing to his kinsman.

'I think whatever Nash thinks. I have no opinion today but his.'

Even this last ironic remark is, in its way, as true an analysis of the theatre as everything else James says. For the live drama, as an art form, is very much dependent on temporary contagious moods: on the audience's after-dinner mood, on the culture's after-television mood, on the mood created by a particular auditorium arranged in a particular style during a particular moment in history – even (as James suggests in that reference to the 'sweltering' crowd) on the notoriously moody weather. If I myself appear at this juncture to think whatever Daldry thinks, having 'no opinion today but his', that too may be seen as a version of mood. In the theatre, who knows what will happen tomorrow?

The final verdict about Stephen Daldry's art is still to come. It rests on what Daldry will do with his own career, both within and beyond the Royal Court. He is scheduled to step down as artistic director shortly after the theatre moves back into its Sloane Square building, at which point he will begin making independent films under the Working Title branch of Polygon films. In addition, he plans to maintain strong ties with at least two theatrical institutions, the Royal Court and the Royal National Theatre. As a freelance director, Daldry will have many choices open to him – between theatre and film, between old plays and new scripts, between English drama and more international work. Much will depend on the plays he chooses to interpret, and on the fact that they really *are* plays (as was pointedly illustrated by the superiority of *An Inspector Calls* over *Body Talk*), for Daldry's is a responsive, collaborative intelligence – it needs something to build on. And much else will depend on Daldry's usual collaborators, including not only the designers, musicians, actors, and technicians he works with, not only the buildings he works in and the producers he works under, not only the audiences he lures in and conjures for, but also the more abstract collaborators every director contends with: chance, history, the undiscovered parts of himself. A great deal depends on these other factors. But ultimately it will have to be Stephen Daldry himself who takes responsibility for making his work into – not lasting art, since nothing lasts in the theatre, but valuable art that endures as long as the memories of people who once saw it.

Bibliography

Artaud, Antonin, *The Theater and Its Double*, trans. Mary Caroline Richards, New York: Grove Press, 1958.

Austin, J. L., *Philosophical Papers*, Oxford: Oxford University Press, 1961.

– *Sense and Sensibilia*, Oxford: Oxford University Press, 1962.

Banks, Iain, *The Wasp Factory*, London: Abacus, 1990.

Beckett, Samuel, *The Lost Ones*, New York: Grove Press, 1972.

Billington, Michael, *One Night Stands*, London: Nick Hern Books, 1993.

Brecht, Bertolt, *Brecht on Theatre*, ed. and trans. John Willett, New York: Farrar, Straus & Giroux, 1964.

– *The Messingkauf Dialogues*, trans. John Willett, London: Eyre Methuen, 1965.

Brook, Peter, *The Empty Stage*, New York: Atheneum, 1968.

– *The Open Door*, New York: Pantheon Books, 1993.

Bulman, James C. (ed.), *Shakespeare, Theory and Performance*, New York: Routledge, 1996.

Butterworth, Jez, *Mojo*, London: Nick Hern Books, 1995.

Cavell, Stanley, *A Pitch of Philosophy*, Cambridge, Massachusetts: Harvard University Press, 1994.

– *Must We Mean What We Say?*, Cambridge: Cambridge University Press, 1976.

Clurman, Harold, *The Divine Pastime*, New York: Macmillan, 1974.

– *The Fervent Years: The Group Theatre and the Thirties*, New York: Da Capo, 1983.

Cole, Susan Letzler, *Directors in Rehearsal*, New York: Routledge, 1992.

Designers: Bob Crowley, Jocelyn Herbert, John Napier, London: Royal National Theatre Platform Papers, 1993.

Dickens, Charles, *Bleak House*, Boston: Houghton Mifflin, 1956.

Directors: Stephen Daldry, Nicholas Hytner, Robert LePage, London: Royal National Theatre Platform Papers, 1993.

Findlater, Richard (ed.), *At the Royal Court: 25 Years of the English Stage Company*, Derbyshire: Amber Lane Press, 1981.

Fleisser, Marieluise, *Purgatory in Ingolstadt* and *Pioneers in Ingolstadt*, trans. Elisabeth Bond-Pablé and Tinch Minter, in *Plays by Women: Nine*, selected and introduced by Annie Castledine, London: Methuen, 1991.

Fo, Dario, *The Tricks of the Trade*, trans. Joe Farrell, New York: Routledge, 1991.

Fried, Michael, *Absorption and Theatricality*, Chicago: University of Chicago Press, 1988.

Gaskill, William, *A Sense of Direction,* New York: Limelight Editions, 1990.

Gielgud, John, *An Actor and His Time*, Harmondsworth: Penguin Books, 1981.

– *Stage Directions,* New York: Capricorn Books, 1966.

Greenblatt, Stephen, *Shakespearean Negotiations*, Berkeley: University of California Press, 1988.

Guthrie, Tyrone, Robertson Davies and Grant Macdonald, *Twice Have the Trumpets Sounded: A Record of the Stratford Shakespeare Festival in Canada, 1954,* Toronto: Clarke, Irwin & Company Limited, 1954.

Hapgood, David, *Year of the Pearl*, New York: Alfred A. Knopf, 1993.

Hart, Moss, *Act One*, New York: Random House, 1959.

Hutchinson, Ron, *Rat in the Skull*, London: Methuen, 1995.

James, Henry, *The Tragic Muse*, Harmondsworth: Penguin Books, 1978.

Jones, David Richards, *Great Directors at Work*, Berkeley: University of California Press, 1986.

Korder, Howard, *Search and Destroy*, New York: Dramatists' Play Service, 1992.

Kott, Jan, *Shakespeare Our Contemporary*, London: Methuen, 1967.

– *The Theater of Essence*, Evanston: Northwestern University Press, 1984.

Lumet, Sidney, *Making Movies*, New York: Alfred A. Knopf, 1995.

Mackintosh, Iain, *Architecture, Actor and Audience*, London: Routledge, 1993.

Miles-Brown, John, *Directing Drama*, London: Peter Owen, 1994.

Miller, Jonathan, *Subsequent Performances*, London: Faber & Faber, 1986.

Molina, Tirso de, *El condenado por desconfiado (Damned for Despair)*, bilingual edition with trans. by Nicholas G. Round, Warminster: Aris & Phillips (no date given).

Oakes, Meredith, *The Editing Process*, London: Oberon Books, 1994.

Payne, Darwin Reid, *The Scenographic Imagination*, Carbondale: Southern Illinois University Press, 1981.

Peter Brook, London: Royal National Theatre Platform Papers, 1994.

Phillips, Adam, *Terrors and Experts*, Cambridge, Massachusetts: Harvard University Press, 1996.

Plato, *The Republic*, trans. Allan Bloom, New York: Basic Books, 1968.

Priestley, J. B., *An Inspector Calls*, in *Time and the Conways & Other Plays*, London: Penguin Books, 1969.

– *Theatre Outlook*, London: Nicholson & Watson, 1947.

Saltz, David Z.,*The Reality of the Theater Event: Logical Foundations of Dramatic Performance*, a doctoral dissertation submitted to the Stanford University Department of Drama, Palo Alto: 1992.

Stanislavski, Constantin, *An Actor Prepares*, trans. Elizabeth Reynolds Hapgood, New York: Theatre Arts Books, 1948.

Treadwell, Sophie, *Machinal*, in *Plays by American Women: 1900–1930*, ed. Judith E. Barlow, New York: Applause Theatre Book Publishers, 1981.

Tushingham, David, 'Interview with Stephen Daldry: There is a new audience out there', in *Live: Food for the Soul*, London: Methuen, 1994.

von Horváth, Ödön, *Figaro Gets Divorced*, trans. Ian Huish, in *Two Plays by Ödön von Horváth*, Bath: Absolute Classics, 1991.

Wesker, Arnold, *The Kitchen and Other Plays*, London: Penguin Books, 1990.

Williams, Raymond, *Drama in Performance*, Milton Keynes: Open University Press, 1991.

Wilson, Edmund, *The Wound and the Bow*, Boston: Houghton Mifflin, 1941.

Winnicott, D. W., *Playing and Reality*, New York: Routledge, 1989.

– *Psycho-Analytic Explorations*, ed. Clare Winnicott, Ray Shepherd and Madeleine Davis, Cambridge, Massachusetts: Harvard University Press, 1989.

Index

['NT' and 'RNT' indicate
National Theatre and Royal
National Theatre; 'RCT' indi-
cates Royal Court Theatre; 'D'
indicates Stephen Daldry, and
'*AIC*' indicates *An Inspector
Calls*.]

Act One (Hart), 96
actor-managers, 4
actors: affected by audience
    response, 11; D's tendency to
    confer privately with, 144–5;
    entrances, 27; resistance to D's
    melodrama, 236–7; as
    'shadows' or shades, 27;
    unpaid at the Gate, 91
Aldwych Theatre, London, 13
All That Fall (Beckett), 100, 105
Ambassadors Theatre, London,
    200
Anderson, Lindsay, 91, 109, 113,
    117
Andrews, Julie, 184
Angels in America (Kushner),
    8–9, 224
Antony and Cleopatra
    (Shakespeare), 4
Arcadia (Stoppard), 144
Architecture, Actor and Audience
    (Mackintosh), 202–3, 224–5
Arditti, Michael *Evening
    Standard*, 46, 52–3
Arditti, Paul, 71, 124, 172, 173,
    182, 217
Artaud, Antonin, 5
Arts Council, 44, 93, 94, 106

assistant directors, 228
At the Royal Court (Findlater),
    110–11, 112
audience: and *Body Talk*, 190,
    192, 193; as both witness and
    jury, 21–2; D on a young audi-
    ence, 90; as D's final collabo-
    rator, 239; as free agents,
    10–11; at the Gate Theatre, 84;
    Goffman on, 193, 194; indi-
    vidual responses of, 8; inspec-
    tion by, 21, 27; invited to share
    in the emotion of guilt for
    Eva's death, 35; and its role in
    events onstage, 84; and
    Machinal, 84; as part of the
    play, 11; and *Rat in the Skull*,
    180; sharing a communal expe-
    rience, 8, 36, 134; and the silent
    figures in *AIC*, 23, 84; spotlit,
    21; takes the place of the
    Birlings, 21; the theatre's need
    for collaboration, 195
Audrey Skirball-Kenis
    Foundation, 94
Austin, J. L., 5, 28, 29
Australia, 100

Bach, Johann Sebastian, 189
Bacon, Francis, 122, 156
Bacon, Nicola, 224
Banks, Iain, 105, 198
Barclays Bank, 94
Barclays New Stages Festival, 96,
    100, 181–2
Barry, Sebastian, 115
Barton, Chris, 30–31, 199, 228
Basilico, Emma, 171–2
Bates, Alan, 109

band, 215; and *Body Talk*, 186;
as Brechtian, 215; and *The
Canterbury Tales*, 43, 44–5;
and *The Editing Process*, 71,
75, 79, 80, 86, 95, 216;
European allegiance, 215; at
the Gate, 46–7; and *An
Inspector Calls*, 16, 30, 34,
2131, 214, 216; and *Judgement
Day*, 43; and *Machinal*, 56, 57,
58, 216; and *Manon Lescaut*,
212; pub story, 218; and *Rat in
the Skull*, 124, 139, 172, 173,
177, 216, 217–18; Rickson on,
216
Warner, Deborah, 117
Washington, Joan, 148
The Wasp Factory (Banks), 105,
181, 198
Webber, Julian, 96, 102, 104, 114,
218, 227, 229–30, 237
Weill, Kurt, 34, 224
Welfare State, 12
Wertenbaker, Timberlake, 59

Wesker, Arnold, 60, 91, 109,
112–13, 118, 141
W. H. Smith, 94
Whybrow, Graham, 101, 182
Wilde, Oscar, 4, 20
Wilson, Angus, 109
Wilson, Edmund, 148
Wilson, Robert, 177
Winn, Steven, 38
Winnicott, D. W., 3, 8, 77, 146
The Winter's Tale (Shakespeare),
195
Wittgenstein, Ludwig, 3
Woodeson, Nicholas, 105,
229–30, 237–8
writer/director relationship: D
speaks through and with the
writer's voice, 13–14; D's
respect for the playwright's
words and intentions, 12

York (*AIC* in), 54–5, 118
Young People's Theatre
Programme, 101